D1579379

The British Building Industry
Since 1800

LEEDS COLLEGE OF BUILDING
WITHDRAWN FROM STOCK

JOIN US ON THE INTERNET VIA WWW, GOPHER, FTP OR EMAIL:

WWW: http://www.thomson.com
GOPHER: gopher.thomson.com
FTP: ftp.thomson.com   A service of I**T**P®
EMAIL: findit@kiosk.thomson.com

LEEDS COLLEGE OF BUILDING

T11853

LEEDS COLLEGE OF BUILDING LIBRARY
NORTH STREET
LEEDS LS2 7QT
TEL: 0532 430765

Also available from E & FN Spon

The Idea of Building
Steven Groak

The Buildings Around Us
Thom Gorst

Emerging Concepts in Urban Space Design
Geoffrey Broadbent

Economics: A foundation course for the built environment
Jose Manser

Design and the Economics of Construction
Ralph Morton and David Jaggar

Value Management in Design and Construction
Steven Male and John Kelly

The Rise of Modern Urban Planning 1800–1914
Anthony Sutcliffe

From Garden Cities to New Towns 1899–1946
Dennis Hardy

From New Towns to Green Politics 1946–1990
Dennis Hardy

The British Building Industry Since 1800:

An Economic History

Christopher Powell

LEEDS COLLEGE OF BUILDING
Classmark 690.09

E & FN SPON
An Imprint of Chapman & Hall

London · Weinheim · New York · Tokyo · Melbourne · Madras

Published by
E & FN Spon, an imprint of Chapman & Hall, 2–6 Boundary Row,
London SE1 8HN, UK

Chapman & Hall, 2–6 Boundary Row, London SE1 8HN, UK

Chapman & Hall GmbH, Pappelallee 3, 69469 Weinheim, Germany

Chapman & Hall USA, Fourth Floor, 115 Fifth Avenue, New York
NY 10003, USA

Chapman & Hall Japan, ITP-Japan, Kyowa Building, 3F, 2-2-1
Hirakawacho, Chiyoda-ku, Tokyo 102, Japan

Chapman & Hall Australia, 102 Dodds Street, South Melbourne, Victoria 3205,
Australia

Chapman & Hall India, R. Seshadri, 32 Second Main Road, CIT East,
Madras 600 035, India

First edition 1980
Second edition 1996

© 1980, 1996 C.G. Powell

Typeset in Great Britain by Cambrian Typesetters

Printed in Great Britain by St Edmundsbury Press, Bury St Edmunds, Suffolk

ISBN 0 419 207309

Apart from any fair dealing for the purposes of research or private study, or
criticism or review, as permitted under the UK Copyright Designs and Patents
Act, 1988, this publication may not be reproduced, stored, or transmitted, in
any form or by any means, without the prior permission in writing of the
publishers, or in the case of reprographic reproduction only in accordance with
the terms of the licences issued by the Copyright Licensing Agency in the UK,
or in accordance with the terms of licences issued by the appropriate
Reproduction Rights Organization outside the UK. Enquiries concerning
reproduction outside the terms stated here should be sent to the publishers at
the London address printed on this page.

The publisher makes no representation, express or implied, with regard to
the accuracy of the information contained in this book and cannot accept any
legal responsibility or liability for any errors or omissions that may be made.

A catalogue record for this book is available from the British Library

Library of Congress Catalog Card Number: 96–84233

∞ Printed on acid-free text paper, manufactured in accordance with ANSI/
NISO Z39.48-1992 (Permanence of Paper).

Contents

Foreword

The history of the building industry over the past two centuries is the history of Britain, for building, as architecture, reflects the society of the time.

In 1800 London and the northern cities were only just beginning to grow. People rarely travelled far from their homes. There were no railways and roads were poor. Materials for building were still mainly locally produced, sash windows and doors were made on site. The enormous gap between the very poor and the well-off was reflected in the difference between the artisans' dwellings and merchants' houses.

Then came the population explosion, industrial growth and prosperity leading to massive urbanization and rising living standards. The railways and improved roads made possible the movement of materials and labour. Local materials became regional and then national. Windows, doors and joinery were manufactured off-site and delivered ready for fixing. There was the birth of the specialist subcontractor. As society became more complex so did the buildings it required. The landmark building dominating the urban scene, historically the church, began to be replaced by the bank, the factory and the town hall.

Society demanded better, healthier buildings, not just for the rich but also for the poor – sanitation laws; building by-laws; planning and open spaces and daylight; new materials resulted in steel frames replacing load bearing masonry and cast iron. There were bigger windows and more glass. Lifts meant the walk-up, the natural limit on building height, no longer applied; economic forces determined height and density, not limitations of building materials.

Increased prosperity meant more money to spend and invest in buildings with higher space and amenity standards than ever before. National pride and confidence were reflected in civic buildings, town halls, hospitals and office buildings.

Mirroring this was the growth of the big contractor, the voluntary divorce of the designers – architects and engineers – from the building process, and the growth of the single contract rather than individual trades and then standard forms of contract. Then there was the rapid expansion of prefabricated components against the hit-and-miss development of fully prefabricated buildings.

If much has changed over those two centuries some things have not. Bust always followed boom in the 1800s just as it does now. Building was, and still is, a barometer of the economy. The secret of success then, as now, is to be ahead of the growth and get out before the crash.

This book chronicles all this and much more. It is both fascinating and informative for the interested bystander as well as the historical researcher. It should be compulsory reading for developers, politicians, planners and all those involved in construction.

Owen Luder CBE
President, Royal Institute of British Architects

Preface

At the beginning of the nineteenth century the national stock of buildings was small and mainly scattered. Individual buildings, too, were mainly small and they were simple and built of natural materials. Today the reverse is true: a vastly larger and more urban stock of bigger and more complicated buildings made of heavily processed goods. The agency which wrought this massive transformation, the building industry, is the subject of this book. The industry was always a very large one, made up of many different parts, which gave it a fragmented and loosely defined quality. Despite this it has always appeared to outsiders as an entity. That they saw it thus is taken as a justification for the wide scope of this study.

The industry, being so large and meaning so many different things to so many people, has been viewed in many different ways. Some people in the industry have viewed it as a saga, the romantic celebration of a series of immense challenges leading to heroic triumphs against crippling odds. Company histories often follow this pattern. Other people (probably no fewer in numbers) have viewed it more as a tragedy, in which resourceful players are condemned to an eternal cycle of hope succeeded by struggle and then disappointment. Some pay-masters of the industry follow this pattern. Each specialism and each successive age brings to the industry its own assumptions and preoccupations, and sees a different image: economic mainstay or business opportunity to some, maker of visual pleasure or battleground to others (and maybe comedy to a few). The historical development of the building industry is about all of these, and more.

The aim of the study is to introduce and describe nearly two centuries of building as an agency of change in the national building stock. Two related groups of simple questions are addressed. First, who decided to build, why, and what was built? Second, who built and how did they do so? A hope (easier expressed than achieved) is to help focus and unify a fragmented historical picture.

The approach is empirical and descriptive, drawing mainly on a growing wealth of secondary sources. Building is taken to be the provision of shelter, meaning roofed enclosure, so purely engineering construction is excluded. The scope is confined to England and Wales, except where otherwise stated. In the interests of space, which press heavily on such a wide subject as this, the rich and distinctive pattern of events in Scotland is regretfully left to others. The term 'building industry' is taken in a broad sense to embrace allied professions as well as firms and people engaged on site and in yard and workshop.

The book is an extensively revised and enlarged version of the same author's *An Economic History of the British Building Industry 1815–1979*, first published in 1980 by Architectural Press, and again as a Methuen University Paperback in 1982. The opportunity has been taken to add two entirely new chapters, to incorporate new material wherever possible elsewhere and to provide many new illustrations.

The study is divided into five historical periods, each of which is treated semi-independently although, of course, common threads may be traced through them all. Two chapters are devoted to each period. The first chapter of each pair takes a broadly external view of building activity. Demand for building arising from society is considered here, and so is the response of the industry in terms of what was built. The second of each pair of chapters goes on to take an internal view of building activity. The means of production of buildings, in terms of industry structure, organization and operation, are considered here. In order to facilitate comparisons between periods, the structure of alternate chapters is similar throughout the book. The five chapters on demand and response (Chapters 1, 3, 5, 7 and 9) begin with a view of building demand and the people who decided to build. A review follows of additions to the stock of buildings, taking each of the main building types in turn. The chapters conclude with brief consideration of losses from the stock, and lengthier treatment of physical building form. The five remaining chapters, on the building industry (Chapters 2, 4, 6, 8, and 10), each begin with a view of the character of the industry and influences upon it. After that, professions, firms and labour are considered in turn and the chapters conclude with treatment of building materials, components and processes. The structure of the book reflects its subject in being subdivided; it is hoped that any resulting loss of narrative flow is balanced by ease of reference.

In the text, building costs refer to finished buildings

including profit, but excluding land, except where otherwise stated. The term 'promoter', by which is meant the person or organization with responsibility for initiating and paying for a building project, has been adopted for reasons of consistency. Equally suitable terms would have been 'client', 'customer', 'employer' or 'owner'.

The author would like to thank the many people who have helped him with his task. No evidence whatever was found here of the adversarialism said to characterize the industry. Particular thanks are due to: Professor Robert Macleod for the initial idea; Professor Richard Silverman of the University of Wales Cardiff for arranging for time to be made available for writing; Stanley Cox for helpfully commenting on part of an early draft; and Roger Wilkes for painstaking work with many of the illustrations. Thanks are also due to Sir Peter Shepherd, Hannah Corlett, Wayne Forster, Sylvia Harris, Lars Jaeger, Paul Jenkins, Pamela Powell, Robert Thorne, Philip Twentyman and to helpful staff at the British Architectural Library RIBA, the Prints and Drawings Department of the British Museum, the Corporation of London Guildhall Library and the University of Wales Cardiff Library. I extend my apologies to those people who also helped, but are not mentioned here by name. Named and unnamed alike are not responsible for any mistakes which follow, which are my own.

1
Building Coketown: 1800–1850

. . . accretions of chaos superimposed on an existing pattern of country lanes . . . .

(E.R. Scoffham (1984) *The Shape of British Housing*)

DEMAND AND BUILDING PROMOTERS

The decision to build
Every building ever built arose from a carefully considered decision, almost always of great concern to those making it. The history of building begins with demand from outside the industry, with the people who decided to build. Who were they, why did they build and how did they set about it? Many of these key initiators and their motives are today lost or only shadowy, especially the promoters of the mass of commonplace and minor buildings. Certainly there was a great variety of people with a matching variety of methods. Sometimes the initial decision was to develop a site, without much early heed to the type of building. At other times it was to erect a particular building before it was known where. Many people were likely to be involved: landowners, investors, developers and builders, though not all of them in every case. Often one person combined the roles of several, while methods changed from place to place and over time. The decision to build was elusive and can seldom be pinned down to a single person or moment. Rather, it was likely to be a staged process involving at least several people. Between them they possessed a building need, the will and resources to procure a building and a preparedness to shoulder the risk of an often-hazardous undertaking.

Custom builders and developers

In the simplest decisions to build, individuals decided to do so on their own land, using their own labour and materials. A peasant smallholder was such a case. The example of a country landowner improving his estate was slightly complicated by the probable need to pay others for labour and materials. More involved cases required land transactions, either sale or lease; examples included traders and industrialists seeking expansion who bought land for new business premises, and groups of artisans in building clubs and terminating societies [1, 2]. The motives of building promoters ranged from capital gain from sale, revenue from rent, expansion of business or other activity and occasionally the personal satisfaction of a leisured individual. Promoters' decisions to build might depend on landowners' decisions to develop or dispose of land. Here another interest, the developer, was likely to be involved. Independent developers, acting as intermediaries between landowners and people with interests in completed buildings, were well established by 1800. An early (and notorious) example had been Nicholas Barbon, active in the late seventeenth century where the market was largest, in London. By the early nineteenth century developers ranged from well-connected figures such as architect John Nash to a rather less illustrious group of more-or-less rickety small building tradesmen, retailers and the like. Their differences were more evident than their similarities, of which the most significant was a willingness to take risks. Large projects demanded large developers, while small projects were within the grasp of correspondingly small figures. Many developers were fairly substantial attorneys, merchants, architects, surveyors and building craftsmen, sometimes working in syndicates of complementary skills. They all needed capital or access to credit, which early in the nineteenth century came variously from banks, private individuals, building materials producers (for example, brickmakers) and occasionally insurance companies. The scale and complexity of development probably increased as the century advanced, but the essential function remained the same. It was to assemble land and capital, and provide the organization to create buildings in return for gain. The cases of peasant, estate improver and expanding trader, as well as projects promoted by the State, were all examples of decisions to build after demand became evident. Many of the resulting buildings were of higher quality and fitted closely to the particular needs of their promoters. In this they reflected their custom-built origins.

Speculative builders

The common alternative to custom building was to build in advance of demand, for disposal on the open market. In this case of speculative building the decision to build was more complicated and events could take a number of courses. Landowners could act as builders by employing their own labour or, instead, employing one or more builders under contract. Rather more common was the intervention of the developer to relieve the landowner of some risk and responsibility. Developers might either purchase land outright for development, or lease it, in which case the landowner often imposed legal controls on what could be built [3, 4]. These were intended to protect the landowner's long-term interests from the possible effects of poor quality building. Having secured the land, developers could either develop it themselves, subcontract the work to others, or resell it. Some complicated arrangements involved large sums and a pace of events which lurched from precariously fast to agonisingly slow. When building began, if not before, other interests became important. One was the source of money reaching the builders to pay for labour and materials. Builders raised loans for this working capital where they could, from private creditors, materials suppliers and others. Another important financial interest was that of people and institutions who bought finished buildings as investments or to occupy. At one extreme were small investors such as widows and retired small shopkeepers who might own a pair of cottages and live off the rents which they produced. At the other extreme were wealthier private investors and bankers. Great and small investors shared earnest hopes of reliable income from their new properties, in an age when safe outlets for investment were often local and could be scarce.

The roles of those who decided to build, whether landowner, developer, builder or investor, overlapped and there was great diversity among the tangle of aims and methods. Treen [5] has characterized these roles in the following way:

1. *Pre-development landowners*: agricultural estate landowners; land speculators.
2. *Developers*: agricultural estate landowners; builders; associated professions of lawyer, surveyor, estate agent; entrepreneur.
3. *Builders*: speculative builders; contractors.
4. *Building owners*: landlords; owner-occupiers.
5. *Residents*: tenants; owner-occupiers.

Early decisions and procedures adopted by these figures strongly influenced the later use and physical forms of buildings and hence remained stamped on them for life.

Building stock in 1800

Promoters' demand for new buildings arose in a context of variable human needs and fixed existing buildings. The national building stock, from nobleman's castle down to dilapidated byre, had always been gradually adapted. By 1800 it stood on the eve of a quickening transformation. What were the main features of this stock which was to meet and influence approaching future demand?

In geographical distribution the stock reflected a predominantly rural population. With two-thirds or more of the population living in scattered villages and farms, it followed that urban buildings were the exception. At the same time migration to the towns had been filling and extending them. Greater London was by far the largest in 1801, with a population of 1,117,000. Next was Liverpool (82,000), followed by Manchester (75,000).

The dominant building type was housing. In 1801 the census recorded 1,623,000 houses, ranging pyramid fashion from the few very grand at the apex down to the humble majority near the base. The second great category of buildings was for agriculture, where there were various types of animal shelter, crop stores and the like. Beyond domestic and farm buildings were relatively small numbers of more-or-less specialised buildings: workshops, mills, maltings, breweries, tanneries and so on for manufacturing and processing; warehouses, stables and markets for trading; churches and chapels; schools; and an assortment of rarities such as theatres, barracks, gaols and hospitals. Altogether their numbers were quite small. Just how small is uncertain, but Chalklin [6] thought that expenditure on new eighteenth century amenity buildings was 10–20%, at most, of expenditure on housing. For many outside London the building stock probably meant little more than a church clustered about with mostly small houses, an inn and shop or two, backed by some nondescript workaday structures near the marketplace and farms.

Most individual buildings were quite small, although there were exceptions, by any standards, in cathedrals, aristocrats' houses and emerging industry. Proud new textile mills were being insured for £12,000 or more, but as yet their numbers were few. Generally small institutions and small businesses had no need for much more than small accommodation.

Capital in, and from, nascent industry was accumulating, but had not so far filtered through to deeply affect the building stock. Because buildings for an agrarian economy had traditionally appeared only one or two at a time, standardisation in appearance was unusual. The stock was composed of a high proportion of unique buildings and few groups of repetitive ones. As ever in such a vast field, exceptions were to be found. Parts of Georgian London, Bath and a few other places, where demand had been intense and building codes enforced, displayed repetition in superior terraced housing.

While the physical form in most building groups was varied, visible specialisation for particular purposes was quite small: form was not much differentiated according to the activities going on inside. This was because the modest scale of most enterprises allowed them to be carried out in general purpose buildings. An example was the prevalence of cottage industry where such diverse goods as gloves, nails and chairs were made in non-specialized buildings. Similarly, administrative and trading functions were carried out largely in general purpose spaces and buildings. At the same time another sort of variety was flourishing. This was the use of buildings for symbolic display of wealth, taste and power. Here was an architectural stylistic vocabulary with a potent influence on the variety of physical form.

Many old high-quality buildings survived because of their inherent durability and the slow advance of obsolescence in a slow-changing pre-industrial society. In contrast, many low-quality buildings were short-lived because low incomes permitted only very flimsy construction [7]. The condition of much of the stock was quite poor for the same reason, that low incomes deferred maintenance and replacement. Further, there was little effective official concern with structural safety or the public wellbeing. Appalling conditions were not difficult to find. This description came from Dorset in the 1840s [8], but the content was timeless:

> I have often seen the springs bursting through the mud floor of some of the cottages, and little channels cut from the centre under the doorways to carry off the waste . . .

That conditions could be as bad in the towns is well-known. There the evils of sodden thatch and collapsing mud walls were exchanged for those of uncollected refuse and poor ventilation.

Methods of building construction were enormously varied.

Some of the variety stemmed from time, with ancient surviving buildings still embodying archaic ways of building. Other variety stemmed from location, with vernacular buildings reflecting local materials availability, climate and level of prosperity. By 1800 vernacular building was in its twilight, with local materials and skills for new building yielding to regional and national markets. Yet local character had not yet been eroded very far in the stock. Practice in one district might still contrast very strongly with that in its neighbours: here chalk blocks walls, there brick and there again timber boarding or rubble. One further source of variety was in the range of quality between costliest and cheapest forms of building. Just as the difference in wealth between rich and poor people has narrowed since 1800 so, too, has the difference between high building quality and low. Certainly the gulf between land-owner's country house and miserable squatter turf hut is difficult to match today.

Increasing demand

Economic and social change in pre-industrial society had been quite slow. The building stock (the supply of shelter) was likely to have fairly closly reflected effective demand for buildings. Most annual alterations to the stock were limited to the few buildings which wore out and were replaced by new ones for the same purposes. The stock reflected, more or less, the social, economic and political structure of the society which created and occupied it. When changes became quicker with the onset of industrialization an effect was soon felt on the building stock. The hitherto close fit between stock and society altered to become tighter in some places and slacker in others; this meant over-use and stress here and redundancy there. Some demand for new buildings went unmet for a while and some established demand for existing buildings melted away to leave them without their original purpose. The growing lag between demand and the building stock gave rise to several responses.

One common response was to alter parts of the existing stock to meet new demands. Alterations had the great merits of being cheap and easy and maybe appealing to that fondness for improvisation said to be a national characteristic. Instances of reuse and rebuild abounded in pre-industrial society (and archaeology); now their occurrence increased. Examples included cellars pressed into use as dwellings, handlooms installed in former bedrooms, and merchants' houses sub-divided into multiple occupancies. Where demand was intense, or opportunities offered by an existing building were attractive, alterations could be ingenious and varied. By the early nineteenth century the large Norman castle at Chepstow had been used variously not only residentially, but also as a sailcloth and bark store, malthouse, cider mill, wine cellar, nailery, glass factory and lime kiln. For all their benefits, alterations usually proceeded without celebration; they lacked the appeal of the grand gesture conveyed by a new building.

The more grand and visible response to mismatch between stock and society was a combination of new construction and demolition, of town growth and renewal. New building began to change from being primarily a means of conserving a near static building stock to becoming in itself an agent of change in society.

The foregoing discussion has been concerned with effective demand. That is to say, the only buildings considered were those for which there was the will and sufficient supply of scarce resources to create. This is to disregard a widespread and deep social need for buildings among those who could not afford them. An illustration of the distinction between social need and effective demand comes from the lethally over-crowded slums. Social need there was demonstrably great, but low incomes prevented its translation into effective demand.

Growth and fluctuations

The driving force behind changing demand for buildings was economic growth. The total gross national income in Great Britain at current prices increased from £232 m. in 1801 to £253 m. in 1851. Sustained growth occurred in all major sectors of the economy, particularly in mining, manufacturing

Gross domestic fixed capital formation by type of asset, Great Britain, 1801–1860 (% of total g.d.f.c, decade averages at 1851–60 prices)

	(1) Dwellings	(2) Industrial & commercial bldgs.	(3) Other non-residential bldgs. & works	(4) Total buildings & works	(5) Cols (1) + (2)
1801–10	23.9	12.4	37.2	73.6	36.3
1811–20	26.9	14.0	33.8	74.7	40.9
1821–30	28.7	16.7	27.9	73.4	45.4
1831–40	25.0	15.3	32.3	72.6	40.3
1841–50	13.5	10.8	47.3	71.7	24.3
1851–60	16.2	10.2	37.0	63.4	26.4

(Table calculated from Feinstein, C.H. and Pollard, S. (eds) (1980) *Studies in Capital Formation in the UK 1750–1920* Clarendon, Table X p. 446.)

and building, and trade and transport. The scale of growth was sufficient to surpass the rate of population increase. The importance of building in this expansionary picture is seen by calculating from Feinstein and Pollard's figures of gross domestic fixed capital formation in Great Britain [9] the approximate percentage of the buildings-related component.

A sizable proportion of non-building items is included in Column (3). Taking Columns (1) and (2) alone, which include a very large proportion of all building, it is seen that building advanced from about 36.3% of g.d.f.c. formation in 1801–10 to a peak of 45.4% in 1821–30. It declined thereafter, a victim of competition with railway and other investment, to 24.3% in 1841–50. The decline occurred in the context of a total of g.d.f.c. formation which advanced powerfully with each decade from £16.0 m. (1801–10) to £46.9 m. (1841–50), and more in the succeeding decade.

The rate of building activity varied very widely from year to year, so that it moved in a series of cycles of boom and slump about a rising trend. These fluctuations, which had occurred at least since the early eighteenth century, have been the subject of much study [10] and debate. Their origins have been described memorably by Parry Lewis [11] in the words 'population change, the credit situation, and stochastic events are the Punch, Judy and Hangman of our show.' In more mundane language what happened at first was that demand

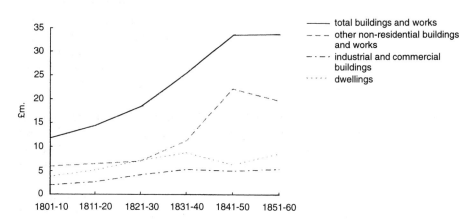

Figure 1 Building-related gross domestic fixed capital formation by type of asset, GB 1801–1860 (£m. per annum, decade averages, at constant 1851–60 prices). (Source: C.H. Feinstein and S. Pollard (eds) *Studies in Capital Formation in the UK 1750–1920* by permission of Oxford University Press.)

for buildings would increase with population growth. Rising business confidence would make money for building purposes readily available so that more and more speculators would become ever more bold in their ventures, to the point of recklessness. Then, just as the market for buildings was replete, an external shock, such as war or poor harvest would trigger a collapse. Working capital would dry up, completed buildings would become unsaleable, and incomplete buildings would be left as overstretched speculators failed. With an overprovision of buildings, activity slumped until the population eventually increased to mop up the surplus stock. The growth part of the cycle would then restart, tentatively at first, then with increasing confidence.

The pattern of cycles which took place from 1800 was recovery to about 1811, followed by decline to 1816, due to wartime difficulties, then further growth to a peak in 1825. Another decline then ensued until a trough was reached about 1832. Events after that are complicated by heavy railway construction (which used many bricks, upon which understanding of building fluctuations largely depends). In London, at least, there appears to have been slow recovery to a peak in 1847. Nationally, recovery from the 1832 trough appears to have been more vigorous, only to be checked by falls in 1835 and again in 1840 [12]. This highly simplified account of fluctuations expresses national aggregate figures of activity which provide only one side of the picture. What remains concealed are the wide differences in building activity in different places at a given time. When one town (or trade) was up, another might well be down; while Lancashire flourished, East Anglia languished. In this sense the national economy operated much as a loosely linked group of local and regional economies, without the integration assumed today.

Urbanization Economic growth stimulated demand for buildings, and the building industry responded. The result was spectacular town growth, urbanization without precedent. The age-old dominance of rural population over urban was challenged, despite some growth in the rural total. New industrial towns were the centre of activity. The populations of Manchester and Leeds grew by as much as 47% in the inter-censal period 1821 to 1831. Elsewhere, too, the pace of population growth and building activity was relentless. By the 1851 census, the five largest towns, in descending order of size, were London, Liverpool, Manchester, Birmingham and Leeds [13]. The dominance of London was reinforced, with a population of 2,491,000. Liverpool had reached 376,000 and Manchester 303,000. Other fast-growing places were Bradford, Sheffield, Salford, Newcastle upon Tyne, Preston and Brighton.

ADDITIONS TO BUILDING STOCK

Housing

Houses continued to be the most numerous buildings in the new settlements. Between 1801 and 1810 of the order of 454,000 were built in Great Britain. The totals for succeeding decades were: 1811–20, 443,000; 1821–30, 600,000; 1831–40, 711,000; 1841–50, 480,000. As a proportion of g.d.f.c., housebuilding in Great Britain stood at about 23.9% in the decade 1801–10. It then climbed to a peak of 28.7% in 1821–30, before declining to 13.5% in 1841–50. Feinstein and Pollard's index of dwelling size and quality (1900 = 100) stood at 50.9 in the decade 1801–10 and advanced gradually, but unfalteringly to reach 58.2 in 1841–50 [14].

The rapidity of housebuilding is seen in the example of Liverpool [15] where, according to the census, there were about 160,000 houses standing in 1811, more than another 4,000 10 years later and 38,600 altogether in 1851. During a boom in the mid-1840s, set off by the prospect of higher costs due to impending by-law legislation, new houses appeared in the town at a rate of over 3,500 a year. This equivalent to 60 or 70 houses a week was impossible for contemporary observers to miss. The Rev. J.R. Stevens exclaimed in 1849 about another northern boom town, Ashton-under-Lyne [16]:

> Within a narrow ring of what a few years ago was . . . moorland with stretch of hill and a sweep of lovely dale, now swarm not less than a hundred thousand souls. Suddenly, as if by spell of fairy or fiend, stray hamlet, scattered township and straggling parish have run together and have become one vast unbroken wilderness of mills and houses, a teeming town . . . .

Neither was 'fairy or fiend' confined to Lancashire. The *Morning Herald* saw the inexorable spread of London in 1848 like this [17]:

> No one who has recently travelled . . . in the environs of this overgrown metropolis, can have failed to observe that houses are springing up in all quarters . . . Money is scarce; the whole nation is in difficulties; but houses spring up

everywhere, as though capital were abundant – as though one-half of the world were on the look out for investments, and the other half continually in search of eligible family residencies, desirable villas, and aristocratic cottages . . . .

The *Morning Herald* seems to have been writing about middle class houses, but there was a world of difference between those houses and the cheapest. Some of the very poorest examples were like those at Lye, between Stourbridge and Dudley. There, it was said [18], Black Country nailers squatted in one-room huts made of fire-clay mixed with straw and stubble, with thatched roofs, no windows, no gardens and with smoke issuing from the doorways. Here was the tail-end of a long-standing tradition of do-it-yourself housing which included flimsy agricultural 'cottages' built for as little as £5 or £10 in the 1840s. At the opposite extreme of quality were vast new country houses. The random example of architect S.S. Teulon's Tortworth Court, Gloucestershire cost as much as £45,000 in 1849, had accommodation on three floors, and 30 rooms on the ground floor alone. Between the standards at Lye and Tortworth was an infinitely varied gradation to suit all pockets: agricultural cottages of the 1840s and earlier often cost between £40 and £60 for two rooms and between £60 and £100 for four [19]. At the same time typical working-class houses in Sheffield, consisting of cellar, living room, bedroom, attic, privy and yard ranged from £60 to £75 [20]. In the remote Ebbw Vale ironworks colony in 1811 cottages cost £55 each, while better quality examples built 30 years later by Ashworth to serve his mill at Turton, Lancashire, cost £120 each [21]. The trend of unit building costs, at least for industrialists' cottages, appears to have been downward from about 55p per cu.m around 1815, perhaps to 37p per cu.m by the 1830s and 29p per cu.m at mid-century [22]. At about that time it was possible to build a respectable terraced house for £200 with ground floor accommodation consisting of 20 sq.m parlour, 16 sq.m living room, 10 sq.m scullery, hall, pantry and privy; on the first floor were three bedrooms. The design had pretensions enough for the front elevation to be graced by an ornamental door surround, string course and plinth [23]. A great improvement on this was a parsonage costing £670 which appeared in a mid-century builders' pattern book and offered on the ground floor a 19 sq.m drawing room, 18 sq.m dinning room, 12 sq.m library, 14 sq.m kitchen, 9 sq.m scullery, pantry, china pantry, WC, stable and gig house. Further again up the social scale was an ornate villa for £1,550, the ground floor of which included 36 sq.m drawing room, 33 sq.m dining room, breakfast room, kitchen, scullery, vestibule, cellars, larder, china pantry, coal store, two WCs, yard, stable and gig house.

The vast majority of houses cost less than £1,000 and not very many exceeded £300, but the pattern of distribution by cost remains open to conjecture. The number of working-class families increased very greatly over the period and many required new houses in hitherto thinly populated districts. Equally, it is apparent that not much of the great increase in national wealth trickled through to manual workers before mid-century. This implies that the middle class received a disproportionately large number of the new houses. Flinn [24] has suggested that the increase in income per person, together with a fairly constant average number of people per inhabited house (5.67 in 1801, 5.46 in 1851), implied improved housing conditions at the upper end of the social scale and deteriorating ones at the lower end. If this is tentatively translated into terms of quality of houses built, then the emphasis clearly lay with superior houses. Yet generalizations are bedevilled (or enriched) by local exceptions and peculiarities. For example, house quality and cost in, say, South London are unlikely to have resembled closely those in the pit villages of County Durham or the insalubrious courts of Leeds.

Industrial buildings

Although prosperous, farming was overhauled in economic importance by industry in the earlier decades of the century. Where economic strength moved, so the provision of buildings followed. Early staple industries of textiles, coal and iron all thrust ahead, not only requiring buildings directly in order to produce goods, but also generating wealth and stimulating the whole economy. In this way they became an ultimate source of demand for all sorts of buildings. Most evident was their effect on housing, both for the labour employed in new manufacturing concerns and as an investment outlet for newly created wealth. The textile and dress industries alone employed in 1851 no fewer than 10% of the total population and over 20% of the occupied population in Great Britain. The industry expanded from a United Kingdom real net output of 100 in the year 1800 to 127 in 1815 and 803 in 1852 [25]. This greatly stimulated industrial building activity, both in total and in the imposing size of its constituent parts. For example, Sedgwick Mill, Manchester, built in 1818, was eight storeys high, and Fishwick Mill, Preston, built about 1830 was seven storeys high and had 42 bays. Traditional cotton factories of that time cost about 90p per sq.m although the most advanced iron-framed examples cost well over double that figure [26]. A similar pattern of expansion was shown by the coal industry, which more than quadrupled United Kingdom annual output between 1800 and 1850. Here considerable pit-head capital investment in the form of engine houses and the like was overshadowed by engineering expenditure. Production of iron, the other staple, rose from 0.3 m. tons a year in about 1818 to 2.8 m. tons in the early 1850s, and the number of blast-furnaces erected in England and Wales during the boom years of the 1820s approached 100. As with coal mining, much investment was in engineering, but casting shops, engine houses and so on were also important.

A major new source of building demand came from the railways, in which the peak of activity occurred in the 1840s mania, when house building, it was noted, was quite light. Route mileage more than tripled between 1843, when it was nearly 2,000 miles, and 1850. Again, much expenditure was on civil and mechanical engineering (itself a stimulus to factory building), but there was heavy investment also in building. The field 'became an engineer's paradise – sometimes a megalomania – with elaborate stone-built bridges, stations, engine sheds' [27]. Principal passenger termini were the most impressive buildings; there appears to have been little hesitation in spending, say, £30,000 on the Liverpool Lime Street station of 1846. The South Eastern Railway terminus at Dover cost about the same in 1843, while a smaller installation at Windsor in 1850 cost £7,000. Less architecturally impressive, but probably amounting to much more in total, were the numerous small wayside station buildings. Tender prices for the five intermediate stations on 20 miles of line north of Bristol amounted to a total of £6,600 in 1843. It may be relevant to add that the contractor for two of them, one George Hawkins, bankrupted himself, perhaps by underestimating for the job.

Large and innovative industries attracted attention because their likes had never before been seen, but they were far from the whole industrial story. To a surprising degree the industrial revolution was forged also in smaller, simpler enterprises. For every blast-furnace or steam pumping house there were many less obtrusive industrial yards, stores, sheds and workshops. Some were for the specialized technological forefront, many were for the general supporting cast. Modest buildings in unprecedented numbers were needed for an infinity of smiths, millwrights, hauliers, coal gas producers, distillers, wheelwrights, turners, blenders of paints and oils, workers in wood and wire and all the rest. Many had once been cottage industries or carried on out of doors; some had not existed before. Their aggregate building needs were very great.

Commercial buildings

Business meant money and numbers and these meant counting houses. Before long, the new building types of commercial office emerged and evolved. Banks, insurance offices and allied businesses increasingly built new premises in the City

Figure 2 Making a London shopfront, June 1834. George Scharf's sketch of 23 Francis Street being converted into a shop. Heavy timber lintel is being lifted by rope and tackle. Shop facia lies ready (foreground). (Source: British Museum.)

and leading provincial towns. As with railway buildings, many of these manifestations of Victorian commercial spirit were imposing and costly, expressing power, prestige and dependability. A leading example was Cockerell's four-storey Sun Assurance offices in Threadneedle Street, which cost £18,500 in the early 1840s. At about the same time the same architect designed the Bank of England branch at Liverpool which cost £23,000. These big and costly buildings may be compared with much smaller examples of similar function built for less than £1,500 each. Related buildings which appeared in response to industrialization included warehouses, shops and a few exchange and market buildings. The ranges of size and cost were wide and defy generalization: in 1850 £7,400 provided Northampton with a quite ambitious corn exchange, while the more parsimonious citizens of Worksop got theirs complete

Figure 3 Plasterwork applied to a public house. George Scharf's sketch of Francis Street – Alfred Street corner, spring 1843. Decorative plaster cast consoles are being applied. (Source: British Museum.)

with assembly rooms and markets for £2,500. Nascent consumerism gave rise to some high street shops, and increasing personal mobility led to the novel building type seen in hotels such as the Regent, Leamington of 1817 and Royal Victoria, St Leonards of 1827. Less architecturally pretentious but far more numerous were the new and extended coaching inns and stables for services which prospered until curtailed by railway competition.

Agricultural buildings

The rise of industry and commerce should not distract attention from agriculture, where landlords and their more progressive tenants were keenly interested in providing a variety of buildings. Among them were shelter for farm stock, machinery, crops and processes such as threshing corn, cider and butter making, chaff cutting and oil-cake breaking. A plan for a small farmstead which was estimated to cost £230 in 1843 included a barn bay, threshing floor, open shed, small fold, cart implement shed, stable, cow shed, pig bed and run, dairy, fuel store, brewery and small house complete with cellar. This was cheap compared with a mid-century figure of £770 for farm buildings and house near Grimsby, and no less than £2,300 for very ambitious proposals at Feltwell, Norfolk.

Churches

It was the opinion of *The Builder* in 1843 that the distinguishing features of building operations were, in addition to housing, the construction of churches, workhouses, gaols and barracks. Runaway urbanization had led to belated attempts by the State and by public subscription among wealthy benefactors to equip the raw new towns with some social provisions. This gave rise to a range of new buildings which, in view of attitudes towards public spending, was remarkable for size, variety and high quality. Places of worship were prominent and possessed economic importance in several ways. Being charged with religious and cultural significance, most had great care lavished on their design, which often meant that they were costly. In stylistic terms and quality of craftsmanship they had considerable influence on other building types: 'Churches are the main and engrossing feature of building operations now-a-days; churches are the determining influence in the question of taste in design, &c.' [28]. A major spur came from the Church Building Act of 1818, which led within 12 years to completion of 134 'Commissioners' Churches'. The eventual total of 214 [29] was dismissed by Cobbett characteristically (and unfairly) as 'heaps of white rubbish that the parsons have lately stuck up.' The Catholic Emancipation Act of 1829 added further impulse to building activity and in addition there was intensive building by nonconformists. At mid-century perhaps one half of church seating capacity was in churches and the remainder in other places of worship. By that time the quantity of church building and restoration had grown to remarkable proportions. There were at least 13 new churches in Manchester in the seven years before 1843, and in the Diocese of Salisbury were 15 new churches, 14 rebuilds and 40 enlargements. Church building costs, as much as those of other buildings, varied widely. In Chalklin's view [30] Anglican churches between about 1800 and 1830 cost £2,000 or £3,000 for small examples and £15,000 or £20,000 for large, with occasional ones as much as £50,000. The average cost of an architecturally significant group of 20 or so discussed by Hitchcock [31] was around £10,000 and the typical size was less than 1,000 places. Twelve churches commenced by contractor George Myers between 1837 and 1849 ranged from £20,000 down to £3,633, with an average of £8,934 [32]. No doubt some of the new places of worship were too small to require the services of national contractors. Among these buildings were the likes of the one at Penrhos, Caernarfon, where 80 sittings cost only £205 in the early 1840s.

Schools

School building, like church building, was strongly stimulated as a consequence of urbanization. The first government grant for education was made in 1833, and between 1839 and 1859 more than £1 m. was spent on building, enlarging, repairing and furnishing elementary schools. Before then, the explicitly named National Society for Promoting the Education of the Poor in the Principles of the Established Church reported in 1816 on the cost of some recently built schools [33]. They ranged from £122 for one with 120 places at Ightham, to £599 for one of two-thirds that number of places at North Creake. The average cost for nine schools was £258, compared with an average of £340 for ten larger schools referred to in a report of 1835. In that year the list ranged from £65 for a 40-place school at Tinwell up to £718 for a 640-place school at Burnley. The customary space allowance was 0.56 sq.m per child and the average cost per place in the Durham area, at least, between 1832 and 1850 was about £2, rather more than the averages of the schools in lists referred to above. As with churches, the range of costs was wide: the 600 pupils of

Hoxton Ragged School got their Tudor-style building for only £750, while the same number of pupils at Wicker Parish School, Sheffield, luxuriated in a building which cost £1,300.

Workhouses etc.
Other recipients of heavy public expenditure were the workhouses which were a result of the Poor Law Act of 1834, grouping parishes into unions to deal with the destitute. Many of the buildings were very substantial, consisting of chapel, administrative block and several large symmetrically disposed wings of accommodation, graced with the popular nickname 'bastilles'. Liverpool planned one in 1843 with a frontage of 244 m for as much as £30,000. In Sculcoates, Hull, the lowest tender for a less dramatic building was £8,300, while the paupers of Bromley had to make do with an edifice costing £5,800. The Liverpool and Bromley examples as well as many others of these imposing complexes were in an Elizabethan style. Architect Sir George Gilbert Scott specialized in the type to the extent that he designed more than 50 of them.

All too closely associated in the public mind with workhouses were lunatic asylums and gaols. Both were expensive building types, with examples in Northampton costing £19,000 and at Reading (another Gilbert Scott job) £33,000 in 1843. Twenty years earlier a design by Richard Elsam for a county courthouse and prison was estimated at £70,000. The court buildings consisted of a large domed hall, civil and criminal courtrooms each measuring about 15 × 12 m; jury, judges', and witnesses' rooms; clerk's offices and WCs. The adjoining prison accommodated 300 prisoners together with gaoler and turnkeys, and its cruciform plan had wings about 9 m in breadth and almost 91 m in length [34]. Among the more important prisons built towards mid-century were Holloway (which cost £100,000), Pentonville and Wandsworth. Not all were as large as these, with tenders for the charmingly named Lincoln and Lincolnshire Penitent Females Home in 1850 ranging down to as little as £1,770. Institutional accommodation was also provided by the Lunacy Commissioners whose concerns in the 1840s ranged from a £200,000 asylum for 1,300 inmates at Colney Hatch [35] to one at Northampton for a paltry £1,500. Another arm of heavy state spending, and an important one in the age of Napoleon and Chartist protest, was barrack building. One at Portsea was estimated at £35,000 in 1848 and another on a four hectare site at Newport was estimated five years earlier at around £45,000.

Health and welfare buildings

Hospital building relied on philanthropy and appears to have been moderately large in volume. London had many, including the West London Hospital, inaugurated in 1818, and University College and King's College teaching hospitals. The Royal Orthopaedic Hospital was founded in 1838 and the Hospital for Consumption and Diseases of the Chest followed in 1841. There were also smaller examples such as the British Lying-In Hospital, Long Acre, which cost £5,000 in 1848. Another category of welfare buildings in the larger towns was public baths and washhouses which were promoted from 1846 by Local Bath and Wash Houses Boards. In 1850 Preston town council voted £8,000 towards one with 100 baths and 100 washing compartments. This was a little more than one in Westminster, of about the same time, but the great unwashed of Miles Platting had to make do with premises costing only £2,000.

A comprehensive treatment of all parts of the national stock is prevented by lack of space and the sheer diversity of minor building types. Many buildings remain to be mentioned, among them libraries, newsrooms, learned institutes and museums, a group of ten of which averaged £7,300 each. Beyond that were an infinite variety of public houses, bandstands, greenhouses and the rest.

BUILDING FORM

Densities

Another way of considering additions to stock is by physical form, without reference to function or user. The remainder of this chapter is about the general characteristics of building geometry. Movement from rural to urban living meant that the number of buildings erected in tightly packed groups increased, while those built freestanding, surrounded by open space, diminished in proportion. Building densities became higher in established towns as well as new ones due to the practice of infilling new buildings among the old. New houses and workshops were ingeniously inserted in existing gardens and yards and old premises were subdivided and extended in a search for more accommodation. In these ways remarkably large total floor areas were squeezed into the pre-existing framework of many towns, pre-eminent (or notorious) among which were Nottingham and Liverpool. Building by-laws did not much inhibit such development, either because they were ineffective (no new Metropolitan Acts were passed between 1774 and 1844) or because in many places they did not exist at all. While the resulting densely packed warrens used building materials very sparingly, the intolerable price of private economy was paid in lethal and well-known consequences for public health. Amounts of party wall were relatively great and those of external wall were small; public open space, or indeed any open space, was minimal while the amount of revenue-earning rooms was as large as possible. Construction was likely to be piecemeal and scanty, with interlocking plans, varied storey heights, short floor spans and tangled roof planes. As improvisations succeeded one another, standards of structural adequacy and weather exclusion are likely to have declined. Conditions perhaps were approaching their worst and densities their greatest by mid-century in the oldest quarters of the largest towns. Here, arguably at its most tangible was the kind of world which followed the unbridled pursuit by each individual of his own interest. As Mumford [36] wrote, 'the devil, if he did not take the hindmost, at least reserved for himself the privilege of building the cities.'

To condemn the characteristic building forms of the industrial town in hindsight is easy. Before joining the 'enormous condescension of posterity' it is worth momentarily suspending judgement of the undoubted human costs and taking another view. One of the things which the centre of coketown did was to support small concerns at a stage of economic development when resources were particularly scarce. Coketown enabled risk-taking and growth at an early phase of capital formation. The high-density town minimized use of expensive building materials and transport (distances between allied producers, and between producers and consumers were short). Coketown also brought together suppliers of complementary goods and services, aiding trade, innovation and diffusion in an age of slow communication. It was the classic entrepreneurial environment of cheap, *ad hoc*, unrestricted buildings. Where high densities so lamentably failed was in restraint of inputs and outputs: air, light and waste. When a reaction to dense development eventually came it affected all subsequent urban form and remains evident even today.

While slums became more dense, a reaction began in newer and better-off development, so that some housing layouts became more ordered and open. Instead of middle class terraces, semi-detached pairs and detached villas began to be more favoured. Lower down the social scale something similar was sometimes evident. In earlier times, when buildings had

been added mostly in only ones and twos, the resulting pattern
had been irregular and jumbled. To borrow Engels' words,
'More recently another different method of building was
adopted . . . Working men's cottages are almost never built
singly, but always by the dozen or score; a single contractor
building up one or two streets at a time.' The horrific example
of the poorest areas must have served as a warning against
excessive density and unplanned irregularity, even where by-
laws had little influence. Yet the quality of individual houses
was not necessarily rising everywhere, rather the meandering
and informal character of old streets was giving way to greater
spatial formality and regimentation.

ANNO TERTIO

VICTORIÆ REGINÆ.

****

Cap. lxxvii.

An Act for regulating the Buildings and Party Walls
within the City and County of *Bristol*, and for
widening and improving several Streets within
the same.   [19th *June* 1840.]

Figure 4 Not all *laissez-faire* for builders. Title page of an Act 'for
regulating the buildings and party walls' of Bristol 1840. This was
restrictive legislation near the height of unbridled industrial growth.
Many other places were less regulated.

Scale and complexity

That the ever-growing building stock was serving an increasingly complicated society was seen in several ways, one of which was an increasing number of large buildings. As industrialization advanced, they were needed more and more to house large institutions and manufacturing processes, to store great quantities of goods and for purposes of conspicuous expenditure. In examining the design of large buildings, distinctions are difficult to draw between architectural expression of display (arising from desire to impress) and necessity arising from function (unavoidable or unselfconscious largeness). In the affairs of any one promoter, where capital formation reached a minimum critical level, there arose opportunities for architectural display. Great size was accompanied often by corresponding complexity where large spaces, or numbers of spaces, gave rise to technical problems not soluble by simple traditional means. Wide floor and roof spans and heavy floor loadings required resort to (and sometimes celebration of) advanced technology; buildings with heavy flows of people or goods demanded well thought out patterns of circulation, perhaps on several levels; the many servants needed to run a major country house required to be segregated from owners and guests and this meant duplicated staircases and corridors. The prevailing economic preoccupation was with the division of labour, of splitting into component parts. So it was that buildings frequently were planned to provide specialized accommodation for each activity or function. A society characterized by hierarchy and differentiation of the parts preferred its buildings to express this where possible [37].

Diversity

Pevsner [38] has noted growing diversification of building function among major architectural works, which took place at least from the Middle Ages. This process accelerated in the nineteenth century, when new institutions and activities demanded new functions of buildings. This led to close investigation of functions and resulted in novel building forms as well as development of older ones. Unfamiliar shapes such as multi-storey framed buildings, wide spans, factory chimneys, massive public institutions like workhouses, and revived Gothic forms are evidence enough of diversification; where it was not the shape which was new, it was often the scale. Many unfamiliar forms appeared to evolve incrementally from one project to another, rather than springing fully fledged into existence. This gradualism was, of course, to be a fundamental characteristic of change in the building stock; while the pace of growth might produce surprises of a quantitative kind, qualitative impact was less common. Diversification was most prominent among purpose-built and unique buildings, yet it was also visible elsewhere. At the level of commonplace buildings as varied as workshops, railway goods sheds and plate glass fronted shops it could also be seen. However, the extent of diversification among many speculatively produced buildings is less clear. For example, the upper end of the housing market was a fairly conservative one in which continuity in design was more evident than cumulative change and increasing variety.

Lower down the housing market there may well have been convergence and more repetition in design, rather than diversification. Certainly strong regional differences (some of mysterious origins) persisted, with distinctive characteristics such as cellar dwellings in Liverpool and back-to-backs in Leeds. Yet the increasing increments of town growth favoured repetition, if not on a national scale, at least locally where it made building easier and quicker. Bigger towns meant that more and more individual buildings looked similar, even if the total number of building types was also increasing. Awareness of monotony of increased repetition may have been a reason for growing application of ornament to buildings. Many questions about innovations in building form, about origins, diffusion and advantages conferred, must remain open at present.

Technology

Details of the technology of building are outside the scope of this chapter except to the extent that they influenced physical form. A prominent example of such influence was the growing adoption of skeletal structures. Increased use of cast iron for structural purposes after about 1830, despite higher costs, gave improved resistance to fire and vibration. Equally, if not more important, it reflected growing admiration for bold engineering innovations in general.

In building design there were circumstances in which it was thought appropriate not only to divide and compartmentalize (as noted above), but also to break down barriers and call into question established practice. Among the barriers were walls which obstructed daylight and inhibited workplace tasks, both sedentary and active. Windows and wall openings in general appear to have been made larger and more numerous by mid-century. If so, this was not, as sometimes mistakenly thought,

LEEDS COLLEGE OF BUILDING

due to the abatement of the window tax on residential buildings, since this lasted until 1851 and anyway did not apply to small houses with fewer than six, later seven, windows. Rather, the reasons for more numerous openings may be surmised as a combination of greater resources, cost-saving technology (beam materials, cheaper glazing, etc.) and changing needs of occupants.

Although impressive constructional possibilities were suggested by innovations in wide span structures and the like, no ingenious engineers, or anyone else, came forward to revolutionize common building technology. There were, to be sure, developments in say prefabrication [39], fireproof floors and factory gas lighting, but technical change nowhere amounted to dramatic transformation.

While there was far more building activity than ever, most of the technology used was not very different from that which it had long been, an assortment of methods involving the fashioning and assembly of small parts in their finished positions. Where new building forms emerged, whether locomotive roundhouse or panopticon gaol, they seem to have been due as much to demand 'pull' from functional needs, as to supply 'push' from availability of new technology.

2

The industry forges the means: 1800–1850

. . . . every person who could obtain the means became builders; carpenters, retired publicans, persons working in leather, haymakers and even the keepers of private houses for the reception of lunatics, each contrived to raise his house or houses . . . .

(J.P. Malcolm, *c.* 1802)

CHARACTER AND INFLUENCES

Magnitude The building industry was big and strong: it occupied a prominent position in the national economy. Not only was it a source of products which underpinned economic growth and sustained the comfort and convenience of the people, but it was also a means of support for very many. Yet the great size of the industry was concealed by dispersal and fragmentation, in contrast to the new textile and heavy industries. Even at major building sites, activity was only transitory and the men engaged there soon scattered to new locations. Although it was seldom possible to be far from building activity, if only small scale, only in a few places such as large slate quarries was there a hint of the total size of the industry.

The size of the industry is difficult to define precisely because its boundaries were so indistinct. Workload and labour force fluctuated with the building cycle, and unskilled labourers and, to a lesser extent, craftsmen were employed casually, with frequent unemployment and under-employment. Building was carried out to an unmeasured extent by farmers during slack times, and by agricultural labourers. Those at Stonesfield, Oxfordshire occupied the lull after the harvest by

quarrying stone slates [1]. Primitive do-it-yourself accommodation built in poor rural areas is difficult to give a clear
economic definition. So, too, are the cases of flexible men,
such as joiner-undertakers, who straddled boundaries in a
society where division of labour still had far to go. Because of
these problems only a general indication of the size of the
industry may be gained from the numbers of people employed
in it. In 1831 the census showed that there were 203,000 men
of 20 years of more in Great Britain who were either masons,
carpenters, bricklayers, plasterers, plumbers, house-painters,
slaters or glaziers; Clapham considered that this number was
very nearly doubled by the inclusion of boys, apprentices and
labourers [2]. Twenty years later, in 1851, there were 497,000
people (including 1,000 women) occupied in building and
construction out of a total occupied workforce of 9.4 m. (of
whom 6.5 m. were male). It was the largest trade group for
men outside agriculture. In addition to the 497,000 building
workers there was an unknown number of people connected
with building, but listed in census categories of mining,
quarrying, wood, furniture, fittings, bricks, cement, pottery
and glass. Even by the strictest definition of occupations, one
person in every 19 in the workforce was occupied in building
and, if male workers alone are considered, the proportion was
as many as one in 13.

**National
influences**

An industry of such economic importance was bound to be
tied in many ways to the national and international fortunes of
the country. When rates of interest changed, not only were
promoters' decisions to build affected, but so was the ease (or
lack of it) with which builders operated. An example of
national influence on local building decisions was the effect of
taxes on some materials. Another example was that of local
building labour shortage which resulted from rival work
opportunities opened up by, say, the railway mania. Most
major events in the economic and social life of the nation
sooner or later were likely to have repercussions on the
building industry. Not all of them were necessarily bad for it
either, as any 1830s Chartist rioter might have reflected when
incarcerated in one of the new and very costly gaols.

The sequence of cause and effect which linked society and
building industry was not all in one direction. Building activity
influenced to some degree all manner of other trades connected
with raw materials and finished goods: workers in innumerable
quarries, processors of lead and copper, glass makers and

those who worked or traded in bricks, tiles, pipes, nails, plaster, lime, paint, wallpaper, timber and the rest. The industry also created a demand for coal for firing a majority of the goods on this list, and was a great (and growing) user of transport. Baltic softwood and West Indian hardwood arrived by ocean-going vessels, while joinery and ironmongery found its way from shop and yard to site by horse-drawn wagon. Canals competed with railways for carriage of bulk materials, from timber and sand to bricks and tiles. Building also demanded a variety of skilled white collar services such as transactions and loans involving land, materials and buildings and, it must be said, disputes and bankruptcies which provided sustenance for lawyers, bankers, accountants, surveyors and clerks of all kinds.

Procurement As the rising industrialized society toppled the old Georgian agrarian one, so the vast building industry and its straggling ramifications gradually evolved. Built products and technology changed, as will be shown below, but the greatest effects were elsewhere. It was in the procedures of building and the organization of business units that transformation took place. Here competition within the industry and the division of labour between firms was paramount. In Pollard's words, there were 'substantial increases in productivity, at least for long runs of work, by better organisation, even without an improved technology' [3].

Roles and responsibilities in building were traditionally fluid. Shifts and overlaps made for flexibility, but serve to confuse modern readers. Roles of, say, craftsman and architect varied and were combined according to preference and circumstance. The generally favoured approach to procurement near the beginning of the period was known as measure and value. In essence, its variants involved advancing money, usually to separate master tradesmen, as the work proceeded or at its conclusion. Payments covered current labour and materials costs at generally agreed rates, often from published price books, plus a customary allowance of 15% for profit. Measurement of completed work prior to payment caused great difficulties and frequent disputes. Not for nothing had Dr Johnson pronounced a generation earlier that to build was to be robbed. There was the 'distressful, often the ruinous, uncertainty of common estimates' by measurers who were 'seldom or ever right in their conjectures' [4]. Methods used with measure and value were often special to individuals and there were marked differences between London and country practices. One merit of measure and value was that it allowed an early start to be made on site and could accept changes as the work proceeded. Overwhelmingly against this, it was 'quite incapable of providing any real means of managing the financial consequences of the building process' [5]. Promoters had little idea at the outset what their final commitment would be.

An incentive for improvement emerged, as so often, from the stress of war. The Napoleonic conflict united two strands of public life: a pressing need for big new military buildings, and growing concern about corruption and public accountability. Not far behind, no doubt, were the thoughts of the rising class of entrepreneurs needing new mills and blast-furnaces and keen to buy in the cheapest market before going on to sell in the dearest. Here were fertile grounds for the idea of competition, of getting buildings built by men who offered to do it, not at a prevailing rate, but demonstrably cheaper than anyone else. Competitive tendering for works, or bidding based on cost estimates sometimes for a part of the building (but increasingly for the whole) promised several benefits. One was an opportunity to avoid some of the shortcomings of measure and value, with its risk of sharp practice and incompetence and its uncertainty of outcome of cost. Where a contract could be signed with one builder responsible for all the works 'in gross', instead of with a series of master tradesmen, better coordination and control were possible and completion could be quicker. Not everyone favoured competition and single contracts. Builders working under competitive pressure were tempted to scamp the work. Promoters were in danger of accepting unrealistically low tenders, which led to financial dispute and difficulty. Some architects resented losing freedom to make late alterations to their designs, arising from need for detailed design and specification at the outset of projects. Worst affected were the independent tradesmen who bitterly opposed builders contracting for the whole of the works since it undermined their livelihoods. Their resistance was strongly felt in London, the Midlands and the North in the 1830s.

A form of contract which was to remain influential for a long time was introduced for government barrack building in 1805. Official use of competitive tendering increased (having already been used for procurement of stores for over 20 years by the Board of Ordnance). It was further strengthened by

Commissioners reporting to the public Office of Works in 1812–13. Another official inquiry in 1828 concluded in favour of contracts for whole buildings rather than separate contracts for each trade of bricklayer, carpenter and so on. Opinion, especially outside the industry and for contracts for smaller and simpler buildings, continued to move in the same direction. By mid-century and despite reservations, contracting in gross prevailed widely, although it would not become universal for a very long time [6, 7, 8, 9]. Meanwhile a confused mix of varied practices continued, with innovation often originating in London and only slowly diffusing to outlying parts. Given the extent of the industry it could hardly have been otherwise.

Business units

Further changes were connected with the three ideas of competition, cost estimation in advance, and single responsibility for whole projects. They centred on division of labour between business units or firms: who specialized in what. The industry in 1800 consisted of a mass of firms, each with its own assets, skills and practices. Firms were related in intricate and sensitive networks which, through the period, evolved new relationships and restructured roles and responsibilities. Whether solitary rural carpenter-cum-jobbing builder or powerful London contractor, each was linked to other business units. Links could be of dependency, where one firm was the source of another's work; often they were cash relationships, of payment for services rendered; or they might be voluntary, where knowledge was shared in a trade or professional association. Business units were subject to constraints of size, with the exigencies of both economies and diseconomies of scale. The degree of specialization of business units also was subject to external influences, among them the overall extent of the market.

The whole mass of firms may be seen as a status hierarchy (nineteenth century citizens often saw things this way). At the top was a handful of mostly large firms standing highest in public esteem. Below was a larger number of firms, as likely as not of diminishing size down the hierarchy, held in progressively lower regard. Firms related laterally would mostly perform broadly similar functions. At the foot were many low-status firms. What conferred or withheld public esteem? No doubt it was a combination of factors. A leading influence was proximity to demand from promoters. Firms working remotely from direct demand (brickmakers for example) depended on firms nearer the ultimate source of work. Their dependency gave them lower status. A related influence was prestige through association. For instance a firm working for a large landowner was more highly regarded than one working for, say, a lowly glue boiler. Another influence was capital accumulation. The comfortably-off proprietor ranked above his under-capitalized, marginal brother. Again, firm size, quality of output and business ethics were influential. Positions in the hierarchy were restless and unstable, as fortunes and influence waxed and waned.

PROFESSIONS

At or near the top were the architects. Initially they were hardly distinguishable from builders and measurers and their skill was commonly combined with those of others. From around the 1820s they gradually began to divorce themselves from direct involvement in building. Urged by Sir John Soane, they sought to represent and protect promoters' interests (an influential position in the hierarchy). The emerging building procurement method required firm cost estimates (and hence firm design) at the outset. Consequently architects were employed to provide increasingly detailed drawings, specifications and tender documents. At the same time closer alliance with promoters was achieved at cost of greater distance from practical building production. The foundation of the Institute of British Architects in 1834 enhanced professional standing and helped to discourage older style builder-architects. This early professional grouping followed that of the Institute of Civil Engineers in 1818.

Related changes occurred in the measurement of building work, where measuring after completion was being replaced by more precise measurement before work began. The method was for a group of competing contractors, who had been invited to submit tenders, to appoint a surveyor. He took from the architect's drawings the quantities of materials required. Sometimes two surveyors were employed, one to serve contractors' interests and the other those of the promoter [10]. The new profession of quantity surveyor began to emerge in the 1820s at about the same time that architects started to relinquish direct commercial interest in building. One of the earliest prominent quantity surveyors was Henry Hunt, a well-established figure involved in work on the new Houses of Parliament and other central governments works [11, 12].

FIRMS

Big contractors

Overlapping in the hierarchy with the emerging professionals were the pioneering big building contractors. Although many were better off than professionals, their status was limited by their being engaged in 'trade'. Few in number, they worked mainly on major public works, contracting for whole buildings and employing more or less permanently most of their labour. They were likely to confine subcontracting to busy times and to minor specialized trades for which there was little continuity of work. One of the earliest was Alexander Copland, who earned over £1.3 m. for barrack building between 1796 and 1806. Large firms like this (Copland once employed 700) needed comprehensive establishments and substantial capital, or access to credit.

Thomas Cubitt pioneered one of the first recognisably modern firms [13]. Starting as a London journeyman he set up on his own as a master carpenter about 1809 and in 1815 he contracted to build the London Institution in Finsbury Circus. He soon decided to escape the mercies of subcontractors and invested heavily in workshops and yard and engaged trades-men semi-permanently. In order to support this costly establishment Cubitt depended on continuity of work, which he achieved by large, high-quality housing speculations in Bloomsbury, Belgravia and elsewhere. His exceptional organization consisted of three parts, one for law business and another for financial affairs under the direction of a confid-ential clerk. The third part was a general office staffed by builders' clerks. These versatile jacks-of-all-trades were 'expected to be fully competent to fulfil the several duties of architects, builders, and artisans, to be thorough draughtsmen and accountants and yet to be practically acquainted with work.' Operations were large enough for each trade to be controlled by a principal foreman in charge of other foremen. The firm employed 1,000 men by 1828 and later occupied a 4.5 hectare works. Cubitt died in 1855, to be long outlived by the firm he created.

George Myers was another well-documented London contractor [14]. Born in 1803 in Hull, he started as a stonemason and soon joined Richard Wilson to build houses and carry out paving contracts in their home city. In the late 1830s they won sizeable building contracts in Derby and Loughborough. Myers left Wilson (who later became bank-rupt) and set up in London with works, yard and wharf at

Belvedere Road on the South Bank. He proceeded to complete
many large, high-quality buildings throughout the country. He
built many of A.W.N. Pugin's designs, who preferred to
appoint Myers for contracts rather than go to tender. Myers is
left for the moment, approaching the height of his powers at
mid-century.

Myers' leading rivals were the likes of Grissell, Kelk, Lee and
Piper. Such men who had proved themselves in a tough
testing ground, met and formed the Builders' Society in 1834.
Here was evidence of a maturing sense of the building industry
as an entity, rather than a loose aggregation of craft trades.
Equally it was a sign of group identity among the new calling
of building contractors.

Other firms   Ranking below such men in the hierarchy was a host of lesser
contractors, speculative builders and single trade contractors.
An example who overlapped with the preceeding group was
John Johnson who built up a very large London business in
the early decades of the century. He undertook a variety of
works including brickmaking, housebuilding and property
development in Somers Town, Earls Court, the Grosvenor
Estate, Westminster and elsewhere. He was also a big paving
contractor, regularly earning well over £3,000 a year, and as
much as £12,400 in 1820 from Westminster Paving Commissioners. His increasingly far-flung activities about that time
were based in workshops and dock near Horseferry Road,
Westminster, though vertical integration also led to Dartmoor
quarrying interests [15].

Not many carried on business on Johnson's scale. Below
him were many lesser figures, mostly lost to historical view.
The 1831 census provides an incomplete picture with 871
London builders, and proportionately many fewer in the
country where older, single trade concerns were likely to
survive longest. Only seven builders were listed in the
agricultural county of Berkshire, and nine in Bedfordshire.
Many firms worked partly on contracts for external promoters
and partly on their own speculative housing. Very many
cheaper houses were created by speculative firms, although
this is not to suggest that all speculative work was cheap. Other
firms worked solely on speculation and in doing so ranked
rather below their contractor fellows. These smaller men were
conservative in outlook, doubtless preoccupied with mere
survival in a fiercely competitive world of violent fluctuations.
London housebuilders seldom ventured more than a mile or

two from their yards or, elsewhere, put up more than ten houses a year. On the Mercer's Company estate in Stepney between 1811 and 1850 one builder erected 570 houses, but only two others reached 100 houses each. In 1845 in North Kensington, where it took 31 firms to build 137 houses, two firms built 26 and 28 houses each, but none of the others exceeded 11. The sizeable London firm of Thomas Burton employed an average of 170 men between 1825 and 1832, mostly on repairs and alterations. At the time of the 1851 census nine London firms were said to employ more than 200 men each, and 57 firms each employed 50 or more. Outside London a builder employing more than ten men was regarded as large.

Another stratum of firms in the hierarchy was the single trade concern, either bricklayer, carpenter and joiner, mason, plumber, plasterer, slater, glazier or painter, as the case might be. Some were old-style master craftsmen who might employ a few journeymen, apprentices and labourers. Some would be capable of high-quality work and, together with other trades,

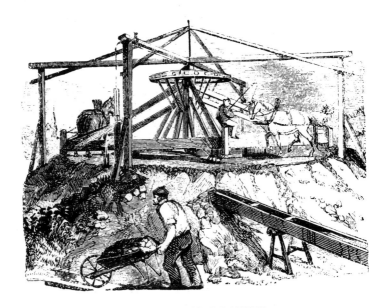

THE BRICKMAKER.

Figure 5 The brickmakers. Pug mill preparing clay for moulding and firing. It looks quite a heavy investment by the standards of materials processing. From *Book of Trades* 1862. (Source: Guildhall Library/ Corporation of London.)

The Plumbers.

Figure 6 The plumbers. Aproned figures melt lead (foreground), carry pipes (left), sheet (upper centre) and fit it in place apparently on balcony or cornice (top right). From *Book of English Trades* 1823. (Source: Guildhall Library/Corporation of London.)

would complete large and prestigious projects. Others had evolved into more capitalistic concerns, employing more men, and undertaking single trade contracts. When the owner of Black Dyke Mills began a £4,700 building in Queensbury in 1835 he let separate contracts for masonry (£585 for stone, £627 for labour), glazing, 'plaistering' and so on. Like some other promoters used his own direct labour for part of the work, in this case the excavations [16].

The life of small firms could be precarious. An instance was 23-year-old James Diment's Bristol painting and plastering firm, founded in 1839. Two years later he moved premises to an adjacent street and then worked for two years with John Grimes, a 41-year-old Derby-born plasterer who lived nearby. The working relationship did not long survive another move in 1843, after which the firm disappeared. Diment reappeared, working alone, from yet another address in 1848. He moved once more in 1851, by which time he employed 35 men. Soon, if not already, he was contracting for whole buildings [17]. Many others followed, or aspired to, the same path, though often into speculative housebuilding rather than contracting. Where single trade firms, usually bricklayers or carpenters, diversified into speculative building they often employed only workmen in their own trade. They subcontracted with others for the remainder of the work in other trades.

The lowest stratum of firms in the hierarchy was likely to be small jobbing builders or tradesmen of various (or few) skills, subsisting on repairs, maintenance and small works. Proprietors were likely to slip in and out of self-employment and, indeed, the industry quite frequently. Of the lowest end Olsen [18] has noted that no one of the time had anything very good to say about the speculative builders, who were themselves generally too busy building (as well as too poorly educated) to speak for themselves. Some subcontractors were so unreliable that general contractors had to pay men direct to ensure that wages reached the right pockets. The ease with which people could enter (and leave) building contrasted with experience in some other industries which required heavier initial investment. That firms could be set up quickly in an ill-considered way was an attraction to men of straw; inevitably there was a heavy harvest of failure.

It was financial and constructional malpractice which often set the tone and reputation of the whole industry. Yet this oversimplified: rogues and incompetents there were, but there were also talented and energetic people who painstakingly founded firms capable of excellent work. They did so under exacting conditions of sharp competition and profound un-certainty. In short the industry embraced an enormous span of ability, from highest to lowest levels of achievement. It is the misfortune of the industry that, with exceptions such as Dove Brothers and some of the examples named above, their memory has been all but lost.

Industry in operation

Having outlined the range of firms, so extraordinarily varied in capability, it is possible, in a sense, to set them in motion. Firms are seen to spring up from humble origins, join forces, split apart and grow and shrink in skill and size. Many acquire new functions, just as Diment did when progressing from lowly painting and plastering to loftier contracting. Some, probably many, overreach themselves at the optimistic peak of the trade cycle and are brought low in the ensuing slump. Some are doomed to end thus (as Wilson was in Hull), but others re-start afresh. So the industry evolved and expanded with effective (or lucky) firms growing and others sinking. The odds were fairly long, so that of one group of firms extant in 1825, 65% survived five years, 47% survived ten years and 16% still existed in 1851. This gave these and slightly later firms a 'half-life' of perhaps ten years [19], short enough, but probably longer than for the average of all new firms in the economy [20].

Amid the frenetic movement of indistinct firms struggling to survive in sharpening competition, patterns are dimly visible. Contractors and builders, undertaking to build whole buildings, emerged, if not triumphant, at least dominant. Old-style master craftsmen already approaching eclipse by 1800 lost further ground. A proliferation of medium-sized and small firms was the main way by which total output of the industry was increased (in contrast to some other more capital intensive and technically innovative industries). A major achievement of the period was the development of business units which could adapt to fluctuating workloads and deliver large, complicated buildings to a minimum price, speedily, anywhere in the country. The scale of this managerial invention, the big contractor, was obscured by innumerable smaller firms doing simpler things.

LABOUR

Trades and skills

The men who worked on site, in shop or yard, possessed a great range of skills which conferred a matching variety of status and wages. At the top were skilled craftsmen, trade specialists who were journeymen having served apprenticeships and from whose ranks small masters arose. Below them were apprentices who learned craft skills while assisting the journeymen, and at the foot of the pyramid, overlapping in income, were a great number of unskilled and semi-skilled labourers who provided the brute force essential to building. A good proportion of the 367,000 unspecified labourers recorded in the 1851 census were connected with building. Here was the casual, tough, and often rough labour which cut foundations, shifted muck and performed the hundred and one heavy tasks in unmechanized construction. The field was a favourite entry point into employment for migrants and particularly for Irish fugitives from famine.

The skills and rewards of masons reflected their eminence among craft tradesmen, particularly in high-quality building work, although elsewhere 'stone cutters' were identified with the less prestigious bricklayers. Carpenters and joiners also held a high place among trades and were numerous. Bricklayers were needed on most sites, too, but seem to have had a slightly lower standing, perhaps reflecting involvement with cheap building. The plastering trade had a lower popular reputation because of a high proportion of men with moderate or low skill. Other trades were the plumbers, slaters, painters, and, in smaller numbers, glaziers and paviors. Trades in materials supply rather than site work included quarrymen, limeburners, sawyers (who suffered with the introduction of steam power), and brickmakers, an unruly group about to face similar change.

The quality of craftsmanship was a cause of anxiety in some quarters. One origin of this was the erosion of craftsmen's autonomy by the growing practice of drawing up full building details in advance of construction. This effectively moved decisions from site and workshop to the designer's office. Once, the craftsmen had decided the details of ornament, staircase and dormer, but now they yielded responsibility to designers. The level of skill exercised on the best work probably remained at least as high as ever. Elsewhere competition may have encouraged short cuts and scamping, while keeping down costs.

Wages

An understanding of wages is hindered by variations from place to place and time to time, depending on local labour market and workload. In the early decades wage-fixing by J.P.s was abolished and piece-rates undermined. The Phelps Brown index of real wages [21] shows a small rise from 1813 to 1820 during a time when prices generally were rising. Between 1820 and 1840 wages were fairly stable, with small gains for those fortunate enough to remain in full employment, and from 1840 to 1849 wages improved somewhat while prices fell slowly. The average London price in 1826 for 'day work', which included nearly 20% allowance for profit, ranged from 40p for well-paid stone carvers (few masons got this much), 32.5p for carpenters and joiners, slightly less for bricklayers and plasterers, down to 27.5p for slaters, plumbers, painters and glaziers [22]. About 10p below were bricklayers' and plasterers' labourers, and at the foot were unskilled labourers. According to Postgate [23] the rate of wages computed on the basis of a ten-hour day between 1826 and 1847 for major trades was 25p. The average wage of operative builders in 1834 was said to be between £1.35 and £1.50 for a 60-hour week. The working week was reduced by one-and-a-half hours in 1847, at which time the hourly rate stood at about 2.3p to 2.5p.

Unemployment due to bad weather or slack trade could at any time reduce earnings. Allowance for loss of earnings due to unemployment among Leeds bricklayers in the late 1830s was said to reduce average wages of £1.15 a week to average earnings of 86.2p [24]. Average figures could conceal wide differences between one place and another, as when unskilled London labourers received 15p a day while those in depressed rural areas had to make do with no more than 8.75p. In general, wages (if not always earnings) in building compared reasonably well with those in other industries. Building craftsmen, if not among the labour 'aristocrats', at least were among the 'respectable' skilled workers. In the 1840s near the top of the income scale, skilled Manchester engineering ironmoulders earned £1.70 to £1.80 a week, which was only about 25p more than the major building trades [25]. It was less than the best-paid masons and bricklayers working on intricate oven-work and the like. Near the bottom of the scale, where agricultural labourers could expect about 51.5p a week, semi-skilled building labourers earned about 80p, incentive enough to forsake the land for a new life building the town.

Working conditions

The working life of highly skilled craftsmen was quite good by the robust standards of the times and as yet sheltered from many of the effects of industrialization. Helped in part by combination, they were fairly secure and quite well rewarded, unlike the unskilled labourers and apprentices, whose lot was more bleak. Their lives and those of the elderly were often threatened by loss of livelihood. Slackening activity, flood of migrant labour, introduction of new machinery, faltering health, a capricious master or merely a spell of bad weather could bring loss of income. An example comes from Bolton during the severe depression of 1841–2, when two-thirds of the masons were said to be without work, together with well over four-fifths of the carpenters and bricklayers. When work was available it was sometimes dangerous, often strenuous and always prolonged, though not necessarily any more so than in other industries. When work was not to be found there was the prospect of tramping in the hope of finding it elsewhere. The leading trades had a system of providing cheap temporary lodgings in major towns for use by tramping journeymen [26]. By mid-century the masons' system, which had allowed men 2.5p a day, was in decay and those of other trades soon followed.

Another possible escape from the unemployment which even skilled men could expect in winter was to try speculative building on their own account [27]. The inexperience and unsuitability of some men, driven by desperation, may well explain some of the frequent business failures.

Organization The Combination Laws of the time around 1800 were repealed in 1824 and trade union growth followed. The collective organization of building labour appears to have been patchy,

The Stone Mason.

Figure 7 The stone mason. Aristocrat of craftsmen suitably well turned out working on ornate moulding. Seated figure (left background) wields an impressive saw on a large stone block. From *Book of English Trades* 1823. (Source: Guildhall Library/Corporation of London.)

The Carpenter.

Figure 8 The carpenter. Unmechanized labour in full swing. Variety of hand tools are visible. Panelled door awaits delivery while carpenter's mate is seen through unglazed window aperture precariously placing rafters. From *Book of English Trades* 1823. (Source: Guildhall Library/Corporation of London.)

all the more so because surviving evidence is fragmentary. Some local groups of skilled men formed builders' operatives' clubs, which seem to have led relatively quiet existences free from much conflict with masters. Such clubs suffered the disruptions of violent fluctuations in activity which alternately flooded trades with new semi-skilled recruits and then plunged many into unemployment. Early trade union activity, typically at local rather than national level, included some strikes staged by the journeymen carpenters' society [28]. In 1832, the ambitious, but shortlived Operative Builders' Union was formed and developed a connection with Robert Owen, but it collapsed within two years. Although it took with it some craft organizations and weakened others, the masons' union survived to remain one of the most stable in a harsh and turbulent climate. In 1841 and 1842, the Operative Stone-masons' Society was embroiled in a stoppage on the site of the new Houses of Parliament. The conflict serves to exemplify the bitter relations between employers and men which often arose in the period. When the dispute was eventually resolved the Stonemasons' Society went on under Richard Harnott to construct a centralized and forward-looking union [29, 30].

MATERIALS, COMPONENTS AND PROCESSES

Stone

Building materials are relevant here for two reasons: first, many were the responsibility of builders to fashion into the finished forms in buildings and as such were not the products of a separate industry; second, materials were a major factor input into building, alongside labour costs. In general, materials prices rose during the Napoleonic War and fell in the era of ever-freer trade to the 1840s. Despite this fall, however, overall building prices fell less than prices generally.

The atmosphere of change and experiment in business units scarcely went as far as site work, where most operatives used similar skills to those of their forefathers. The example of stone well illustrates the changelessness of much building work. The walls of many high-quality buildings were of ashlar; many cheaper examples were of rubble (which embodied less labour), and stone flags were widely used. Sources of stone included a few large quarries trading nationally in high-quality materials, such as the Portland group, where 800 people produced 25,000 tons annually. Elsewhere there were many small and intermittently used quarries, for example, in most Cotswold villages. Nationally, stones ranged from prestigious granites to lowly sandstone rubble and chalk. In the mid-1820s, Portland and Painswick limestones cost about £8.83 per cu.m including transport to London, but excluding carriage to site. In country districts, rough rubble walling cost as little as 88p per cu.m. This great differential partly reflected high transport costs of all bulk materials. For example, in 1839 Ketton stone at the quarry near Stamford cost £3.01 per cu.m but delivered to London it was £5.89. Inland waterways could bring down rates to about one-third of overland charges [31], and had the important effect of reducing local price differences. Railways began to accentuate the same trend.

Some stones were also used as roof finishes, particularly during the early decades. After that they ceased to be competitive with other materials, some of which benefited from lifting of taxes in the early 1830s. North Wales slate cost in the mid-1820s between £2 and £3.35 for 9.3 sq.m (100 sq.ft) of roof complete with boarding and nails; rather more than clay tiles. The decline of stone and rise of slate exemplified a general trend in materials use. Early in the period typical roofs (where not thatched) were finished with variably sized units of considerable weight and thickness. At mid-century typical roofs had regular sized units of some precision and weighing perhaps only one-fifth of earlier types. Similar, or better, performance was being achieved with less material and site labour, using goods brought further from their sources.

Brick and tile

Bricks possessed the attractive property of cheapness, provided there were local supplies of fire-clay. A result of this and other practical advantages was that their use increased greatly, so that quinquennial average production beginning in 1845 (1,749 m.) was more than double that beginning in 1800 (711 m.). More building (and civil engineering) appears to have been carried out in brick than ever before, but it is not easy to be sure whether brick was maintaining or increasing its share of the walling market. Observation suggests that brick increased its share for cheaper work, although it may not have made equal progress in higher-quality building.

Brickwork made up a large proportion of total costs of typical buildings, estimated [32], together with carpentry and joinery, at not less than two-thirds in new houses in the first decade of the century. In a large house built at Deal, the bricklaying and plastering amounted to 42% (£362) of the total cost, carpentry 50%, and painting and glazing about 4%. The cost of completed brickwork was mainly in the materials, with labour charges considerably less. An estimate for new houses near Birmingham in 1810 showed the proportion spent on brickwork materials was 27%, and timber materials 23%, while main labour charges were only 23% altogether. Until 1850 there was a tax on bricks, which must have prolonged the competitiveness of various alternatives such as stone and timber cladding. The rate of duty payable from 1803 was 25 p per thousand bricks, rising to 29.2p from 1833. This was a sizeable proportion of the prime cost, which in the mid-1820s ranged from about £1.60p per thousand for cheap London place bricks for foundations and party walls, up to £6.50 for best stocks. High-quality brick walling, including lime, sand, labour, use of scaffolding and 15% profit, was estimated at £4.86 per cu.m, considerably cheaper than good stonework.

There were many brickworks and their average size was small with activity local, technically simple and often transitory. Clay was dug direct from the building site if possible and where not, a brickfield nearby was sometimes leased to supply a contract. Elsewhere independent brickmakers acted as suppliers on a more permanent basis for series of projects. In London, the largest single market, demand exceeded local capacity and supplies were brought from outlying Essex, Kent and Middlesex to add to the products of Islington, Fulham and Hammersmith. Brickmakers, working in an expanding market in which competition was limited by transport costs, increased output by multiplying the numbers of suppliers. Early attempts at mechanization in the 1830s were sometimes violently opposed by labourers whose jobs were threatened [33].

Many clay tiles were made alongside bricks. The two main types of tile were plain and the larger pantiles. The estimated cost in London in the mid-1820s of 9.3 sq.m (100 sq.ft) of roof, including laths, nails and labour, was £2.94 for plain tiles and £1.82 for pantiles. Among other clay products were floor tiles and chimney pots.

Cob and thatch

In inaccessible places with high transport costs, old building practices [34] survived. Cheap materials were not only taken directly from the site itself, or nearly so, but avoided as far as possible the use of heat in processing. There is little record of quantities or costs of such materials, but by their nature they were labour- and skill-intensive. Among the walling materials were mud, pisé and clay lump using various combinations of earth, lime, chalk, chopped straw, gravel and sand [35]. For roofing the choice was likely to be reed, straw or heather thatch. It is probable that the use of these materials fell relatively and absolutely, quickest in areas of population growth, slowest in remote upland areas.

Timber

Timber had many uses, in few of which it could be substituted by other materials. It also recycled easily from demolished buildings into new ones, a practice much favoured among poor, small buildings (and usually ended by terminal recycling into the fireplace). Nearly all roof structures used timber, and so did suspended foors, doors and fittings. Other uses included stud walls, lintels, claddings, window frames and stairs; there were also important temporary uses such as scaffolding and arch centring. Building, as well as other uses, were heavily dependent on imports, which climbed accordingly. The average annual value of imports for the five years from 1846 was over one-and-a-half times that for the five years from

1826. Following great increases during the Napoleonic Wars, timber prices were relatively steady, with softwood around 1815 at £6 or £7 for a 1.4 cu.m (50 cu.ft) load, including duty. Cheapest pine at £4.50 a load contrasted sharply with West Indian mahogany at over ten times that figure. English oak, where it could be found near the site, was competitive with best imported softwood, but elsewhere transport costs pushed up the price. Where there were no navigable waterways, and before the railways were built, overland timber transport often added a sixth or a quarter to costs, encouraging reuse of old timbers (and other materials) wherever possible. When the prime cost of softwood stood at £6.67 a load, the price on site in London used in lintels and bonding timbers was estimated at £8.10 per cu.m, and planed on all faces £8.98 per cu.m. Powered machines for sawing and planing had been pioneered in the eighteenth century and new machines gradually began to supplant the work of skilled craftsmen, especially towards mid-century [36].

Cement, plaster and other materials

Some product development took place with masonry bonding agents and surface finishes. Traditional lime mortar [37] began to be replaced on a small scale where conditions were onerous by the stronger Parker's hydraulic Roman cement and, later, Portland cement, production of which expanded in the 1840s [38]. Renderings for external walls, encouraged by the first London Building Act (which was concerned with incombustibility) and by fashion, increasingly embodied patent products such as Dehl's mastic, patented in 1815. Internal walls were finished generally in plaster, sometimes decorated with paper costing in 1825 from 1.7p to 5p or more for 0.91 m length, 0.5 m wide (36 × 20 in.), with extra for labour. This could cost more than four coats of paint on woodwork of the same area, costing about 4.87p per sq.m.

A miscellany of materials remains, most of which were quite highly processed, carried far and used in relatively small quantities. Glass production became concentrated and excise duty was repealed in the 1840s, reducing prices. Other materials included lead, fairly widely used for roofing, flashings, pipework and cisterns, despite high and fluctuating costs; copper, for some of the same applications; and zinc, a cost-saving substitute for lead from about 1830 [39]. In the still rudimentary field of services, glazed ware and cast iron increasinlgy replaced wooden pipes; WCs were a rarity, costing up to £6.30 complete with valve apparatus in the 1820s; and various patterns of kitchen range costing about £1 for every 300 mm of width, in the 1840s. Cast iron was used for balconies, balustrades and window frames [40], gradually replacing the more costly wrought product. Among heavy iron items in the 1820s were structural columns and beams, costing from 75p per 51 kg (1 cwt), and helical stairs. Among remaining products, concluding this chapter at the basement floor, were mastic asphalt, introduced in 1837, and bitumen pavings.

3

Building and the triumph of urbanization: 1851–1914

The increase in population has led to a brick-and-mortar crusade which is defiling every green spot near the town.

(*The Builder*, 1862)

DEMAND AND BUILDING PROMOTERS

Growth of stock

The growing national economy vigorously generated a need for new buildings, suburbs and whole towns, on a scale never before seen in Britain. Expansion of manufacture, trade and social institutions always meant investment in buildings; the two were mutually dependent. Sometimes expansion was in large increments, giving rise to large and costly buildings, but more often it was in numerous smaller increments, giving rise to appropriately small and commonplace buildings. Today, the only reminder of many of the people and methods underlying the provision of terraces, industrial sheds, small shops and cottages is a shrinking stock of obsolescent buildings.

Speculative building

As markets expanded so did opportunities for speculative building and the scale which it could be carried out. It is likely that more larger developers were able to systematize their activities; not that small men were forced out. One example of making decisions to build in later Victorian towns comes from Cardiff during a phase of spectacularly rapid growth after 1870 [1]. Most building land was owned by three large estates, whose development policy was to lease building sites for 99 years. This practice resembled that in London prior to the exhaustion of major estate land supplies by about 1870 [2], and in some other districts; in many other places land was sold freehold. Strict control of the quality of Cardiff development was enforced by estate officials whose activity in this way approximated to modern town planning control. Most building was by small firms which built houses as speculation, hoping to sell quickly to pay off debts and move on to fresh ventures. Their sources of short-term credit are uncertain, but included mortgages given by solicitors (at least before the 1890s), insurance companies and building societies. Buyers of new houses, who thereby provided the necessary long-term investment, were local people seeking safe outlets for small amounts of capital. They chose to keep an eye on their assets, rather than invest in other places where returns could be higher. Such investors appear hardly ever to have been in short supply; when building flagged it was likely to be due to problems with short-term credit or finding tenants able to pay economic rents. About nine out of ten houses were let rather than owner-occupied, and ownership was widely spread. Only about a quarter to a third of houses were owned by investors holding more than ten houses each, and only six men held more than 50 houses each.

Custom building

A contrasting approach to the decision to build was at Bromborough, near Birkenhead [3], where the Wilson brothers decided to move part of the Price's Patent Candle Company in 1853. Their motives were several: their Battersea site was unhealthy and fully developed; and they wished to reduce transport costs both to their principal market in Lancashire, and from their raw materials source, which was imports through Liverpool docks. A new works, houses, school and other facilities were built, one example among many of 'footloose' capital searching for a suitable site after the decision to build had been taken. In this case site choice was based on economics of industrial location, but there were innumerable other cases in which promoters also decided what to build in advance of where to build it. For example, many schools and tenement blocks had locations determined by social need and chance factors such as the availability of sites. This sequence of building decision before site decision was the reverse of that in Cardiff where estate owners took the first step in development before it was known what sort of buildings eventually would appear. Another distinction was that Bromborough was a case in which buildings were likely (though not necessarily) to be custom-built under contract. Cardiff, on the other hand, was a case in which buildings were likely (again not necessarily) to be speculatively built. It was the speculative approach which continued to be dominant throughout the country.

Institutional investment

Although most promoters continued to be local people operating in their home towns, changes were afoot. The average scale of projects probably increased in sympathy with capital accumulation and the size of organizations which were accommodated. Decisions to build began to migrate, as it were from drawing room to board room. The shift, where it occurred, was from entrepreneur and principal to members of the board and management committee, from individual to collective decisions. While capital continued to flow into building from private individuals, much in the form of advances to speculative builders from landlords, there were also institutional sources. For better quality London housing, particularly before the 1880s, insurance companies made capital available [4], and building societies were widely active. Older terminating societies gave way to permanent ones, although the primitive pattern persisted for some time. The evolution of societies was gradual, hampered by financially doubtful forms such as the Starr-Bowkett societies, falling property values in the 1880s and occasional dishonesty. Acts of Parliament intended to regulate the societies were passed in 1874 and 1894, at which time total assets of incorporated societies were £42 m. [5].

Another of the institutional sources of capital were the early property companies such as the City of London Real Property Company founded in 1864. This joint stock concern had property which grew from an original £330,000 to £2.5 m. by 1914 [6]. The activities of such firms formed a relatively small proportion of all building activity, like one other category of promoters, the local authorities. These augmented the efforts of other non-profit-making promoters, namely central authority, churches, individual benefactors and philanthropists, and charitable trusts. Their activities increased in total, particularly late in the period, but did not challenge the established dominance of promoters motivated by profit.

Geographical distribution

The geographical location of building activity was concentrated heavily in towns. At mid-century an approximate numerical balance had been reached between the urban population of 9.0 m. and the rural one of 8.9 m., but by 1911 the figures had changed to 28.2 m. in the towns and only 7.9 m. in the country. The proportions of urban and rural dwellers had been reversed during the course of the century. The largest single concentration of population, and hence buildings, in 1911 was of course London where there were 7,256,000 in the conurbation as a whole. Birmingham was the next largest city (840,000), followed by Liverpool (746,000), Manchester (714,000) and Sheffield (455,000). The order had changed since 1851, but the only newcomer among the largest five was Sheffield. The growing dominance of the largest towns is seen in an index of population growth [7], taking 1851 as the base year with an index of 100. The index for 84 great towns in 1901 was 254, compared with 169 for the rest of England and Wales, and a fall to 95.5 for typical rural counties. The percentage growth rates of the largest towns, despite their quantitative dominance, moderated from the peaks attained before mid-century. To be sure, there was a new generation of very rapidly growing places which sprang up later in the century. One example, the Rhondda Valleys, grew from 8,000 in 1861 to 56,000 in 1881, but later-developing centres such as this did not go on to challenge the size of the older great towns.

Continued growth of some neighbouring centres led to their merging to create huge continuous settlements. London was such a conurbation by the early nineteenth century, and other places followed later. Boundaries were blurred and made meaningless as the scale of apparently limitless growth surpassed all precedent.

Population

One of the most powerful forces which drove demand for new buildings was population growth. Within limits, the more people there were, the more buildings were required. The following table shows the intensity of that stimulus through the century.

Population growth in England and Wales, 1801–1911 (thousands) [8]

1801	8,900	1861	20,100
1811	10,200	1871	22,700
1821	12,000	1881	26,000
1831	13,900	1891	29,000
1841	15,900	1901	32,500
1851	17,900	1911	36,100

Business activity

Another key driving force acting on building demand was business activity. Until about 1873, this was generally high and, as yet, unchallenged by overseas competition to call into question apparently irresistible material progress. After 1873 there were more than two decades of less ebullient prosperity, when the rate of economic growth was retarded. Frustrated expectations led to the overstating sobriquet 'great depression', although optimism eventually revived somewhat to make the years from 1896 to 1914 an Indian summer. A measure of UK expansion is seen in the tripling of gross national income in the half-century after 1851, from £523 m. to £1,643 m. While the long-term trend in building demand was upward, an important shorter-term influence was the attractiveness or otherwise of investment in building. Investment might be made in the light of use value, the utility of the building in furthering dependent ends such as providing goods or services. Or it might be in the light of exchange value, what the building would realize when completed. Potential promoters weighed returns from investment in building with those possible from a growing number of other outlets for capital, such as joint-stock companies and overseas investments. What had once been purely local building investment decisions became more and more bound up with national and eventually international events. In this light, the choice facing a potential promoter might lie between new houses in Hoxton and a railway in Argentina. Better-informed promoters were distributing resources more efficiently, but building was having to compete more strenuously for a share of national wealth.

Health and welfare

Increase in national wealth was unmistakable, with UK gross domestic product per person not far from doubling between 1855 and 1900–1913 (£26 and over £45 respectively, at constant 1913 prices). Rising real incomes, at least until the early twentieth century, meant that some people were able to afford better accommodation than their parents. Although the increment of enhanced spending power was not all that large, it was bound to affect building demand. A wealthier society was able to devote more not only to personal consumption, but also to public provision in health, welfare, education, administration and the like. As a result, promoters diversified and the balance among them began to shift. After about 1870, and particularly in the last decade or so, local authority promotion of various types of building was established alongside that of central government as another source of public sector building. It was a small but significant start to the task of narrowing the abyss between effective demand and social need for buildings.

Volume

The total volume of new building was vast: the estimated value of buildings as a percentage of the national capital of Great Britain went up from 22% in 1885 to 26% in 1912, a proportion almost double that of the early 1830s. UK gross domestic fixed capital formation in dwellings and industrial and commercial buildings expanded from £17.64 m. a year average (at constant 1920 prices) in the quinquennium 1851–55, to a peak of £41.46 m. in 1876–80. After an ensuing fall the next peak was in 1901–05, at £61.26 m. [9]. The proportion of the buildings-related component in g.d.f.c. was calculated in the following table, in which Column (3) includes a sizeable but unknown proportion of non-building items.

Building activity continued to proceed in fluctuations now more influenced by international events than in the first half of the century [10, 11]. While non-residential activity corresponded with fluctuations in the business cycle, the greater part of all building, house building, developed a pattern of its own. House-building cycles were longer and more extreme than the fluctuations in national investment in general. The national

Gross domestic fixed capital formation by type of asset, UK, 1851–1915 (% of total g.d.f.c, quinquennial averages at 1920 prices)

	(1) Dwellings	(2) Industrial & commercial bldgs.	(3) Other non-residential bldgs. & works	(4) Total of buildings & works	(5) Cols (1) + (2)
1851–55	18.4	9.9	39.8	68.2	28.3
1856–60	14.4	11.0	43.7	69.2	25.4
1861–65	14.4	8.8	42.9	66.1	23.2
1866–70	19.9	10.6	36.6	67.2	30.5
1871–75	21.7	12.6	32.7	67.0	34.3
1876–80	23.4	10.5	34.7	68.6	33.9
1881–85	20.1	8.3	36.1	64.6	28.4
1886–90	19.6	9.8	33.3	62.7	29.4
1891–95	18.6	10.0	31.3	59.8	28.6
1896–1900	20.7	10.3	27.3	58.4	31.0
1901–5	18.3	9.3	27.5	55.0	27.6
1906–10	16.9	10.1	25.3	52.4	27.0
1911–15	8.5	12.6	21.4	42.5	21.1

(Table calculated from Feinstein, C.H. and Pollard, S. (eds) (1988) *Studies in Capital Formation in the UK 1750–1920* Clarendon, Table X p. 446.)

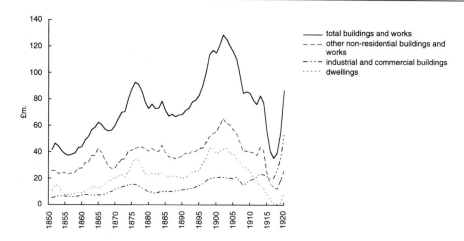

Figure 9 Building-related gross domestic fixed capital formation by type of asset UK 1851–1920 (£m. per annum, at constant 1920 prices). (Source: C.H. Feinstein and S. Pollard (eds) *Studies in Capital Formation in the UK 1750–1920* by permission of Oxford University Press.)

pattern of house building activity, seen in Parry Lewis's index [12], was one of growth to a peak around 1876, after which activity fell away rapidly at first, then more slowly to a trough in 1890. It then picked up to reach a peak in 1898, falling to a very low level before 1914. Local departures from this pattern remained wide [13, 14].

ADDITIONS TO BUILDING STOCK

Housing

The continuing dominance of house building is underlined by comparing the value of output with that of commercial and public building. In 1907 the figure for housing was estimated to be £28 m., compared with £16.5 m. for commercial and public building [15]; and at other times, too, housing generally dwarfed all other types of building together. The great importance of house building may be seen in its percentage of total gross domestic fixed capital formation. For every quinquennium from 1851 in the UK it never fell below 14.4% (in 1856–60 and 1861–65), and the mean for the six decades was 18.9%. This was down slightly (from 21.6%) compared with the period 1801–50. The numbers of dwellings built in Great Britain per decade moved from 579,000 in 1851–60 to a peak of 1,049,000 in 1871–80, followed by a slackening in the ensuing decade, and then on to another peak in 1901–10 of 1,311,000. The mean for the six decades was 942,000. Feinstein and Pollard's index of dwelling size and quality (1900 = 100) stood at 66 in the decade 1851–60 and advanced without break to 101.2 in 1901–10 [16].

Promoters   Most of the considerable output of houses was speculatively built, although there were exceptions in the custom-built houses of the better-off. There was a little non-speculative house building, too, by industrialists whose employees might otherwise have lacked shelter or proved recalcitrant. Pioneering enterprises which were obliged to build houses in remote upland parts such as Merthyr Tydfil early in the century, were joined later by some lowland employers such as those at Swindon and Wolverton. Minor house building inspired by philanthropy mixed to a lesser or greater extent with self-interest took place in the countryside and in industrial colonies such as Saltaire (1851) and New Earswick (1903). Related motives underlay bodies such as the Peabody Trust (1862), at their most active in London from the 1850s to the 1880s. By 1914 they had built about 100,000 rooms for London artisans, little more than enough to absorb the population growth of two years.

More significant were the building societies which, we saw, grew up by degrees into sizeable permanent (or would-be permanent) institutions with interests over quite large districts. In the process they shifted emphasis from direct promotion of specific building projects towards helping individual investors. In doing so they became a major means by which private savings were channelled into speculatively built houses.

A minor source of houses was the local authorities, pioneered by Liverpool with the St Martin's Cottages tenement scheme of 1869. Subsequent national progress was slow despite Housing Acts in 1890 and 1909, although by 1914 Liverpool had completed nearly 3,000 dwellings and there were 12,000 in London. Despite opposition by private interests, many Edwardian local authorities were called upon to supplement the flagging efforts of speculative builders. By 1914 about 5% of house building was said to be in public hands, with a prospect of heavier commitment ahead.

Local authorities built small numbers of dwellings within the reach of the 'respectable' part of the working class. New construction for the cheap end of the housing market was supplied mostly with speculative through terraces, as successors to the court and back-to-back types which appeared in diminishing numbers. Low-cost houses of the third quarter of the century typically cost rather less than £100 each. In Liverpool, three-room cottages with cellars, having 3.7 m frontage and 4.1 m depth, cost from £80 to £110 to build [17]. In the 1850s at Copley, near Halifax, one-bedroom houses were built for £90 and £100 [18], while for £120 there were stone back-to-backs with cellar, generous living room with adjoining scullery, and two bedrooms. Some terraced houses in nearby Saltaire cost £100 to build and gave employees of Titus Salt a cellar and basement pantry, 16.9 sq.m living room, 11.7 sq.m scullery and three bedrooms. Enlightened opinion of the mid-1860s held that this was the lower cost limit for a 'decent cottage' in a town, although many inferior cottages were run up much more cheaply. Well-paid workers, like Salt's overlookers, could expect a terrace house costing about £200 with an ornate frontage, a basement wash-house, pantry and coal cellar, a ground floor parlour (23.0 sq.m) and kitchen (18.9 sq.m), a first floor with three or more bedrooms, and a back yard with separate WC and ashpit.

The average quality of the cheapest new houses improved with time, partly as a result of legislation, so as to resemble increasingly the example above. High quality respecting floor area, room numbers, and provision of services gradually raised average costs. In 1890 some Birmingham municipal cottages consisting of living room (15.7 sq.m), kitchen (10.0 sq. m), pantry, flush WC, two bedrooms and attic, cost £175 each. By 1913 workmen's cottages were said to range from about £150 to £240, and from 60p to £1.00 per cu.m [19].

Artisans' multi-storey tenement blocks were inherently more expensive than houses, but made higher densities possible on valuable urban sites. A six-storey London scheme for the Improved Industrial Dwellings Co. in 1870 had 294 dwellings of three rooms and a scullery each (£162 per dwelling) and 359 dwellings of two rooms and a scullery (£108 each). The equivalent cost per room of £54 was low compared with others in London in the 1890s, which ranged from £83 to £138 per room. Tenement building was estimated in 1913 at £65 to £100 per room (£1.20 to £1.32 per cu.m) in London, and £60 to £90 elsewhere.

Rural house building was generally cheaper than urban, for not only were building wages less (as, indeed, were land costs), but building quality could be lower. This followed lower expectations and purchasing power of rural householders, and less rigorous by-law control outside the towns [20]. At mid-century costs ranged from about £40 for two-room cottages up to £100 for four rooms. Where speculative investment was inadequate, landowners often built, some to higher standards. The Duke of Bedford built four- and five-room estate cottages around mid-century for between £90 and £100 each. In the last quarter of the century Birch [21] thought that rural labourers' cottages of quite high quality, with porch, living room, scullery, pantry, fuel store, privy and three bedrooms, could be built for between £113 and £200 – a wide range, possibly reflecting his desire to impress potential clients. Building activity declined over time, but costs had not changed dramatically in 1913 when attractive examples of four-room cottages in short terraces cost £112 each, perhaps about 66p per cu.m altogether.

The sharpest possible contrast to this sort of residential building was provided by large country houses which each accommodated a small community. Their peak was reached in the early 1870s [22] when, in five years, 74 large houses were begun, more than double the figure for the five years from 1835. For every house of this quality and size, perhaps 6,000 meaner specimens were built in the early 1870s. A particularly impressive example straddling good times and less rosy ones in the 1880s was Eaton Hall, near Chester, on which the Duke of Westminster lavished no less than £600,000. A later example was the smaller, but still considerable Castle Drogo, Devon, begun in 1910, but not finished for 20 years. The owner allowed £50,000 (with another £10,000 for the garden), enough for 300 or more labourers' cottages. This vast gulf in quality was bridged by the houses of the middle class.

New houses for lower middle class families overlapped in quality with those of 'respectable' artisans. Above them came the more costly, but fewer houses of the ever-growing numbers of the comfortably off. A view of the lower end of this market in 1857 was that four- or six-room houses cost about £50 for each room of 4.3 × 3.7 m. It followed that a house with a basement kitchen and scullery, two ground floor rooms and two bedrooms would cost £300 or more. A ten-room house was likely to be more expensive per room, with a cost near the upper limit of speculative building, of the order of £800 to £1,000, although some were less. Houses built around 1860, ranging from the smallest of 176 sq.m costing about £500 up to the largest of over 700 sq.m and most expensive costing up to £2,800, had a typical unit cost per sq.m of £3.75.

A £3,000 'relatively modest country house' of 1899 included a billiard hall, conservatory, veranda, drawing room, dining room, ten bedrooms, two nurseries and servants' quarters. Here was lavishness not available to many; for every house costing that much there were very many similar to an example in Gidea Park, Essex, in 1912. Although termed a cottage it cost £900 and had porch, sitting room, hall, lobby, dining room, kitchen, scullery, larder, two WCs, four bedrooms and a bathroom. In the following year the estimated cost of 'villas' lay between £1.20 and £1.50 per cu.m and the most expensive houses from £1.75 to £2.20.

Industrial and commercial buildings

Building for industry and commerce advanced with generally vigorous business foundation and expansion, with peaks of activity in the early 1870s and early in the new century. In manufacturing and processing, the amount of capital invested per employee increased. Processes once carried out outdoors with only a few simple hand tools and many men now needed workshops, boilerhouse and engine room, equipment and fewer employees, for greater output. The heavy industries of coal, shipbuilding, engineering, iron and steel achieved the commanding position in the economy held by textiles at mid-century. While these industries increased impressively, under-lying the progress from the last quarter of the century was a conservatism which began to prolong the life of obsolescent buildings and equipment. In some other fields more progressive attitudes prevailed: rising real incomes stimulated demand for consumer goods, giving rise to factories for flow production, for example of foodstuffs and clothing; elsewhere scientific approaches were applied to processing dyes, rubber, oil and other products; engineering expanded from basic foundries to precision machine tool shops; chemical works poured forth acid, soda, bleach and fertilizers. Older industries such as papermaking, printing, brewing and milling also benefited from growing markets, and by the turn of the century emerging industries included cycle, electrical and motor concerns.

The unfurling list of manufacturers was matched by commercial and service enterprises which controlled, administered, accounted and marketed. They were stimulated by the number and size of firms and their increasingly complicated and numerous transactions. There were diverse retailing activities, from corner shops to public houses and opulent department stores. Again, there were banks, insurance companies, company headquarters, branches and the offices of a growing number of professions and agencies which provided services to businesses, the public and to each other [23]. Another sector was commercial entertainment, with music halls and extravagant theatres. The variety of building need was almost unending.

Economic and social change was reflected in the types of buildings [24] for which tenders were published in contemporary periodicals. Random examples from the 1860s included industrial projects, in which to manufacture goods, such as an engine house and chimney in Hull costing £1,200; an 'earthenware manufactory' in Great Fenton, Stoke-on-Trent, costing £6,400; and Brighton railway workshops costing about the same. Later, the growth of consumer purchasing power is seen, for example in a tiny aerated water factory in Devizes, Wiltshire, costing £300 in 1886. The continuing rise of consumer spending is suggested by a 1913 Battersea ice factory costing £7,000. The marriage of rising household expenditure and new technology is visible in 1894 electricity generating stations at Great Yarmouth (£2,600) and Wolverhampton (£5,200). Nineteen years later one at Wallasey cost as much as £65,000, by which time they were estimated at 90 p to £1.20 per cu.m. This was little more than both 'plain factories' at 75 p to 90 p and low-cost housing.

Buildings for goods storage could be great, like a group of Cripplegate warehouses in 1876 for £19,000, or small, as in any backyard store. The unit costs of warehouses were considerable, from £1.50 to £1.75 per cu.m. in Edwardian times. Simpler structures could be had down to 80p, and corrugated iron shedding was only 50p to 65p. Impressive structures for large markets and exchanges had matching prices, as in the case of Broderick's Leeds Corn Exchange of 1861, for which tenders ranged upwards from £12,000. Stores and markets were serviced by short-distance transport requiring stables and coach houses, and here a national fondness for animals was reflected in what was paid for their shelter. In 1913, new fitted stables cost from 90p to £1.50 per cu.m compared, it was noted above, with only 60p to £1.00 for workmen's cottages. Not many stables can have rivalled the cost of the London General Omnibus Co. Ltd premises at Bromley, Bow, which cost £3,600 in 1876.

New, bigger commercial buildings were demanded in urban centres to house predominantly locally owned businesses. Banks became key examples, costing for a simple one £2,000 in the 1860s. A larger example was the West of England and South Wales District Bank, Cardiff, with 13.7 × 7.6 m banking room, basement, clerks' rooms, and eight-bedroom manager's accommodation, for £7,000. A sample of eight bank projects carried out between 1860 and 1911 had a mean value of £3,500. Such projects as these were small compared with some high-quality offices priced at £30,000 or £40,000 apiece in the 1860s, though many were far cheaper. Half-a-century later banks with offices or flats over them cost much the same as luxury houses, from £2.00 to £2.28 per cu.m. A few years later offices were said to range widely between £1.30 and £3.50 per cu.m or more; in the third quarter of the nineteenth century major Whitehall government offices had cost around £1.75 per cu.m.

Shop projects ranged upwards from near-domestic unit costs. The mean cost of five shop buildings (three in the West End) by the same contractor late in the century was £8,500. Nearly all promoters were local, but multiple retailers began to emerge in the 1870s and large department stores followed in the 1890s. New standards were set by Selfridge's Oxford Street store of 1909, with eight levels on a 75 × 50 m floor [25].

Hotels, public houses and theatres were more built evidence of the advance of consumers, both humble and conspicuous. Hotels varied as much in size and cost as other building types. A small example in Malvern designed in 1861 cost £5,800, while the much larger Victoria Hotel, Bradford, of a few years later cost £18,600. Even this was thoroughly overshadowed by the mighty Brighton Palace Hotel proposed in 1886 with 250 bedrooms on nine floors and estimated at £120,000. Succeeding schemes vied with each other in size and luxury and by 1913 hotel costs per cu.m. were in about the same range as offices. 'Taverns' ranged from near-domestic scale and unit cost up to £4,000 or more in the 1870s, reaching as much as £30,000 by the turn of the century. Some theatres and music halls were among the most sumptuous of buildings. The 1856 Surrey Gardens Music Hall costing £18,000 paled into insignificance when compared with D'Oyly Carte's Opera House which seated 2,000 (plus 300 standing) in 1891 for a cost of £150,000. Ten theatres built between 1876 and 1897 [26] cost from £65 per place for the lavish example above, down to less than £6 per place at the doubtfully named Grand, Islington, but only three examples exceeded £20 per place. By 1913 increasing numbers of rivals were appearing, with 500 'electric theatres' already in London and suburbs, and new provincial examples costing up to £3,000 each.

Social and welfare buildings

Public buildings such as barracks, workhouses, churches, schools and hospitals formed highly visible additions to stock, but not an overwhelming proportion of total expenditure on building. Mid-Victorian civic pride and identity often found expression by architectural means, as in the celebrated case of rivalry recorded by Asa Briggs and manifested in Leeds Town Hall and St George's Hall, Bradford. Improvement and modernization on a lesser scale were accomplished in many towns such as Middlesbrough where there were 'fine public buildings of the kind that grow up with the development of a municipality: a Town Hall, a Free Library, the various offices of the corporation, churches, schools . . .' [27]. Public buildings were promoted variously by central and local government and voluntary sources, both individual and collective. The purposes served by public buildings were progressively diversified so that monumental examples were increasingly joined by mundane fire stations, tramway depots and the like. The growth of public authority activity is seen by comparing their average annual expenditure with that of consumers: in the 1860s they spent about one-sixteenth that of consumers, rising to one-tenth in the decade after 1900.

A leading field of central government spending was barrack building. At Chatham in 1861, for example, a project for 500 officers and men was estimated at £60,000 and at Albany, Parkhurst, there were building plans for 100 soldiers estimated at £18,000. Large police stations and courts also were costly, with Norman Shaw's design at Kentish Town estimated at £13,000 in 1894, and Great Marlborough Street police court and station costing £29,000 in 1913. Rural and small town law enforcement came cheaper than this.

Care of the sick and destitute in workhouses was surprisingly costly. One in Preston of 1869 for 956 inmates cost £30,000. By 1913 the cost of workhouses was reckoned to be from £160 to £200 per inmate in London, slightly less elsewhere. At that time lunatics emerge as a more expensive cause than the destitute, with asylums costing from £200 to £400 per inmate (at £1.00 to £1.50 per cu.m, much the same as villas) including wards, administrative buildings, chapel, mortuary and roads. Four mid-century asylum contracts earned Myers' firm a total of £258,000. In 1907 Long Grove Asylum, Epsom, housed no less than 2,013 patients at a cost of £243 each.

Figure 10 Site visit 1853. Stovepipe-hatted and female figures in very early site photograph. Strangeways Court, Manchester. Chaos on the ground is timeless. (Source: Manchester Central Library: Local Studies Unit.)

Buildings for human derangement on such a superhuman scale were not everywhere; 100 female patients in Worcester had a paltry £2,500 spent on them in the 1860s. Examples of hospitals of the same decade, when care of the sick poor outside workhouses became compulsory, were St Thomas's, Westminster Bridge, which housed 588 patients for £360,000 and Winchester County Hospital for only £23,000. For over a decade from the mid-1860s cottage hospitals multiplied, at a rate of about one a week. From average expenditure of £115 per patient in 1845, hospital building costs advanced by more complicated buildings to £170 in 1875 and about £300 by 1901 [28]. By 1911 there were nearly 2,200 institutions for the physically ill [29] and a first class urban hospital cost from £300 to £500 per bed (£1.30 to £1.75 per cu.m). Below this

Figure 11 Tense moment in the Gothic Revival. Roof timber is hoisted at Rochdale Town Hall *c.* 1868. Men perched (upper right) look unperturbed. (By permission Metropolitan Borough of Rochdale Community Services Dept.)

were cottage hospitals at £200 to £300 (£1.20 to £1.50 per cu.m) and, not very reassuringly, 'corrugated iron hospitals' at £100 to £150 (75p to 90p per cu.m).

The value of school building advanced greatly, from less than £0.5 m. a year average in the 1850s to well over £4 m. after 1900 [30]. Seaborne [31] gives a picture of mid-century school building with data on 11 schools designed by J. Clarke. The largest was at Leigh, Essex, for 260 children and the smallest at Monk's Horton, Kent, for 50 children. Costs ranged upwards from £2.40 per place at Monk's Horton to £8.20 at Coopersale, Essex. During the 1850s and 1860s school building accelerated and costs of £3 to £4 per place seem to have prevailed. The same source tabulated elementary day schools illustrated in *The Builder* between 1850 and 1870, giving an average cost for 24 schools of £1,859, with a maximum of £5,000 at St Saviour's, Paddington, and a minimum of £600 at Mansel Lacy, Herefordshire. The average cost per place

Figure 12 Building law. Portland stone shell of Cardiff Law Courts is well advanced. Bricks, timber and ironwork lie ready in foreground. An early twentieth century view. (Source: E. Turner & Sons, Cardiff.)

among the 15 schools for which data was published was £5.10 with a maximum of £16.70 at St Saviour's and a minimum of £2.60 at Hythe National School. The 1870 Education Act stimulated a large programme of elementary school building [32] in which were London Board Schools at around £8 per place in the early 1870s, rising to over £20 in 1899, by which time more than 400 existed. In 1913, elementary schools ranged from £7 to £12 per child in the country and up to £15 or £20 in large towns. Overall sizes were often large as, for example at Portlane Road, Croydon, with 1,300 places in 1901. Public school building, as at Marlborough and Lancing, was likely to take the form of quite costly, but few, buildings.

Higher education buildings were promoted by local government, societies, religious bodies and wealthy individuals. Institutions included a thin scatter of university buildings and

Figure 13 Mobile steam cranes at County Hall, London. Light railway also visible in deep excavations (far left). Vaults appear (far right), and Houses of Parliament are glimpsed (top right). A generation or more earlier, Myers' headquarters were near this spot. (Source: Greater London Record Office.)

the technical colleges, of which more than 30 appeared after about 1890. Finsbury Technical School, for instance, housed 150 day and 750 evening students and cost £21,000 for three storeys plus a basement, with another £15,000 for furnishings, appliances and fittings. This was cheap compared with the 300-student Central Technical Institute, South Kensington at £80,000 plus £20,000 for furnishings (£2.20 per cu.m). Many other educational buildings were less than this with, for example, Huddersfield Technical School at about 80p per cu.m, and Oldham School of Science and Art at about £1.20 per cu.m [33].

Church and chapel building held the prestige and vigour gained in the first half of the century, with well over £1 m. spent on them each year. In the Diocese of Manchester, between 1869 and 1885, £730,000 was spent building over 100 new

Figure 14 Sidings in the basement. County Hall structural steel columns rise (right) while bricks (centre) and timber scaffold poles (lower left) wait. Hoardings (left upper) advertise a 'stupendous production' of *Ben Hur* at Drury Lane. (Source: Greater London Record Office.)

churches [34]. In Middlesbrough in 1907, where 100,000 people lived, there were 60 places of worship, 20 of which were nonconformist (compared, incidentally, with 25 elementary schools). Micklethwaite [35], writing of costs in 1874, believed that most churches cost from £5 to £10 per sitting, although there were rare cases of £50 or more. He continued, 'We do indeed hear of churches at £4 and even at £3, but . . . they are nearly always . . . unfit to be called churches at all, every consideration of decency and convenience in performing the service being sacrificed . . .'. From £10 to £12 per sitting was '. . . a fair estimating price for an ordinary well-appointed, but unpretentious parish church, exclusive of the tower', allowing 0.8 or 0.9 sq.m per sitting. In a sample of 22 new churches built by the firms of Diment, and Stephens and Bastow between 1860 and 1911, the mean cost was £9,560. Among them were churches at Portsea (by

Figure 15 Plenty of Lift. Five cranes dominate work by contractors Holland, Hannen & Cubbits. This sort of heavy investment incomparably eased monumental construction with large stone blocks. Posters enjoin passers-by to enlist – 'Remember the Lusitania . . .'. World war has not stopped work on County Hall. (Source: Greater London Record Office.)

Blomfield, 1887) for £35,000 and Earley (by Waterhouse, 1879) for £3,500. The average cost of 29 places of worship built by Myers between 1850 and 1870, mainly in London, was £11,600. By the turn of the century cubic costs were perhaps double that of banks and major offices.

In the less spiritual subject of town halls we find the peak of quality upheld by a few monumental examples such as Liverpool, and a host of lesser buildings. An average cost per town hall project between 1820 and 1914 of about £31,000 emerges for a list of 239 buildings compiled by Cunningham [36]. The range of that sample was from very modest edifices of less than £1,000, up to leviathans costed in hundreds of thousands of pounds such as in Manchester. No clear cost trends emerge. Taking one random example, St George's Vestry and Union Offices, Hanover Square, Mount Street of 1886, the unit cost of the £20,000 building was about £1.70

per cu.m. This cost lay comfortably within the range of £1.50 to £2.65 per cu.m typical for such buildings in 1913.

A novel municipal enterprise was public libraries [37], pioneered in Manchester following an Act of 1850. There were 25 library projects by 1860 and by 1913 typical costs were a moderate £1.10 to £1.50 per cu.m. Swimming baths were built occasionally and cost from £1.75 to £2.00 per cu.m in 1913, the year in which one at Sevenoaks cost £3,000. Heavy Edwardian public authority investment in tramways gave rise to buildings such as large tramway depot sheds by Bradford Corporation for £46,000 in 1912. There appeared also an increasing number of buildings more useful than agreeable, among them mortuaries, refuse destructors, abattoirs, fire stations and, not least, public conveniences.

There remains a category of buildings such as public halls and private clubs which were non-profit-making, but paid for by private interests rather than public authorities. Examples from 1861 included a public hall for 1,000 at Guildford for £2,500, built when nearby Godalming had to be content with one of 'unpretending appearance' for only half that number at a cost of £600. Then there were the likes of Bishop Auckland Temperance Hall, with separate rooms for a Band of Hope, committee assembly and tea preparation, in all 240 sq.m for about £3,000 in 1876. Beyond were Salvation Army barracks, drill halls, working men's clubs, golf club houses and others.

Agricultural buildings

Farm building activity peaked prior to the great depression, at over £7 m. per year average in the 1860s. There followed a crucial turning point in the prosperity of Victorian high farming. Investment in buildings fell, starved of capital so that spending was below £4 m. a year average by the decade from 1911. An example of investment before prosperity waned was a group of buildings at Tranwell, near Morpeth, for the Earl of Carlisle, costing £1,040. The architects, J. & J. Girdwood, were from London, some indication of the importance attached to such ventures. Similarly, when a farm, which included house and cottages, was proposed for a site in Wilsthorpe, Lincoln-shire, tenders were attracted from as far away as London (although the lowest of £1,250 came from neighbouring Baston). This was mere financial chickenfeed, compared with Lord Bateman's Uphampton Farm, Shobdon, Herefordshire planned in 1861, like the previous examples. This was estimated to be nearly four times as costly and was elaborately equipped with a light railway. The small amount of agricultural buildings undertaken later on the eve of the First World War was among the cheapest of all building, from 50p to 60p per cu.m for barns and from 60 p to 90 p per cu.m for cow houses.

LOSSES FROM STOCK

Losses from stock were of two kinds: buildings which had decayed beyond repair and buildings which obstructed opportunities for financial or social gain. Popular tolerance of unsafe buildings gradually diminished as local government took growing reponsibilities for protecting the public interest. Main building losses were among dwellings of the poor, both urban and rural. They were victims of various predatory forces additional to time and the elements. Houses in urban centres were swept away singly or in groups to make room for commercial developments of shops, warehouses, offices, banks and the like. About four-fifths of the buildings standing in the City of London in 1855 were estimated to have been replaced by 1905 [38], although few other places generated comparable pressures for redevelopment. Another source of loss was the railways, relentlessly driven into the towns. In London in the 1860s alone as many as 120,000 people were thought to have been displaced by this onslaught [39]. Further losses stemmed from municipal street improvements such as Victoria Street and High Holborn, clearances for new artisan dwellings, board schools and other public buildings. Urban prosperity brought losses for purpose of redevelopment, while rural depression brought losses through depopulation and suspended maintenance.

BUILDING FORM

Opportunities for novelty New building forms and details, and novel application of the familiar, made their appearance. Two conditions were associated with this: first, new functions which buildings were required to perform (stimulating demand for innovations); and second, availability of new materials, methods and ideas (stimulating supply of innovations). Novel plans, circulation patterns, materials, structures, services and styles were tried in addition to, and in competition with, orthodox solutions. Many offered benefits of cost saving or higher performance, each to take its chance and be pitted against orthodoxy. Some would succeed, others fail to gain acceptance; thus form evolved in the building stock. Many innovations were

LEEDS COLLEGE OF BUILDING

introduced first in high-quality buildings where money restrictions lay lightest and talented people clustered thickest. In some lower-quality buildings there was less dramatic novelty where bulk-produced goods competed increasingly with materials fashioned locally by hand. Here the novelty was less the appearance and performance of the new goods than their near-universal distribution.

Building by-laws

As well as new freedoms there were new constraints, prominent among which was public health legislation. The influence of by-laws joined an emerging national market in materials to push designers towards a common style for cheap buildings. Before the last quarter of the century, the legislative framework of building was unclear, and where regulation applied at all, it differed from place to place, defying generalization. The London Building Act of 1844 was a key piece of legislation [40], but other major cities such as Liverpool and Bristol also were governed by early local Acts dealing with fire, party walls and structural stability. Coaxed and threatened by reformers and cholera, public opinion gradually rejected this minimum and often ineffective control. The Towns Improvement Clauses Act 1847 helped to standardize provisions made in numerous local Acts. The Local Government Act 1858 was centrally significant as a model for many subsequent local Acts, with provisions on new streets, structure of walls respecting fire and stability, ventilation and space around buildings and drainage. Another Act in 1875 extended the scope and in 1877 Model by-laws were published [41]. Even then, some smaller towns appear not to have adopted by-laws at least until 1890; provisions remained very complicated.

For most of the century many crucial points had been left to the discretion of the local boards, thereby permitting loopholes in the application of controls. For example, where new drainage cesspools apparently were prohibited, they might still be permitted where unavoidable. The required standards were not always very onerous: for example in Manchester in 1865 party walls of only 114 mm thickness were permitted. The 1875 Public Health Act helped to achieve a semblance of comprehensive national control over new urban building, rather than profoundly affecting regulation in places already covered. Henceforth smaller and less progressive towns which had not so far troubled themselves with permissive legislation were subject to controls. Rural authorities were granted by the Public Health Amendment Act of 1890 some of the powers already exercised in the towns [42]. By-laws retained similar subject headings to those named above, but their scope and requirements were extended in succeeding versions of the Model form. The erosion of freedom to determine building form, which advanced through the century, was paralleled by falling urban death rates. Less desirable, however, was the obstructive influence of by-laws on technical innovation, particularly late in the period respecting structural steel frames and structural use of concrete [43, 44].

Suburban and urban forms

Public health was one of a number of influences on the physical form and grouping of buildings. Suburban development was spurred by revulsion against high-density slums and freed by mechanized transport to give many sites less enclosed by nearby buildings. Larger plots enabled many new buildings to be a story or two lower than hitherto for a given volume and to have larger frontages. Small enclosed courts became fewer as ventilation became more valued and demanded. The pattern was unmistakable: middle-class households forsook town houses for villas, while artisan households abandoned tight back-to-backs for loose by-law terraces; congested communal courts yielded first to private back yards and then to gardens front and rear. Densities, at least for some of the people some of the time, were in decline from not long after mid-century.

But towns were very far from dissolving: central area renewal has already been noted. Old urban plots were sometimes combined into fewer larger sites, so that the land could be used to the fullest possible extent where rising land values made it desirable. The result was central area buildings of ever greater height, bulk and complexity, in forms which reflected the rising call for ventilation and daylight. The scale of whole streets in major cities increased appreciably after mid-century, as new succeeded old. Massive new offices and hotels began to dominate the eroding townscape of Georgian London. Elsewhere new big hospitals, mills and warehouses had similar effects and, more modestly, so did the increased average size of individual houses.

As urban scale increased so, too, did the diversity of building types and the differentiation of processes taking place within them. Marcus has noted that 'By 1850 there had been a typological explosion: a host of new industrial buildings, railway stations, town halls, bath and wash houses . . . markets, libraries, art galleries and museums . . . [etc.]' [45].

Now these pioneering types proliferated greatly. The different-iation of processes is illustrated by the example of schools where once children were taught in large single classrooms, and where now they might be divided by age group and gender, and have multiple specialized spaces like gymnasia and laboratories. Similarly where textiles had once come from the cottage, now they emerged from vast weaving shed connected to engine house, counting house and warehouse. Time and again new buildings were called upon to meet larger, more complicated and more specialized needs than before.

Standard-ization

While variety blossomed in such ways, largely among more costly buildings, it withered among some lesser ones. Weaken-ing of the considerable local and regional differences in mass housing before 1850 accelerated, particularly after the 1875 Public Health Act. The lowest quality of building was raised, but stereotyped by-law streets spread ever more widely. The idiosyncratic builders of Leeds somehow defied the trend by carrying on building back-to-backs long after they were outlawed elsewhere (right up to 1937), but this was highly exceptional. The trend was towards universal building forms and away from local peculiarities and distinctive regional characteristics. Earlier, the character of cheap buildings had been decided largely by their geographical location, but now their date became more significant. Not that standardization was confined only to cheap housing, for it appeared also in such places as office blocks, warehouses and mills. There was to be found increasing repetition from one floor to the next and from one bay to the next. Nor was standardization confined within single projects. Some railway companies, for example, were big enough to find benefits in standardizing whole buildings across groups of like projects. The Great Western Railway erected standard signal boxes, halts and stations in Edwardian years and earlier [46]. Other standardiz-ation of an unsung sort came from makers of corrugated metal sheeting, patented in 1829 and increasingly evident from mid-century. By 1886 there were at least 23 builders of pre-fabricated sheet metal buildings in London alone [47], making such buildings as churches, mission rooms, cottages and farm buildings, some for export.

Construction of carcass

In many larger and costly buildings the offensive was against obstructive external walls, partitions and columns. For example, workshop floors and shopfronts were freed where possible by spacing supports more widely than hitherto, and minimum sizes for domestic windows were now stipulated in by-laws. Ease of movement for people and goods, flexibility to change functions, greater visibility, daylighting and ventilation were all in the ascendant. The means by which to achieve them included greater use of cast iron frames and the introduction of wrought iron beams and trusses in the 1850s and 1860s. Use of mild steel joists was sluggish, but began to grow in the Edwardian years. Floors of large buildings having concrete infill between wrought iron joists dated from the 1860s, being superseded by reinforced concrete early in the twentieth century [48, 49].

Deeper scientific understanding of the behaviour of some structures and materials made it possible to eliminate functionally redundant material. Materials in their un-processed naturally occurring condition, whether clay, stone or timber, were ousted increasingly where performance requirements were onerous: where a heavy rubble wall once served, now there were slim metal columns and plate glass; where once were uneven hand-made bricks, now were regular machine-pressed ones or terracotta products; where once were hand-crafted wooden window frames, now was manufactured patent glazing. Yet the advance of engineering and processed products at the expense of tradition and natural materials was not the whole story. Reaction was evident from such writers as Ruskin and Morris, with results widely visible in most high-quality buildings. Churches, country houses and other prestigious edifices generally sought to celebrate crafts-manship, revive past techniques and conceal technical innova-tions.

The position was different in lower-quality buildings where choice was restricted by cost and where a more striking feature of form was continuity with the past. A simple coach house or workshop was not likely to profoundly differ whether built in 1860 or 1910; maybe storey heights or window areas increased a little, or construction of the ground floor or roof varied slightly, but essentially the form was the same. At this level of building continuity was strong and craftsmen would not have been unfamiliar with the work of their counterparts a century or more earlier.

Services   Circumstances were different with building services, where all manner of pipes, cisterns, fittings and wires for the first time amounted to more than a trivial afterthought to building work. In the massive new 1860s Foreign Office building lifts, bells and fittings alone amounted to about 5% of total cost [50]. This rising proportion of services in the total cost of building was partly a response to growing concern with public health. Other important influences were growing expectations of convenience and comfort and an enhanced capacity to pay for them, together with new problems of circulation and communication in large buildings. Finally, there were inventions and improvements such as telephones, sprinkler fire-fighting systems, lifts and domestic cookers, which stimulated hitherto unvoiced demand as well as meeting established wants.

Among services and appliances which increasingly replaced builders' work of earlier and technically more simple times were iron ranges and components such as ready-finished ceramic sinks instead of made-up hardwood ones. Services increasingly penetrated throughout buildings rather than being confined to all-too-insalubrious extremities. Where once a combination of bucket and unwashed humanity was enough, now there were basins, tanks, pipes and drains. Householders who once cheerfully endured a garden-long walk to the privy now expected a WC on every floor, and some office workers basked in centrally heated warmth instead of having to take their own coke to work. Where the corridors of business once echoed with messenger boys' footsteps, now they resounded to gadgets such as speaking tube and electric or pneumatic bell. If such services did not yet much influence building form, they increasingly perforated its divisions and linked its spaces, as well as giving people cause to wonder and, usually, be thankful.

Improved space heating was achieved by more open fireplaces in cheaper buildings, and new systems arising from efforts in the 1860s to separate the point of combustion of fuel from occupied rooms. Some costly buildings employed steam or hot water circulation systems connected to boilers carefully sited out of sight and smell [51]. By the early twentieth century advanced systems incorporated underfloor air cleaners, ducts and concealed radiators [52], although well-tried enclosed stoves remained plentiful. While the first gas lighting systems appeared in early nineteenth century mills, it was not much before mid-century that a growing network of mains made possible widespread domestic installations to replace candles and oil lamps. Nearly 1,000 gasworks existed by 1859 [53] and price reduction increased the market so that there were 2 m.

gas consumers by 1885. Electric lighting made slow progress from the 1880s: lower installation costs were offset by high running costs. Electricity supply began to spread to the suburbs from about 1900 and by 1910 about 2% of homes were connected to mains [54].

There was a remarkably varied range of appliances supplying water for kitchen, washing and sanitary purposes [55]. As with space heating, invention was followed by adoption by the wealthy few, then acceptance by the middle class, and finally use in the mass market. This process could take a very long time; decades for purpose-built bathrooms and a century or more for flush WCs. Around mid-century baths began to cease being regarded as portable and gas began to be used for water heating, bringing formidable geysers in the late 1860s and piped water to bedrooms soon after. Earth closets may be said to have lost ground to water closets as the latter became more reliable and hence acceptable inside the house, and as new public systems of water supply and waste disposal replaced old private arrangements (often inadequate and sometimes lethally mixed). Innovations in the various services perhaps proceeded farther than those in other aspects of building; in this field, if anywhere, a builder of mid-century would have had cause for surprise by what was visible by 1914.

4

The industry consolidates: 1851–1914

. . . as it appeared to me that you are simply humbugging me from week to week, with promises that have no result I shall, unless you at once settle this matter, give it into my solicitor's hands . . .

(Subcontractor Ernest Brock seeks payment, 11 July 1895)

CHARACTER AND INFLUENCES

Growth and technology

The most striking change affecting the industry over the period was growth in size and productive capacity. Already a vast and far-flung industry by mid-century, it reached massive proportions by 1914 and retained a key position in the much-enlarged national economy. One aspect of size was the number of people engaged in building. Males occupied in building and construction as a proportion of all occupied males in Great Britain, increased from 1: 13.2 in 1851 to 1: 11.3 in 1911. A peak of 1: 9.5 was recorded in the census of 1901. Numerically the workforce grew from 497,000 at mid-century to 1,219,000 (including 3,000 women) in 1901. Cyclic depression then dragged the total down to 1,145,000 in 1911 [1]. Another aspect of size was total investment in building, which was around 60% of fixed capital formation between 1856 and 1875. Thereafter from 1894 to 1913 there was a slight decline to 56%.

Growth was achieved mainly by duplication of firms, most of which remained quite small. There was some increase in average size of firms later in the period, as will be seen below, but concentration remained limited. On the other hand, as

Adam Smith had observed, where the extent of the market increased, the division of labour was likely to do likewise. So it was that in the largest markets such as London and the North West, division of labour among firms advanced. There, new firms might attempt new types of service and process, some involving new types of product. These firms mostly did so by integrating themselves fully in the prevailing contractual procedures. In structure, organization and procedures the keynotes for the industry were caution and consolidation. In technology also there were similar attitudes, most respecting the building carcass, least with building services and minor components. Where technological advances did occur they were mainly in materials processing rather than on site.

The absence of a revolution in the built product sometimes gave rise to comment (like Sherlock Holmes' curious incident of the dog that did nothing in the night-time). In favour of such a revolution were an enlarged market and the emergence of a possible agency in the shape of the new integrated contracting firms. Yet many forces were ranged against potential innovators. Traditional building crafts had been very fully developed over a long period, making cost-reducing substitutes exceedingly difficult to find. Further, contracting firms were routinely separated from specialist designers, who might otherwise have combined their skills creatively. Probably more importantly, although aggregate demand for building was enormous, it was critically fragmented by being immovably tied to fixed sites and always prone to fierce fluctuations of activity. The latter ever threatened to turn boom-time capital investment in plant into recession-time liability; would-be innovators so seldom faced the same challenges and opportunities for any length of time. In a volatile business climate builders were forced to take as their core skills the amassing and safe deployment of resources of capital, labour and materials. Survival favoured firms which sought to minimize dangerous demand-side uncertainty and risk, rather than add to them by attempting to supply innovatory products. In this light, firms behaved in ways that were more economically rational than blindly averse to technology.

PROFESSIONS

Contract procedure

The open and changeable roles and relationships in the industry in the first half of the century became less fluid in the

second half. Here, too, procedures were refined and consolid-
ated and widely accepted practice emerged for the non-
speculative, generally high quality, minority of work. There a
promoter would typically commission and accept a design
from a professional architect, whereupon general building
contractors were invited to submit competitive tenders on the
basis of detailed drawings, and specification. The successful
contractor, usually the one with the lowest tender, was chosen
to carry out the work under contract to the promoter and
under the architect's supervision. Standard guidance documents for contracts began to appear in 1870, subsequently
developing into simple standard forms [2].

Architects   After the person who paid for the building, the central figure
in this procedure was the architect. The profession developed
significantly in nature and size, largely in consequence of
heavy building activity and increasing numbers of commercial
clients. The underlying concerns which directed professional
development were prospects of public approval, movement
towards legalized closure to non-professional outsiders, and a
plea for a code of ethics [3]. With evident emotion, Micklethwaite stigmatized professional circumstances of the 1870s in
which

> Any man worth a brass plate and a door to put it on may
> dub himself an architect, and a very large number of
> surveyors, auctioneers, house-agents, upholsterers, &c.,
> with a sprinkling of bankrupt builders and retired clerks of
> works, find it in their interest to do so. [4]

Some leading practitioners had long fought this state of
affairs so that by the 1860s the professional institute was
elevated to a position of some distinction, with the broad mass
of the profession, who did not yet belong, gradually following.
Old direct links with craft trades became more tenuous and,
for members of the minority Royal Institute of British
Architects at least, were severed entirely in 1887. Numbers
grew from 3,000 'architects' recorded in the 1851 census
(many of whom were also builders and so on) to over 10,000
by 1901. During the same interval the proportion who were
members of the RIBA increased from 8% to 15%. A slightly
more businesslike approach began to supplement earlier
artistic leanings and somewhat routine work took on a fair
proportion of the total carried out in architects' offices. Where
commissions had once been confined to the few superior

buildings, now some quite commonplace housing and similar projects were also designed by people calling themselves architects [5]. Summerson observed that the profession of the 1860s was a gentleman's profession — but only just [6]. The rise of contracting and large projects emphasized a host of legal and financial matters such as contract procedure, insurance, costs and arbitration. There was increasing need to draw and specify details of ever more complicted buildings, to facilitate estimating and replace the ebbing autonomy of individual craftsmen. Again, the need for by-law approval helped to create work. These new responsibilities which gathered round central creative and aesthetic skills perhaps made more hard-earned the customary fee of 5% of building cost.

Quantity surveyors and engineers

Quantity surveying practice and techniques in compiling bills of quantities varied over the country, but slowly evolved in ways first set in London. There the issue of the 1860s and 1870s was whether two quantity surveyors, one for the architect and one for the contractor, or only one, were needed for each project. The Surveyors' Institution (which included quantity surveyors among land surveyors) was founded in 1868, and the professional standing of quantity surveyors slowly grew. By the Edwardian years, when forms of contract were jointly agreed between architects and contractors, and quantities became part of the contract, the quantity surveyors were fully-fledged professionals standing above the more commercial builders' estimators [7]. Occupying a position somewhere between architects and quantity surveyors were civil engineers, who contributed to some larger and technically advanced projects. Retaining some direct links with contractors, engineers were concerned mainly with heavy structural elements such as deep foundations and wide roof spans.

FIRMS

Sizes

The hierarchy of firms which had emerged before mid-century was sustained and probably gained in definition. Within it some changes were evolving. One was the trend towards more and rather bigger firms [8]. According to the 1851 census there were five firms employing more than 350 people and 19 firms employing more than 200, while smaller firms employing fewer than 20 people amounted to at least 65% of the total. In the large market of the North West, firms with over 50 employees accounted for 8 or 9% of the total, approaching the proportion in London. There, a firm with 150 employees was regarded as large. In many other parts of the country the proportion of firms of over 50 employees was only 3 to 5% [9]. Shortly before mid-century about half of all London house builders had built only one or two houses a year, and about four-fifths of them built six or fewer houses a year. There appears to have been little change in firm size for another 30 years or so. In Sheffield between 1865 and 1900 half of the house building firms put up no more than three houses each and three-quarters no more than eight houses. The pattern in London began to change in the booming late 1870s and early 1880s, when the number of small firms increased less than the number of larger ones. Small firms suffered more heavily

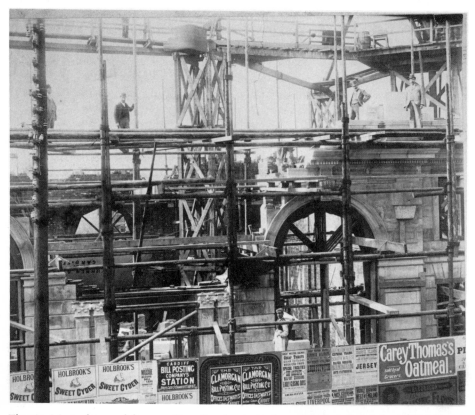

Figure 16 Arches and figures. Four bowler-hatted gents are aloft on the scaffolding *c.* 1895. Temporary timber centring is seen on this unidentified high-quality masonry shell. (Source: E. Turner & Sons, Cardiff.)

when the boom ended and when the next one came in the late 1890s some really large firms benefited. In 1899 17 firms, less than 3% of the total, put up over 40% of new houses [10]. Doughty [11] has suggested the advantages of size as economies of scale and development of a diversity of business interests in other sectors of the economy, perhaps property ownership and rental. Bowley [12], on the other hand, has questioned economies of scale for firms in respect of the numerous small projects. House builders aside, an indication of the upper end of size among contractors comes from the firm of Myers. He employed a nucleus of 100 men at Ordnance Wharf yard and works, but on sites country-wide he employed up to several thousand others, engaged more casually on particular contracts.

Contractors Firms such as Myers' were the elite of the industry. They engaged in work anywhere in the country, directed by professional architects and engineers, under contract to promoters, many of whom were wealthy and influential. The majority of their work was won through competitive tender.

Figure 17 Stonemasons in the Library. Part of an elite near the end of their heyday. Building Cardiff Central Library extension *c.* 1894. Cut stone is moved on trolleys. Timber scaffolding abounds with lashed joints (top left). (Source: South Glamorgan County Library.)

Figure 18 Manchester hod-carriers. Three figures have trouser leg straps, all have headgear and neckerchiefs. Houses rise without scaffolding. (Source: Manchester Central Library: Local Studies Unit.)

Myers' success rate appears to have been of the order of 16% of projects for which he tendered [13]. Short-term fluctuations in materials and labour markets, with 15% or more movements after tenders were accepted, could sometimes make for difficulties [14]. Some high-quality projects, at least, continued to be the result of non-competitive appointment on architects' nomination, where contractors had built up a favoured relationship with a particular designer. In some parts, particularly the North, general contractors appear not to have won so dominant a position and the practice persisted of tendering separately for each trade.

Leading firms associated in order to share experience and protect their collective interests by presenting a united front in dealing with organized labour. Various organizations, some purely local, of different strength and longevity appeared, the more important being the Institute of Builders, which succeeded the Builders' Society in 1884, and the National

Figure 19 Early electrification. Cardiff City Hall begun 1901. Electric cranes by Joseph Booth Bros. Ltd. Leeds were said to be a pioneering installation. (Source: E. Turner & Sons, Cardiff.)

Association of Master Builders of Great Britain. This dated from 1878 and led in 1899 to the foundation of the National Federation of Building Trade Employers (NFBTE).

Examples of contracting firms

The example of Myers, chronicled by Spencer-Silver, is presumed to provide a picture of a top-ranking contractor in the third quarter of the century. At management level he relied in part on various of his relatives, including one son as a clerk, another as a site overseer and a brother-in-law as cashier. This would have reduced Myers' risk inherent in delegation to otherwise unknown managers; a common enough problem for the nineteenth century entrepreneur. Day-to-day responsibility for large contracts, some very many miles from headquarters, must have been decentralized. Site craftsmen were recruited locally by a general foreman who coordinated separate trade foremen for bricklaying, masonry and so on. Unskilled labour for excavating and other heavy work was recruited by the gang. Myers engaged in diverse support activities, among them running a railway rolling stock fleet connected with limestone quarrying, and supplying temporary hutting and catering for remotely sited workforces. The South Bank headquarters were well equipped with up-to-date steam-powered machinery for stone and woodworking. Raw materials arrived by water, as they did for neighbouring firms Grissell and Peto, and Holland and Hannen, as well as many others elsewhere. Myers worked on well over 100 each of churches, mansions and houses, and he worked on warehouses together with associated docks and railways. The firm seems to have been almost as at home with heavy civil engineering as with finely-wrought Gothic revival buildings. The firm also built many banks and offices, schools and colleges, hospitals, and other buildings, sometimes as many as ten projects concurrently. To win such a volume of work required tendering on average once every two weeks. The names of several respectable figures prepared to stand surety in the event of failure to meet the contract were often required. Myers sometimes quoted his materials suppliers, who were substantial men, for this purpose. Once a project was running, stage payments whose value was certified by the architect were made, with a defects liability period after practical completion. Many projects were large and could be carried out rapidly. While the 250-patient Lincolnshire Asylum worth £35,500 took three years altogether, Colney Hatch Asylum, cost £138,000, employed 1,300 men and took only about 18 months. Myers retired in 1873 aged 70 and the firm ceased to exist shortly afterwards.

Aspects of another prestigious firm, that of William Higgs and Joseph Hill, over the last quarter of the century have been recorded by Cooney [15]. They each began with a capital of £15,000 consisting of plant, machinery and stock. Their profits fluctuated widely, averaging £10,500 a year, from which they withdrew an average of £9,100 a year. They built public, social and commercial buildings and some houses, usually with between six and 20 contracts concurrent. The workforce was about 500 men in summer and fewer in winter. Cooney concluded that such proprietors were unlikely to become millionaires, but their return on capital was far greater than that obtainable as *rentiers* from secure, fixed-interest investment. They were comfortably among the affluent businessmen of their time.

An example of a firm engaged on high-class work, but at a smaller scale, was Stephens and Bastow [16]. It grew out of

Diment's Bristol contracting firm which, it was seen above, employed 35 in 1851. Diment undertook a succession of local churches and other prestigious buildings in the 1860s and extended into Wales and Devon on similar work in the 1870s. Diment's managing foreman John Bastow, born in 1827, joined forces with George Stephens, a Gloucester joiner of humble 1846 birth, who was employed by Diment as 'accountant'. They took over from the now-elderly Diment, re-styled themselves Stephens and Bastow and moved to larger premises in 1874. Contracts followed in London, the home counties and as far afield as Lancashire. The partnership split about 1880 and Bastow subsequently employed about ten men while Stephens continued to trade as Stephens and Bastow, later as a limited company. In 1881 the firm employed 359 men and 18 boys and about the same time invested heavily in steam-powered joinery working. As Myers had already found, the heavily-ornamented architectural style of the day encouraged such a move, an investment which plain house builders could more readily do without. Projects included New Court, Lincoln's Inn (£80,000), the Lyric Theatre, Shaftesbury Avenue (£30,000 in ten months), and many churches. About 1910 the developers of a £100,000 commercial project in Hans Crescent, Knightsbridge, over-reached themselves. Stephens reluctantly took a financial half interest in the crippled venture, in return for labour and materials expended. In 1911 he retired, auctioning off head-quarters premises with five cranes, three timber carriages, three portable engines, mortar mills, steam drilling machines, timber stocks and other goods. Stephens and Bastow, and Diment, together undertook at least 290 projects of which half are of known value, totalling £1,495,000. The firm effectively operated in two markets, a nation-wide one for large and high-quality work, and a local one for more mundane work.

Examples of smaller contractors relying on local work are George Roylance of Macclesfield and Walter Mason of Haverhill, Suffolk. Roylance was born in 1836 and built many important public and private buildings in Macclesfield where he began in the mid-1850s with small jobbing work [17]. He flourished in the 1880s, with vertical integration through brickworks ownership. His brother succeeded him in the business in 1892, taking limited liability company formation in 1898 with interests as joiners, builders, timber dealers, wheelwrights, smiths, plumbers and dealers in building materials. The Haverhill firm was founded by the son of a

builder who also kept a beerhouse and who was born in
1833 [18]. Walter Mason built up the business, employing 50
men and two boys by 1871. Like Stephens, he invested in
woodworking machinery and the firm became by far the
largest builders in Haverhill with builders' merchant and
brickmaking activities. By 1881 as many as 102 men and 16
boys were employed (his nearest rival had 12) and the firm
would undertake a range of industrial, domestic, agricultural,
church restoration and public building projects. Mason died
early in the new century, though a reduced firm survived until
the 1940s. The firm in its heyday, with diverse materials
supply interests, must have held something of a local
monopoly.

Taken together these five examples of contracting firms
show some common experiences. Vertical integration into
brickmaking was common, as were investment in woodworking machinery [19] and diversification into merchanting
activities. Successful proprietors advanced by gradual
accumulation leading to larger projects and, often, limited
liability (although there appears to have been little separation
of ownership and management of firm). The perils of succession when founders withdrew were sharpened in at least three
cases by second generation indifference to continuity. This was
when, in D. S. Landes' words, offspring of business founders
became 'tired of the tedium of trade and flushed with the
bucolic aspirations of the country gentleman . . .'.

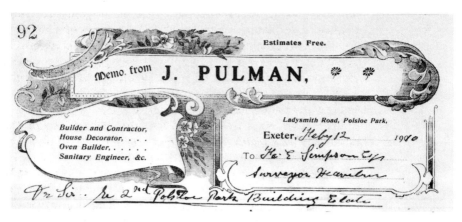

Figure 20 Mr Pulman's business letterhead. How to create a good impression in Exeter
1910. Firm advertises services as 'Builder and Contractor, House Decorator, Oven
Builder, Sanitary Engineer &c.'

Figure 21 Works entrance. Stephens & Bastow, Bristol, *c.* 1910. Through these gates joinery was sent as far afield as York Minster, Aden and Durban.

Speculative builders and sub-contractors

The superior status of general contractors did not prevent some of them engaging also in speculative building. The degree of involvement depended on market conditions and the inclination of proprietors. Below these part-contractor-part-speculative-builder firms in public esteem were the wholly speculative builders [20], greatly outnumbering contractors and mostly engaged in commonplace buildings. It may be conjectured that the building managerial skills needed for speculative projects were less than those for contracts of similar value, contracts typically being less constructionally repetitive and more replete with risky features such as wide spans and deep groundworks, than were speculative housing projects. Speculative builders appear to have been more prone to failure than the big contractors, with bankruptcy sometimes an end to unrealistic hopes nurtured in boom times, abetted by easy access to credit and doomed by under-pricing of work. An example from North Kensington represents a tragically large number of failures. One George Ingersent undertook to build 90 houses around Westbourne Grove in the heady atmosphere of the early 1850s, but had run into financial difficulties by

1854. Soon he came down in the world and was to be found building a mere four houses in Palace Gardens Terrace. One of them was the Mall Tavern, of which he was licensee by 1856 [21], no doubt a sadder but wiser man. A tale of rags to riches was that of Edward Yates who arrived in London from the North early in the 1850s to build houses in South London. He began with small numbers, but after 1870 worked on a steadily growing scale. Dyos showed that between 1867 and 1895 Yates borrowed over £280,000 to finance his ventures, mostly at the normal rate of 4.5 to 5%. Activity peaked around 1890 at about 150 houses a year. He died in 1907, a millionaire responsible for over 2,500 houses [22], showing that at least some speculative builders won positions of considerable social standing. Another firm which made a handsome living for its proprietors was C. A. Daw and Son Ltd, active at the same time as Yates, though in a higher-class West London market. The eponymous founder came from Devon in the early 1860s and was soon engaged in speculative building with his two brothers. The partnership was broken up in 1871 and C.A. Daw was joined by his son William, with whom a formal partnership was eventually drawn up in 1886. From the mid-1870s father and son built 28 very substantial houses in De Vere Gardens, Kensington, which they disposed of only slowly. Expansion came in the mid-1880s with more than 150 large houses over the next 20 years in Kensington and elsewhere. C.A. Daw retired in 1894, and the partnership dissolved, although the name was retained. William died suddenly in 1908 leaving effects valued at £190,000. After completing sizeable current commitments the firm trans-formed itself into property management [23]. Just as there were contractors who sometimes engaged in speculative building, so there were speculative builders who sometimes engaged in subcontracting. At the level of the smallest speculative ventures in smaller markets were many 'penny capitalists' who moved quite freely between paid employment (say as carpenter), subcontracting, jobbing and repairs, and small speculations [24].

Subcontractors were a loosely defined group which included firms of highly skilled craftsmen such as ornamental masons, up-to-date technicians such as electricians and lift engineers, down to more or less disreputable tradesmen such as low-skilled painters. Between these extremes was a growing range of specialist subcontractors who contributed only small parts to any one project. An index of 1886 [25] listed over 400 trades, from alabaster warehouses to zinc workers, offering such arcane services as well-sinking and weathervane making. In London alone there were 83 firms listed as shop-front builders, 10 laundry fitters and 19 plasterers' hair merchants. Many such specialists were obliged to seek continuity of work on numerous widely spread projects. The more specialized the firm, the further it was likely to travel to get work. Examples were specialists in design and fabrication of metal frames, and makers and installers of patent glazing on high-quality work. Architects often nominated such subcontractors in order to assure the quality of intricate work.

Peripheral firms

Contractors and subcontractors alike obtained many of their materials from specialist suppliers and builders' merchants. These acted as a major source of short-term credit for firms on site, in addition to their function as wholesale stockists. Kelly listed 100 builders' merchants in 1870 and by 1910 there were 1,300, the largest of which had outlets in three or four cities [26]. Suppliers and merchants in turn were kept stocked by manufacturers and processors who, in some cases, also supplied builders direct. At the same time, as seen above, some builders owned their own sources of materials.

Thus materials processing and supplying firms were partly within the building industry and partly outside it. Where, say, a brickworks was owned by a builder (such as Roylance), it was still within the building industry. Yet where a brickworks was owned by someone who identified primarily with other brickmakers, and to whom builders were customers, it had effectively ceased to be in the building industry. Building was stimulating new industries adjacent to, but separate from, it (and as such beyond the scope of this book). The industry was increasingly turning from processing to assembly by acquiring pre-finished components and branded goods from other industries. As yet the goods were mostly small and quite light, but varied and numerous: metal bolts from Birmingham as substitutes for painstakingly cut carpentry joints in roof timbers; iron pipes brought from afar, but quicker to fix in position than time-consuming brick flue building; fencing wire; factory-made panelled doors and bay windows; branded varnishes and paints, and so on. Such developments brought into existence a network of makers, dealers and stockists complete with a system of publicity, sales, deliveries and accounts. One result of the increase of branded goods, as well as subcontracting, was to intensify the demands made on builders and designers. An understanding of building crafts alone was ceasing to be enough; skills in administration and management were in the ascendant. This raises the question of training: for the trades, apprenticeships on site and in yard and workshop; specialist technical training appears to have had origins in evening classes. More formalized syllabuses and examinations were in place late in the century. All were supported by price and pattern books and later more technical works, catalogues and weekly periodicals, starting with *The Builder* (1842) and *Building News* (1855) and later flowering to include *Illustrated Carpenter and Builder* and many others.

New ways and firms gradually emerged, but the old ones died hard in the country. Survival of an archaic village firm in Haddenham, Buckinghamshire, into the 1890s was recorded by Rose [27]. There, and no doubt elsewhere, were three independent concerns: carpenter, 'masoner', and a combined plumber, glazier and decorator. They were owned by three close relatives who worked informally in unison as required, though by the nineties they recognized the arrangement as inconvenient and outdated. By then craft joinery and other skills were yielding to cheaper machine-made products. The carpenter succumbed before 1914 and became a commercial traveller. His was a surrender to implacable forces which had destroyed a timeless tradition of local self-sufficiency, to give cheaper and often better-performing products and higher wages.

LABOUR

Variety and numbers

Edwardian building workers were described as ragged-trousered philanthropists, exploited men who handed over the results of their labour to others [28]. In fact the arduous and sometimes physically dangerous life on site was probably no worse, or better, than in many other industries. In building, the worst off were the unskilled labourers, the heavy workers and shifters of muck, of whom there were perhaps a quarter of a million in the 1870s and 1880s [29], a large proportion of all labourers. For them, more than among skilled men, employment was at best intermittent and vulnerable. Casual employment and surplus labour meant that movement in and out of jobs was frequent, as it was between trades and between building and other industries. Instances of mobility were carpenter-greengrocers and smallholders-cum-brickmakers. Some adaptable individuals took on jobbing building on a casual basis interspersed with gardening [30]. The contribution of these versatile and unclassifiable figures remains unquantified.

The circumstances of skilled tradesmen are better recorded. Carpentry and joinery was the largest trade, with 177,000 at the time of the 1861 census, rising to 270,000 by 1901. A typical mid-century figure was the young carpenter and joiner working for a London speculative builder, having left the countryside in search of improvement. No doubt some found it, for Clapham noted that foremen were recruited generally from their trade. Bricklayers displaced the masons as the second largest trade by 1871, growing from 79,000 in 1861 to 213,000 by 1901. Like the carpenters, the total fell back during the ensuing slump [31]. The 86,000 masons recorded in 1861 remained largely unchanged in number for the rest of the century, with expansion arrested by changing materials usage. The painting trade was large, but had low levels of skill, casual employment, and indistinct boundaries. Combined with the glaziers, over 100,000 painters were recorded in 1881, along with 37,000 plumbers, 29,000 plasterers and 7,000 slaters and tilers.

Wages

The trend of building wages was upward and broadly in sympathy with levels of activity, with a slow rise from the 1850s accelerating towards the beginning of the last quarter of the century. Increases then levelled off until the boom of the 1890s took wages to a peak, followed by stagnation until shortly before the outbreak of war [32]. In the 1850s wages in southern England were of the order of 22.5p for a ten-hour day for craftsmen and 14p for labourers [33]. In 1867 Levi [34] thought that London wages were about 3.3p an hour for first-class men. He noted wide regional differences, such as that between 2.7p and 3.3p an hour in Yorkshire and 1.9p and 2.0p in Norfolk. The national average rates were estimated at about 2.9p an hour, £1.50 to £1.60 a week for skilled adults, 60p to £1.25 a week for labourers and 25p a week for boys and lads. As well as losses due to bad weather and slack trade, allowance had to be made for payments for tools. For bricklayers this was only about £1 initially and 25p annually, but for some joiners it was £20 or more initially and £1.75 annually. Between 1873 and 1892 typical craftsmen's wages were 30p for a ten-hour day and labourers 19p or more. In the mid-1880s the highest rates were for decorators, grainers and plaster modellers. Next were slate masons followed by plumbers and smiths, then stonemasons, bellhangers, plasterers, gasfitters and glaziers. Slightly lower were excavator gangers, slaters, carpenters and joiners, painters and paperhangers, slightly ahead of bricklayers and tilers. Below these skilled men were their respective labourers [35]. By 1914 craftsmen's wages had advanced to about 35p for a ten-hour day; those of labourers were about 25p. On the basis of annual earnings in 1906, building craftsmen were paid slightly more than the average for all skilled manual workers, although labourers did less well. Carpenters were said to earn about £98 and bricklayers a few pounds less, while the respected railway engine drivers earned £119, engineering fitters £90 and bakers £75 [36].

Organization   Wages were related in part to the organization of building trade unions, hampered as they were by fragmentation of the industry into many mostly small firms offering largely casual work on dispersed sites. Identity of interest between men of different trades and districts was hard to perceive. Disputes between employers and labour usually remained confined by the relative insularity and lack of organization of the men. Nevertheless some skilled workers combined into effective unions, prominent among which was the Operative Stone-masons Society, in its heyday in the late 1870s. As other leading trades also organized themselves, local branches began to become more centralized, but the process was slow and the number of unions very large.

   Building unions of the 1860s were for that minority of skilled men who could afford high contributions in exchange for large benefits. Policies were based on the moderate belief that the best way to share growing prosperity was by a conciliatory posture towards employers [37]. This attitude was epitomized by Robert Applegarth, influential leader of the Amalgamated Society of Carpenters and Joiners. The two main aims were to reduce working hours and resist employers seeking to replace payment by the day by payment by the hour. These issues were central to a conflict with London builders in 1859–60 when there were inflamed feelings and rousing talk of a 'tyranny of fustian'. However, payment by the hour, and with it one hour's notice of dismissal, was gradually accepted, and shorter hours did not come until the early 1870s. By that time London masons, with a 51-hour week, enjoyed one of the most favoured positions, but very wide variations long persisted over the country.

Militancy was discouraged by slack building activity during the 1880s and early 1890s, although there were said to be more than 100,000 union members in 1885, perhaps an eighth of the building labour force. Returning prosperity in the 1890s brought a near-doubling in the proportion of craftsmen, approaching one in five, belonging to unions. Neither this growth nor more radical leadership much changed their decentralized ways and structure. Key issues besides pay and hours were piecework and apprenticeship. National conciliation boards, on which employers and unions met, began to appear near the end of the century, by which time the main basis of working rules was becoming established.

Very gradual improvement in living and working conditions was halted by economic adversity in the new century. Employment was scarce (there was 12% unemployment among carpenters in 1909), while wages were stationary and

Figure 22 The men (and boys) who did the work. Building was a mass employer when this opening ceremony took place at Cardiff Civic Centre, *c.* 1904. Headgear was *de rigeur*: flat caps, or bowlers for higher status. (Source: E. Turner & Sons, Cardiff.)

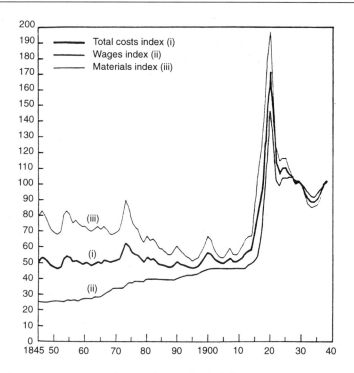

Figure 23 Maiwald's index of building costs 1845–1938 (1900 = 100). (Source: K. Maiwald (1954–55) 'An Index of Building Costs in the UK 1845–1938', *Economic History Review* 2nd series (7).

prices rising. Technological obsolescence began to threaten parts of certain trades, calling for adaptation: less stone was used; joinery work was mechanized; brick and timber began to yield to steel and concrete; and some lead roofing was replaced by asphalt. Here, if anywhere, were fertile grounds for demarcation disputes among unions [38]. In the last few years of peace, union membership declined and active members' thoughts shifted from reform to more profound change.

MATERIALS, COMPONENTS AND PROCESSES

Costs   While labour cost trends were upward, those of materials and components generally fell gradually in sympathy with whole-sale prices. The most notable exceptions to the downward trend were peaks around 1873 and 1900, and a rise after 1909. The effect of rising labour and falling materials costs was to keep total building costs fairly stable; at the same time labour assumed a greater proportion of total costs than materials. Around mid-century the proportion of total cost represented by materials on a typical project probably was about two-thirds or more, but this appears to have fallen to about one half by early Edwardian times [39]. The fall was due largely to productivity and efficiency gains from mechanization in workshop and yard and from improved transport. The circumstances of each trade varied so that those with high materials costs were plumbing, bricklaying and carpentry, and those with high labour costs were plastering, painting, masonry and joinery.

An example of a project giving orders of magnitude for the costs of different trades in house building comes from Huddersfield in 1888. Percentages were calculated from Springett's figures for building 13 lower middle class houses costing an average of £359 each [40].

Masons	61%	Slater	3%
Joiners	20%	Water, gas &	
Plasterers	5%	sanitary	2%
Plumbers	4%	Painter	1%
Whitesmiths	4%	TOTAL	100%

Coastal and inland water transport was the mainstay for large users of bulky raw materials. Delivery to inevitably scattered sites was likely to be by horse-drawn vehicles. The new railways were more help for raw material delivery to headquarters than for supplying sites, although some big projects had their own temporary lines and sidings. General rail freight tonnage increased eight-fold between mid-century and 1914, and typical rates were 21p per ton-mile up to 20 miles and less for greater distances. The new century brought another competitor to the field, with the number of goods road vehicles in the UK swelling from 2,000 to 84,000 between 1902 and 1914 [41]. This sharpened competition among hitherto sheltered materials producers. When large brickmakers and others added steam or motor traction to horse ownership, many vulnerable local producers like small quarries were unable to adapt to the new competition. As the old gave way to rising regional and national concerns, many local building characteristics were eliminated and uniformity spread.

Brick

Foremost among materials was brick: once only one of several alternative walling materials, it advanced to near-domination and became synonymous with building itself. It accounted for a large proportion of the total cost of materials, often not far short of one half. Even where suitable stone was plentiful, brick began to be preferred for most uses. Output by 1907 (4,800 m.) was well over double that of 1845. Uniform-looking machine-made bricks often ousted uneven hand-made ones, and decorative colours and shapes, as well as terracotta work, gained popularity. The Fletton brick industry emerged in the 1880s, expanded strongly in the London market around the turn of the century, and eroded cost advantages held by small yards. Brick prices were relatively stable and not so very different from those of the 1820s. In London, in the mid-1890s, they ranged from about £6 per thousand for very high-quality products, down to £1.15 for place bricks for use in concealed positions [42]. The average price at Fletton works was rather less than the latter, although subsequent cut-throat competition brought some prices so low as to close higher-cost makers.

Stone

The fortunes of stone were the reverse of brick, with a general decline except in monumental architectural uses. Many quarries which survived were ones which managed to find outlets in high-quality work or which avoided costly transport. The economic problem with stone was that of bringing closely together irregular shapes and sizes to make walls as quickly and cheaply as was possible with bricks. Stone cutting was mechanized increasingly and carried out at the quarry rather than on site, so as to minimize transport cost. The cost of stone remained steady from mid-century, having fallen somewhat since the 1820s, but rising labour costs counted against it. Rough rubble walling cost about £1.01 per cu.m in the eighties and nineties, when the cost of rubble delivered to site was 33p per cu.m. For higher-quality work, typical prices at the quarry were about 6.5p per cu.m for Corsham and Doulting stones and triple that for harder Hopton Wood stone.

Timber

Timber was the next most important material after brick, with carpentry and joinery costs on typical small buildings of the 1860s amounting to about a quarter or a third of total building costs. The timber import trade was one of the few international contacts for the building industry and one carried out on a greatly increasing scale. The annual value of UK imports fluctuated between £8 m. and £13 m. in the decade from 1854, and between £23 m. and £34 m. in the decade from

1903. There was a downward cost trend until the 1890s, with a slight rise thereafter amid short-term fluctuations. In the 1850s a typical prime cost of softwood was about £4.75 per load, on site in bonding plates and lintels it was £6.20 per cu.m, and more when wrought and framed. By that time English oak was far more expensive at over £12.35 per cu.m. in bonding plates. Joinery items such as doors and windows were imported at that time and within another decade Swedish and American goods were undercutting home-produced ones, despite increasing workshop mechanization [43, 44].

Slate, tile, plaster and cement

If brick was one half of the stereotypical Victorian building, then slate was the other half; its use for roofing peaked towards the end of the century, by which time North Wales output had nearly devastated rival producers. In the third quarter of the century, slaters' work probably accounted for between 5 and 10% of total building cost, and slate prices in London appear to have been lower than they were earlier in the century. In the 1850s a square (9.3 sq.m or 100 sq.ft) of small slates including labour and metal nails cost £1.30, more for larger slates. Having vanquished so many producers of traditional roofing materials, slate itself faced stiffening competition from early Edwardian years when coloured asbestos-cement tiles joined the concrete tiles already in limited use. Pantiles were often rejected in favour of slates, although prices remained fairly stable: a square of pantiles complete with laths, nails and labour in the 1850s cost between £1.20 and £1.75 [45]. Plain tiles cost more at £2.25 per square, falling, like the cost of pantiles, by about 10 p late in the century. Tile-making followed brick-making with gradual mechanization and some concentration into larger businesses.

Plastering costs were typical of others in following a generally downward trend, with lathing plastered with one coat and set costing about 6p per sq. m in the 1850s. Laxton's price for cement was about 12.5p per bushel (about 0.036 cu.m.) while at the same time Portland cement gradually became more reliable and largely superseded the older Roman cement, but use remained cautious. By 1912 reinforced concrete beams and columns were said to be cheaper than steel, brick arches and timber [46], but were not yet widely adopted.

Services

Building services were a relatively fertile field for innovation and proliferation of branded goods. The price range for many goods is notable: a cheap dry earth closet of deal cost £1.42 in the 1880s, compared with £5 for a similar article in mahogany (or slightly less for a WC with valve); hand basins varied from £1.25 to £11 according to size and material; and there were wide differences between cheap japanned cast iron baths and costly zinc and copper ones. Similarly, there was a wide price range among the large array of gas appliances of the 1890s, with stoves from £1 up to £12 or more, and fires from 72p to £4. The cost of electric lighting installations also varied widely, with a typical sum for a 50 lamp system in office or large house about £100. Where affluent householders had no access to public electricity supply, a private generator with dynamo, accumulators and steam, gas or oil engine, could add a further £300, more than double the cost of a small private gasworks. Lifts of the 1890s ranged from about £32, for supplying and fitting a small dinner lift, to ten times that sum or more, for a 400 kg hydraulic passenger lift of 15 m travel.

Miscellaneous goods

Painting and decorating was a minor trade in terms of total building costs, but a ubiquitous one which increased in importance with the standard of living. Glass usage increased and prices fell: in the 1850s small panes of crown glass cost between 40p and 67p per sq.m and polished plate could be had for around £2.50 per sq.m. About 40 years later polished plate was down to a half or two-thirds of its earlier price and crown glass had been superseded by superior sheet glass costing between 20p and 90p per sq.m. By then glass-making had become very centralized and among new products in their infancy were patent glazing, wired glass and glass blocks.

Like glass, iron and steel demanded large capital investment for production and were supplied to other markets as well as building. Iron prices stood relatively high at mid-century and fluctuated thereafter. The cost of rolled iron girders in the 1880s was from 50p to 75p per cwt (approximately 50.8 kg), far cheaper than it had been back in the 1820s. Competition from newer rolled mild steel joists was not intense. Lighter applications of iron included galvanized sheeting, cast window frames and cast kitchen ranges. Among the ever-widening range of other materials and branded goods offering to improve quality and save labour and cost were the likes of metal and wire partitions ('expedition in erecting'),

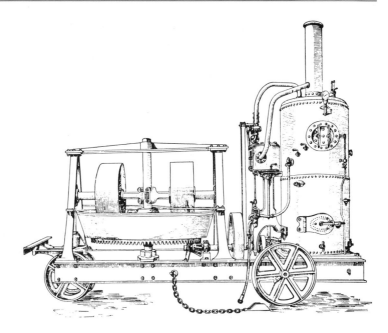

Figure 24 Steam power for builders. Mortar mill, *c.* 1900. From right to left: vertical boiler, vertical cylinder driving horizontal shaft with flywheel, rotating mortar pan with two rollers. Frame is metal channel and wheels are iron. It looks unwieldy to move.

patent ridge tiles ('handsome, neat, artistic and durable'), and patent preparations such as Browning's colourless preservative ('Cleopatra's needle preserved by this solution'). The new century brought new low-cost sheets such as asbestos-cement roofing, fibreboard and millboard.

Plant   Plant required by small builders (and larger ones working on small buildings) was a minimum of craftsmen's hand tools, ladders and odd scraps of timber for scaffolding and shoring. Larger firms working at great heights or depths increasingly bought or hired plant to speed their progress. In larger joinery shops of the 1880s there might be moulding and planing machines, lathes and morticing machines, powered by steam engine. In order to move goods to site, builders could hire a horse, cart and a man at a rate of 7.5p an hour or even use an expensive steam traction engine. Heavy handling might require a portable crane (£34 cost for 1-ton capacity, £120 for 5 tons) and on the largest sites it could be economical to hire a steam excavator at £12 a month. A 600 mm-gauge light railway (£300 a mile) was a far cry from a wheelbarrow (about 75p), but both had parts to play. Other plant included mortar mills (£35 to £90 in the 1890s), and donkey pumps powered by steam or gas engines.

5

Building the suburbs: 1915–1939

Deferred Payments up to 5 years. GARAGES from 61/-d. to 3/9d. down. . . . BUNGALOWS of every size and description priced from £28 carr. pd.

(Advertisement in *Homes and Gardens*, February 1936)

DEMAND AND BUILDING PROMOTERS

Coketown to suburb The old pre-industrial economy had left a distinctive legacy of buildings over the countryside. The succeeding industrial economy superimposed a contrasting legacy of its own; coketowns were added to farm, village and market town. In the interwar years the stock of buildings was further transformed so that the two legacies, rural and urban, merged. The demand was for suburbs. From dense urban centres promoters began to move to the green fields beyond the towns. Demand was marked by vigour, with energetic expansion of those towns and conurbations which managed to escape the heavy industrial depression. Demand also reflected the rise of the public sector, with satisfaction of social need joining profit as a motive for building. The annual average level of public building expenditure increased five-fold between 1920–23 and 1935–38 [1]. Each new responsibility taken on by the State for the well-being of the people brought expansion in public building activity. Efforts to replace slums, improve education, create employment and resist the Nazi threat all led directly or indirectly to public sector building. With the stress and shortages of the First World War the government began to regard building activity as some sort of national priority, a fresh concern which outlived recovery from the war.

**Public
authority and
private
promoters**

The rise of public sector promoters affected many departments of central and local government: during the First World War the Ministry of Munitions and Office of Works, for example, were heavily engaged; after the war came the turn of the local authorities. In the housing field, particularly, policies and public debate moved back and forth between local authorities and private builders and from additions to stock towards replacement. Amid policy changes imposed from above, many of the 1,500 or so local authorities became experienced promoters. Building programmes, consisting of large numbers of small units of building, rather than occasional large units, gave continuity of work in administration and execution. Local authority organizations grew and the provision of houses became almost a matter of routine, although levels of competence were varied [2]. Repetitive procedures applied less to other local authority buildings such as the considerable number of new schools and occasional important buildings like town halls and central libraries, treated as unique ventures. Various departments of central authority also continued after the war to promote a share of buildings, among them post offices, telephone exchanges, labour exchanges, training centres and installations for the armed forces. There was another smaller category of promoters midway between public and private, the newly founded public corporations such as the Central Electricity Board and London Passenger Transport Board.

Private promoters were motivated mainly by profit, although some minor exceptions should not be overlooked. Among them were private trusts and those receiving official subsidies. Private promotion was undertaken for several reasons: to help provide goods or services, as with owner-occupier industrial or commercial promoters developing their own premises; to provide personal satisfaction, as with owners building their own house; to provide income by renting to others, as with a commercial office developer; or to provide a capital gain by outright sale, as with a speculative house builder. The initial act of developers of suburbs, often specialist land or estate agents, was to buy land either for themselves or on behalf of others. Much was bought from land speculators who had originally acquired it to 'hold for a rise', that is to await the reversionary value which would accrue from advancing demand or development of nearby amenities. Having bought the land the developer laid out roads, arranged installation of mains services and offered plots to buyers.

Expensive prime sites might be sold singly for detached houses, otherwise multiples of plots were sold for groups of semi-detached and terraced houses. Occasionally land speculators or original landowners themselves arranged development, employing agents to lay out the site and sell the plots. To attract early buyers many developers erected a few prominently placed houses by means of contracts with builders. The speculative builders, many of them local, who bought or leased the plots often paid only a deposit to the developers; the remainder followed after they had sold the houses which they intended to build. In this they followed the shaky precedent of many of their Victorian forerunners who had survived (if lucky) on the barest minimum of working capital. At some stage, perhaps later rather than sooner, sites were taken by other private interests for shops, and by public interests for church, school and other non-residential buildings. Developers generally hoped to dispose of entire sites within five years and to recover costs plus interest and make a profit of not less than 10%. Speculative builders sometimes kept houses as investments or sold them to other investors, but most were sold to owner occupiers, at which point building societies played a crucial part in lending money to buyers. The growth and concentration of building societies was spectacular, with a nine-fold increase in both shares and deposits over the period, and a five- or six-fold increase in the annual amount advanced on mortgage.

A variation on the method of development, more typical of the South East during the 1930s than the 1920s, was for large building firms themselves to handle all the various stages from site purchase to finished building. A vertically integrated series of development, sales and building companies, with related financial support, carried out much of the work formerly done by the numbers of independent firms [3, 4]. Increase in the size and scope of concerns here was like that in local authorities and other promoters such as high street retailers, manufacturers and railway companies, where there were amalgamations and emergence of large organizations. The larger private and public building promoters increasingly needed large and continuous building programmes instead of intermittent ones. They began to accumulate first-hand knowledge about the nature, cost, timescale and procedures of building; they were becoming experts, less parochial and less at the mercy of suppliers of buildings.

Location

The largest additions to the building stock were made on farmland near the towns. Early in the century the percentage of land area occupied by urban development was just short of 5.5, rising slightly to 6.2 in 1925 and then rapidly to 8.6 in 1939. Towards the end of the period the rate of development was over 25,000 hectares a year [5]. This was fast enough to provoke anxieties which did nothing to redeem the doubtful reputation of speculative builders.

Among the stimuli of surburban growth were repulsion from often unattractive towns, and the magnetism of the countryside, with connotations of health (and cheaper land). A newer influence was increasing mobility brought by mechanized transport and rising incomes. Bigger towns needed bigger centres so that gradual conversion, extension and renewal made in total for a larger, taller and more specialized building stock. Yet by no means was there unbridled growth right across the country, for there were sharp contrasts between the regions. In the South and Midlands, where economic prospects were brightest, new houses and light industry burgeoned. In depressed or 'special' areas of declining old industries in the North and West, there was decay. J.B. Priestley's comparison was between the 'England of arterial and by-pass roads, of filling stations and factories . . . of giant cinemas and dance halls and cafes, bungalows with tiny garages' and sad places of 'cindery waste ground, mill chimneys, slums, fried-fish shops . . . sooty dismal little towns' [6].

Fluctuations

The turning point in the fortunes of older industrial towns was the First World War. For four years non-essential building tapered away as national priorities and resources were redirected from construction to destruction. New work required an official licence and output was drastically curtailed, although not before completion of some sizeable contracts such as Heal's store, Tottenham Court Road, and the academic building in which these words are being written. Uncertainty over the outcome of the war, stagnant incomes and conversion of production to satisfy needs of war all hindered change to the building stock. The exception was building for war purposes, such as armaments factories, hutted camps and hospitals for the armed services.

The armistice was followed by intractable national problems of readjustment, both in building and heavy industries. A brief postwar economic boom brought sizeable, but short-lived,

Figure 25 Impact of war. Innovatory construction to house wartime shipbuilding workers in Chepstow, Gwent, *c.* 1917. Concrete blocks are substituted for scarce bricks. Open-fronted casting shed and yard with finished blocks stacked (foreground). Narrow guage railway serves yard (extreme left). On railway siding behind shed are some Government Office of Works trucks. (Courtesy of Chepstow Museum.)

demand for industrial buildings at about the same time that local authorities struggled with a housing shortage. Collapse in demand soon followed, and with it a fall of prices from high levels. Recovery in building came in 1924 so that gross capital formation in UK building expanded from about £109 m. in 1923 to £201 m. in 1927. Activity then slipped back a little, but remained fairly high, largely due to house building, until a burst of vigorous growth took place from 1932 leading to the interwar peak of £272 m. in 1937. By then not only was the volume of building greater than hitherto, but the old violent extremes of boom and slump had been much reduced. The great overall addition to stock was unmistakable: in Birmingham in 1938, over one-third of all dwellings in the city were less than 19 years old.

Influences on demand

The impressive national performance in meeting building demand was a response to various important forces. High

Figure 26 Modernism arising. Immaculate white architecture emerges from mud and sparse scaffolding. House designed by William Lescaze in Dartington, Devon, 1932. (Source: British Architectural Library, RIBA, London.)

among them were demographic changes, of which the most significant was an increase in the number of families. While population growth was very moderate compared with nineteenth-century levels, the number of families in the UK increased considerably, by 3.5 m. between 1921 and 1938. This meant that although the average family size was much smaller than it had been, the need for separate houses increased greatly. Housing need was stimulated also by movement between regions, mostly by unemployed manual workers from depressed areas seeking jobs in the South East and Midlands, which gained over a million people by immigration between 1921 and 1936. Most of those who found jobs benefited from increases in real income, enabling them to translate housing need into effective demand. Better-paid households could move to better houses, often changing from rental to owner-occupation in the process. Another stimulus for building came from the fashion for suburban living [7], which increased demand for more than houses, for even the most soulless ribbon development eventually generated shops and other amenity buildings. A further source of demand was that arising from replacement of worn-out buildings, although in total this was not as large as the condition of the stock appeared to warrant. Where good accommodation was scarce, people made to with obsolescent buildings and replacements were few, but where emigration eased the shortage, local authorities could demolish and replace, rather than only add to stock.

Most of the sources for demand noted so far concerned occupants (or would-be occupants), but there was demand also from investors who either sold or let. This demand was influenced by the level of return on investment which could be expected. From 1915 house rents were controlled by government and returns generally were smaller than hitherto, although they recovered slowly on average between the wars. Another influence on investment demand was the level of competition from alternative investments and the level of general interest rates: when high, investors put their money in fields outside building in order to get greatest returns; when low, their money flowed into building. Interest rates were very low after 1931 and many investors were attracted by the favourable returns and freedom from risk possible from property and building societies. Swelling with funds, the societies offered mortgages to householders of ever smaller incomes, thereby broadening their market. New industrial and commercial building was determined mainly by level of business activity and technological change. Growth of manufacturing soon led to new building, as did growth and concentration in retailing, insurance, banking and the like, particularly if interest rates on loans available for expansion happened to be low. The volume of building activity was influenced by the cost of building, with cheapness promoting activity. Here, once postwar difficulties were overcome, the pattern was favourable, with costs moving downwards for the most part until the late 1930s. One other influence on activity, and not the least, was government policy, in which efforts to stimulate house building could indirectly affect the cost of all other kinds of building. Subsidies to private house builders had more limited impact, but still were significant and, similarly, municipal non-residential building could exert an influence. This was particularly so where it happened to be close to building for rearmament purposes in the later 1930s.

ADDITIONS TO BUILDING STOCK

Housing

Between the wars a total of 3,998,000 dwellings were built in England and Wales – a large output, maintaining the annual value of new housing at over half that of all building. The peak was reached in 1937 with 347,000 completions, equivalent to over 1,000 every working day. Nearly three-quarters of the total 2,886,000, were built by private agencies, most for sale rather than rent. At the outset private house builders recovered slowly from wartime dislocation, with fewer than 100,000 completions before March 1923. Less than half of these were built with the aid of subsidy introduced by the Housing (Additional Powers) Act 1919, intended to stimulate private house building. This inducement was not long-lived, it being Chamberlain's 1923 Housing Act which triggered more lasting expansion, with a subsidy of £6 per house for up to 20 years, subject to restriction on house size. The rate of house building, subsidized and unsubsidized, increased until the late 1920s when subsidized completions fell away. They subsequently reached 430,000, but were eclipsed by an upsurge in the number of unsubsidized houses. Heavy activity in the late 1920s was interrupted by slight slackening during the slump before the golden years of speculative building after 1932. The threat of the approaching Second World War and market saturation reached intense activity from 1938. As Professor Burnett has written [8], new houses have probably never been so cheap or so widely available as in the mid-thirties.

Typical 1930s speculative houses were known as 'five fifties', their selling price being £550. For this the mortgaged householder could expect a semi-detached 'Tudorbethan'-style house on an estate at a density of 20 or 25 per hectare. Typical accommodation was: hall and stairs; parlour (11.6 sq.m); living room (13.0 sq.m); 'kitchenette' (6.0 sq.m); upstairs bathroom and separate WC; and three bedrooms. The average cost per cu.m was about £1.75. Not all houses cost as much as the 'five fifties'; around London a reasonable minimum was £400 and elsewhere it was £300 or even £250. For a short time after the First World War, when prices generally were high, even the cheapest houses were far above such levels. Around 1920, small London houses cost as much as £1,000, until a steep fall brought unit costs from £10.75 per sq.m to about £5.40 by 1922. Costs drifted slowly downwards thereafter under the influence of low interest rates. The relationship of housing unit costs to those of other major building types now settled into a pattern which was to persist broadly unchanged for many years. However, cost relationships over time necessarily must be approximate, because building types changed their forms, invalidating direct comparisons [9].

The top end of the 1930s suburban speculative market had houses for £1,000 to £1,250 or more. For example, £1,200 semi-detached three-bedroom houses built by A.W. Curton at Edgware each had a dining room 4.1 × 4.5 m; drawing room 3.7 × 5.3 m; kitchen 2.8 × 3.2 m and a garage. Individual architect-designed houses overlapped in cost with the better speculatively built ones, but most were more expensive [10]. The size, and probably number, of new larger private houses was less than before 1914, owing to the effects of higher taxes, economic depression and shortage of domestic servants. The proportion of new houses large enough to have rateable values between £27 and £78 fell from 33% before 1931 to only 13% between that year and 1939. Typical architect-designed detached four-bedroom houses cost over £1,400, about £2.00 per cu.m. Some cost £2,500 and upwards, with unit costs of £3.00 per cu.m, while the wealthiest few could pay £4.40 per cu.m for a mansion or compact town service flat.

Public sector housing [11] was sustained during the First World War by the Ministry of Munitions which erected both temporary and permanent accommodation for war workers. After the armistice local authorities were quickly plunged into action by interventionist central government anxious to reward a weary and fractious people with 'Homes fit for heroes' to meet a severe shortage. They did so, through vicissitudes [12], to the extent of a total of 1,112,000 new dwellings by 1939. Provision was started by Addison's Housing and Town Planning Act 1919 which required (no longer merely permitted) local authorities to ascertain housing need and, with Ministry approval, take action. Soon, new estates showing the influence of the forward-looking Tudor Walters Report [13], began to appear, but so, too, did alarming price increases, reflecting overstretched resources. The housing drive was curtailed after 170,000 completions; the heroes would have to wait [14]. The Chamberlain Housing Act which followed in 1923 stimulated some further local authority activity whilst demanding greater financial responsibility from them. Local authorities were restored fully to their new-found place of importance in housing provision in 1924 by the Wheatley Act. New subsidies revived local authority activity to reach the interwar peak of 104,000 new houses in 1928, a few of which embodied novel prefabricated techniques. Soon official attention turned from additions to stock towards replacement of slums by means of subsidies created by the 1930 Greenwood Housing Act. Eventually this and later measures intended to abate overcrowding led to redirection from houses to flat building. In the late 1930s under the shadow of approaching war, local authority activity expanded almost to its 1928 level.

Addison Act houses were relatively high quality, generous size, short terrace and semi-detached at densities of about 30 per hectare. Floor areas ranged between about 88 sq.m and as much as 130 sq.m. A typical plan by the Ministry of Health for local authority guidance had hall and stairs, living room (16 sq.m), parlour (12 sq.m), scullery (7.5 sq.m), larder and coal store. There were three bedrooms corresponding with the main downstairs rooms and a separate bathroom and WC [15]. In 1920 the cost with parlour was about £955, equivalent to nearly £10.75 per sq.m, and without parlour £870. By 1923 non-parlour three-bedroom houses on average had fallen to £365, or £5.80 per sq.m. Chamberlain and Wheatley Act houses which followed were smaller and cheaper, with most between 70 and 80 sq.m in floor area. Later examples and those built under the Greenwood Act were smaller than earlier ones [16]. When quality was near its lowest in 1936 the average cost of non-parlour three-bedroom houses was £310 and that of parlour houses £487, approaching double the figures of 1913. The number of flats was small compared with houses, at about one in 20 local authority dwellings [17]. They were built in the largest cities and most took the form of four- or five-storey blocks at densities of 110 to 160 dwellings per hectare. With more costly structures, circulation and services they cost about one-third to two-thirds more than equivalent accommodation in houses. By the late 1930s, when costs were beginning to rise, the average was about £600 each, around £2.65 per cu.m.

Industrial buildings

Near many a new outlying estate of semi-detached houses, over an improved arterial road, were the long and mostly low shapes of new factories. In 1935 about 5% of building investment was in industrial or warehouse buildings, and many individual units were imposing ones. They appeared widely during the early 1920s boom, but activity then faded for a decade, until there was fresh growth lasting for about five years. Like new private houses, most factories were located in the South and Midlands where there were effective distribution networks and proximity to the largest consumer markets. Freed from earlier dependence on congested city-centre sites by improved communications and electric power, factories now fitted more spacious suburban sites. The *Architects' Journal* [18] remained sceptical:

> . . . all the terrible signs of pig-headed industrialism . . . at Hayes, Southall and fanwise round the northern suburbs are springing up miles of new factories. Even the Great West Road . . . has, in places, the look of a motor track leading to an absolute fun-fare of comic factories. It is as though London were now the absolutely irresistible magnet for all the money in the country.

While the old staples remained depressed, growth was to be found in motor, electrical, rubber, manufactured foodstuff, furniture, hosiery and other light finished consumer goods industries. Typical new factories were larger than before and some were standard units, rented rather than owned by their occupiers. Earlier in the period, in particular, they might well be multi-storey [19], but the typical 1930s pattern was a single-storey block with saw-tooth bays of north-light roofing concealed at the front by offices. In heavy plants such as those for chemicals, purely engineering aspects often replaced traditional building enclosures, so that tanks, pipes, valves and so on were fully exposed to view and building provision was very basic. Where managements were unadventurous (say, textiles), as well as where growth was hectic (say, motor manufacture), building was often more improvisatory than visionary. Simple buildings such as engine sheds cost £1.30 to £1.40 per cu.m and factories were to be had for £1.75 to £2.35 per cu.m (not much different from housing). Typical warehouses cost from £2.20 per cu.m to £2.95 per cu.m and some examples, like two Southern Railway Company cargo sheds in Southampton Docks in 1934 costing £145,000, serve to remind of the very large scale of some industrial investment.

Not all industrial installations were mundane: there was a handful of new airport terminals as at Heston and Croydon, as well as novel multi-storey garages to house part of the six-fold increase in motor vehicles during the period. Some fast-growing firms serving new consumer markets were happy to pay for showpiece designs which attracted public attention. Sir Bannister Fletcher's Gillette factory, built in 1926 on the Great West Road, was one such. New buildings for rearmament purposes were a different matter. They appeared increasingly in the later 1930s as the Hitler threat intensified. While in 1934 major new RAF works amounted to a modest £900,000, two years later the figure had jumped to £8 m., and in 1938 it was £20 m. [20]. Work for the other armed services was to be added, with one new ordnance factory at Glascoed alone expected to cost £3.7 m. in 1938.

From the military to rural life was a long step; agricultural building remained light and of piecemeal adaptive nature, largely for livestock. Extreme economy drove many farmers to reuse 1914–18 wartime huts and discarded railway rolling stock bodies, but those who could afford better paid about £1.20 per cu.m for new barns and £1.75 per cu.m for cow houses [21].

Commercial buildings

Commercial buildings such as town centre offices, shops and hotels were a category which generally was smaller in value than industrial work. Activity fluctuated uncertainly, with depression in the early 1920s and 1930s offset by periods of growth around 1922 to 1924, 1927 to 1929 and from 1932 to 1934. Promoters who set the pace were non-local development companies, chain stores, insurance companies and the like, building for themselves; private individuals lost their former significance, except as owner-occupiers. As promoter decisions moved from local high street and provincial city centre to nationally centralized sources, funding now came from banks and sale of shares rather than from local capitalists [22]. Top-quality office building cost £3.50 or more per cu.m, but lesser premises for rent on the open market, for branch banks and building societies, down to plain blocks connected with factories and depots, cost of the order of £2.65 per cu.m. Large department stores, costing about the same as the best offices, increased from about 200 in 1914 to over 500 in 1938. Similarly the number of premises occupied by multiple chains such as Marks and Spencer expanded briskly: in 1919 Woolworths had 81 stores, by 1939 the number was 768. Smaller shops and showrooms cost between £2.65 and £2.95 per cu.m, perhaps £10,000 each in total, while minor examples in suburban parades cost from £1,000 to £2,000.

Many new shopping centres soon acquired a cinema: there were about 3,000 in 1926 and another 1,300 within eight years, having a combined seating capacity of 3.8 m; by 1939 the total had reached 4,800 buildings. A suburban example like the Regal, Altrincham cost £27,000 while the exceptional

Figure 27 Cinema building, 1920. Reinforced concrete frame (left centre) and walling (right centre). Steel frame roof by Dawnay. (Source: E. Turner & Sons, Cardiff.)

4,000-seat Gaumont State, Kilburn, cost as much as £345,000 in 1937. In a sense, cinemas carried on where hotels had left off in 1914 in competing with each other in conspicuous expenditure. Some new hotels still appeared, but earlier flamboyance was usually lacking. Costs appear to have advanced from £4.00 per cu.m in 1927 to an upper limit of £7.00 per cu.m in 1936, although few other building types increased by more than about 30p per cu.m. Leisure needs also gave rise to a moderate number of public houses, many in the range of £10,000 to £15,000, and to seaside holiday camps which by 1939 could house half a million pleasure-seekers.

Public and social buildings

A large proportion of all public and social buildings were put up by public authorities and probably only a diminishing minority came from philanthropic individuals and charitable trusts. Public authority building expenditure soon recovered from its low levels of 1918 to reach a size comparable with both industrial and commercial categories. The upward trend

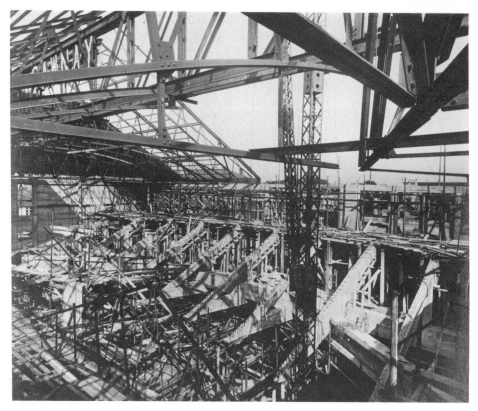

Figure 28 Heavy structures. Large Cardiff cinema has concrete balcony structure and steel roof. (E. Turner & Sons, Cardiff.)

was almost continuous, except for a pause during the slump, in contrast to other sorts of non-residential building which suffered periodic falls. Expenditure on public and social buildings of the order of £5 m. a year (at 1930 prices) shortly after 1918 climbed to over £30 m. by 1938. This expansion is all the more notable since it took place in a period widely regarded as one of government inactivity and lack of resolve, the time of the 'long-weekend' and 'wasted years', with mass unemployment and appeasement. Yet there was another side, with fairly widespread relief projects and municipal building, a key part of which (in addition to ever-dominant housing) was building for education.

This began with a light programme which included reused army huts for classrooms, but later in the 1920s there was steady development of secondary schools, followed by further resurgence after the slump. In 1934 a junior mixed and infant school for 600 children could be built for about £13,000 and a few years later senior schools cost about £50 per pupil. A reasonable cost for cheaper school building was about £2.35 per cu.m, with more for the modest quantity of private and further education building. Only about 5% of children attended private fee-paying schools and the increase in students in full-time higher education between 1924 and 1938 was only 8,000, to a total of 69,000.

Technical institutions and large hospitals, where there was some expansion, had fairly heavy costs of about £3.50 per cu.m. The total number of beds in hospitals and related institutions increased from 200,000 shortly before the First World War to about 260,000 in 1938, while the number of hospital institutions went up from 2,190 to 3,140. The wide variety of medical buildings ranged from small cottage hospitals and clinics complete for around £10,000 up to large hospitals like Chadwell Heath, Essex, for 1,120 patients for about £0.5 m. in 1938. Public expenditure on this heavy scale was not confined to health buildings. New town halls were so conspicuously large and expensive that George Orwell [23] questioned why so many northern towns saw fit to build themselves immense and luxurious examples in times of severe housing shortage. Barnsley spent close on £150,000 on a new town hall (enough for well over 350 council houses), and Southampton Guildhall cost almost the same. A typical cost for such buildings (and also law courts) in the mid-1930s was about £4.10 per cu.m, although London ratepayers found the cost of upholding civic dignity nearer £5.30 per cu.m. A few museums and art galleries and, more frequently, libraries were also built. Smaller branch libraries cost anything between £7,000 (Belsize Branch, Hampstead, 1937) and over £40,000 (Leytonstone Branch, Church Lane, 1934), between £2.95 and £3.25 per cu.m. Central libraries such as Huddersfield, completed in October 1939, cost £3.50 per cu.m; £87,000 altogether. Even this was dwarfed by Manchester, which reached nearly £400,000 in 1934.

Public authorities provided many other far less monumental and more utilitarian building types. Among them were police stations for about £2.95 per cu.m, fire stations for slightly less, crematoria and laundries. Some of the latter were immense; for example, Surrey County Council's Carshalton central laundry was estimated at £186,000 in 1938. New public baths and washhouses also were significant, with over £2.5 m. in loans sanctioned during the three years to 1937, and cubic costs similar to those of police stations. There was also hostel building, such as a home for 220 nurses in Crumpsall, Manchester, for £80,000 in 1930 (incidentally, about enough to have bought each nurse their own house). Many other buildings, most cheaper, were promoted for non-commercial purposes either by public authorities, private interests or combinations of both. They included drill halls at only £1.75 per cu.m, village halls at 35p or so more, sports pavilions and a few community centres. The great impetus behind religious buildings, so strong in the nineteenth century, was now much weaker, although there were more than 2,000 new buildings between 1921 and 1941. In the 1930s the cost of places of worship per cu.m was between £1.50 for plain corrugated iron chapels ('tin tabernacles') and £12.65 for brick, while good quality examples cost about £11 to £14 per seat.

LOSSES FROM STOCK

Slum clearance and obsolescence

The times were not very good ones for the demolition gangs. Clearance must have been reduced by unfettered suburban expansion which would have redirected some development pressure from urban centres. Shortage of low-cost housing also encouraged patching and mending rather than replacement. Limited damage was inflicted by air raids and coastal bombardment during the First World War. In the 1920s, about 179,000 slums were demolished, with a further 258,000 in the 1930s. Many stood, and fell, in the fastest-growing earlier nineteenth century towns. One cycle of activity begat another as building boom eventually led to obsolescence boom. Town centre commercial expansion accounted for further housing losses. Some old industrial buildings also were destroyed, as with redundant textile mills (700 premises closed between 1933 and 1938) and some buildings in the prostrate heavy industries.

Quiet decay proceeded in the country among less competitive farms and workshops of blacksmiths, saddlers and others. With growing concentration and changed markets and products, small bakeries, mills and shops disappeared, their premises finding new owners and uses, or simply being abandoned to ruin. Small beer houses were replaced by large road houses; cramped stables were swept away to make space for filling stations; corner shops came down and department stores went up. Ceaselessly the work of attrition went on as the cherished investments of one generation transmuted into the liabilities of another.

BUILDING FORM

Outward and upward growth

The physical form of typical new buildings changed in numerous ways due to broad economic and social influences. Perhaps the foremost change was the continued growth of maximum and average building size to reflect that of the institutions and organizations which were housed. The tallest buildings were higher, volumes greater and large groups of related buildings more numerous, as seen in imposing new power stations, aircraft hangars and some multi-storey factories. New offices, shops and department stores, and composite versions of them, dwarfed neighbouring older buildings in town centres. Some new giants occupied whole street blocks, so that streets in leading commercial districts became ever more canyon-like.

Escalating urban land values encouraged promoters to redevelop sites to the limit of their capacity, spatial and financial. As town centre building designs were pushed to their limits, physical forms were more determined by regulations governing daylight, ventilation and fire precautions, among the main legally enforceable constraints. Prominent legislation included Factory and Workshop Acts in 1929 and 1937 (following those of 1901 and 1907) and the Public Health Act of 1936. Larger buildings were encouraged by technical advances in services and framed structures, and by an element of rivalry between instigators of succeeding projects.

Beyond the town centres, among more dispersed suburban development, the dominant emphasis of built form was less upward than outward, in the shape of mainly horizontal buildings. There were carpets of one- and two-storey development, punctuated only occasionally by the height of a new cinema (or engulfed old village church). Lower forms and densities were a product of lower site values (probably averaging £16 per m of frontage around London, less elsewhere) than prevailed in town centres. Other practical and economic advantages also favoured lower and more dispersed buildings, since lofty, gravity-defying structures and basements were difficult and expensive to design, construct and maintain, for all their powers to exploit restricted sites and impress onlookers. Where they could be avoided, and in the suburbs they nearly always could, it paid to do so.

Universal space   Differentiation between one building type and another, and between separate parts of the same building in some cases, grew less. Needless to say, built form had always been tailored in size and shape to the specific functions and activities which it contained. Proliferation of building forms and types with the emergence of new functions, already noted in the nineteenth-century context, continued, but now amid signs of a contrary trend. While some forms became more specialized according to function, others became less so by the development of universal space. Increasingly whole floors were provided as unobstructed open spaces, without subdivision by partitions, columns or varied ceiling heights. Similarly, many whole large buildings took the form of repetitive uniform bays, each part indistinguishable from the rest. As well as speeding up building operations, this enabled early decisions about activities and functions to be postponed and, later, in the life of the building, to be changed at will without demanding difficult physical alterations. One instance of need for flexibility arose from expansion in the market for offices, leading to buildings being made without prior knowledge of their occupiers' identity. Another instance came from the Board of Education, increasingly aware that some school activities were hampered by inability to make economical adjustments to the fabric [24]. Similar considerations applied in the retail and shopfitting world.

Some offices were planned to allow space to be let either in single or multiple increments, depending on demand; final choice could be left open. Likewise, in many factories there was need for unobstructed floors capable of meeting a variety of functions. Among many influences which encouraged this were speculative rather than custom-built development, availability of flexible electric power, use of light plant making consumer goods for changeable markets, need to accommodate expansion and adaptation of equipment, and perhaps a desire to maintain factory resale value. A pioneering attempt to accommodate change was the LMSR research laboratories at Derby, in 1935, where partitions were demountable and services specially positioned [25]. The penalty paid in some fields for inflexibility was recognized, and obsolescence within five years or so not unknown.

Range of quality   Building quality, loosely embodied in terms of spaciousness, durability, performance and cost, continued to vary widely. The quality range of new buildings, between highest and lowest, before 1914, may be regarded as a pyramid. At the base were numerous low-quality examples and near the apex a small number of those of high quality. The pyramid broadly reflected the nature of society, with the wealthy minority at the top and the poorer majority below. It is supposed that in the interwar years the pyramid became rather more squat. As social and economic differences between the classes narrowed, so differences between highest- and lowest-quality new buildings also diminished. The quality and number of the best buildings was held down mainly by the economic constraints imposed by their promoters. The quality of the poorest buildings was elevated, if anything, by more effective by-laws, public sector promotion and economic growth.

Nowhere was this process of compression between the two extremes more visible than in housing. Major country house building, already flagging before 1914, became all but extinct, superseded by fewer and less grandiose new houses. At the same time the quality of new rural cottages, traditionally the embodiment of the lowest standards, improved, as hovels yielded to asbestos-sheet chalets and the like. Likewise, new working class housing improved, as makeshift flat conversions and cramped tenements gave way to suburban local authority housing estates.

Form and appearance

Other notable general trends in form and appearance remain. Building mass in proportion to usable floor area diminished as massive load-bearing masonry external walls were increasingly replaced by structural frames and infill. Similarly, solid masonry domestic walls were replaced by cavity brickwork, and stout masonry partitions lost favour to slender concrete block or light sheet substitutes. External appearances were affected by restraint in the use of applied ornament, so that Edwardian spiky roof silhouettes, intricate porches, terracotta work and suchlike were widely sacrificed to modernist simplicity. Lower ceiling heights and generally simpler roofs and chimneys, as well as more generous windows lent greater horizontal emphasis to many domestic buildings. Builders before the First World War having aspired to the heavens, now preferred to convey an impression of speed across the land. In larger buildings wider use of frames in multi-storeys and multi-bays was likely to be concealed behind more traditional claddings. New forms of construction were more likely to be displayed and celebrated in the small minority of overtly modernist buildings and in utilitarian structures such as factories. Exteriors of most other buildings continued to look traditional, often in some dilute variant of the classical style, even if they concealed technical innovations within. In appearance, particularly, the products of the building industry were at their most conservative, being led, it may be supposed, by demand. In building function and performance (and out of sight) it was often different, with rather less reluctance to experiment.

Services   Attitudes to mechanical and electrical services were probably the most progressive of all, with almost everyone happy to forgo the rigours of old heating, lighting, plumbing and sanitation in exchange for modern comfort, convenience (and cost). Much of the money saved by eliminating traditional exterior decorations like plinths, fretted barge boards and ornamental ridge tiles, found its way indoors into improved services. The general directions of development were already clear by 1914, and most later changes were consolidation. By the 1930s services in housing had grown in complexity and their cost amounted to one-third of the total for the building.

The greatest technical advances were in electrical systems, the market for which expanded vigorously such that British consumers increased from 730,000 in 1920 to 2.8 m. in 1929, and nearly 9.0 m. by the 1930s. Gas lighting declined accordingly, although it continued to be installed for this purpose in some houses in the 1920s. Central heating systems, some oil, most coal, appeared more widely in offices and public buildings, but seldom in houses. Large non-residential buildings relied more and more on lifts and were fitted with more telephones and ventilation systems. In houses there were more numerous, and more reliable, plumbing and drainage services, electric and gas water heaters, and fitted fires instead of small open ones. The benefits which services brought to building users were very great. This was a period in which earlier inventions in the field diffused far more widely. In doing so, the luxuries of the Edwardian few became the convenience (figuratively as well as literally) of the many.

6

The industry as a force for stability: 1915–1939

There is rather a tendency for industry nowadays to expect the Government to take the initiative in everything.

(O.W. Roskill *Architects Journal*, 1 December 1938)

CHARACTER AND INFLUENCES

Position in national economy

The position of the building industry between the wars was marked by prosperity and independence. Although building activity was, as ever, ubiquitous and immense in total, it remained aside from the most intense political and economic storm centres which disfigured the period. Fluctuations in activity were not closely similar to fluctuations in other industries, although upward and downward movements in building sometimes led movements in other sectors. Growth of building activity stimulated materials producers and other associated industries and services; what was good for building was likely to be good for transport, public utilities, consumer durables and legal and financial services. If the national economy was not entirely carried forward by the growth of building, at least building seems to have exerted an important stabilizing influence in troubled times [1].

While the exact influence of building on the national economy may be debated, the magnitude of the industry is beyond dispute: the share of building investment in UK gross domestic capital formation generally exceeded 40%. Even at its lowest (38% in 1923), building investment compared well with levels before the First World War. At its highest (58% in 1933) it took on a dominating stature. Moreover the rate of growth of building production was greater than that of industry generally, estimated at 4% and 2% respectively, between 1913 and 1938. Indeed, it may be argued that investment in building was large enough to starve of capital other industries deserving modernization. The significance of building for good or ill was most evident in the capital market, but it was important also as a source of employment. In 1921 the number of males occupied in building in England and Wales (974,000) was barely more than it had been in 1901 and represented a smaller proportion (8.0%) of the total occupied male population. By 1931 the number in building had grown to 1,277,000 and the proportion of the male workforce was 9.6% [2], figures which subsequently grew still further. After recovery from the low levels of output per man which followed the First World War, more men on more sites than ever before each carried out a larger volume of work. By 1937 output was reckoned to exceed by a third or half the levels of 1924, at least in respect of local authority houses.

PROFESSIONS

Contracts   The way in which demand for buildings was formulated and put before the builders remained broadly unchanged. Where promoter and builder were separate concerns, a contract usually was agreed between the two parties and its execution administered by professional designers and their advisers. Many large and experienced promoters, particularly local authorities, permanently employed their own architects, engineers and surveyors, otherwise they commissioned independent consultants. In cases in which promoter and builder were the same, no contract was necessary, although often the services of employee or consultant professionals were still required. The aim of contract procedure and documentation was to minimize scope for disagreement between the parties, but the delicate balance of opposing interests was difficult to strike. The key principles were that the whole works would be carried out by one organization; work would be completed for a predetermined sum; drawings would be complete before work started; and the contract would be the administrative responsibility of an architect. Contract procedures continued to evolve, with the 1909 standard form being superseded, after lengthy negotiations between the representatives of the architects and builders, in 1931 [3]. In the same year the Joint Contracts Tribunal was set up to continue similar work [4].

Architects   Architects were estimated to design about one half of all
building work by value in the late 1930s. Repetitive housing
was the largest field in which the cost of their services might be
avoided and there engineers, surveyors and unqualified
draughtsmen frequently tried their hands. The proportion of
architect-designed speculative houses was said in 1938 to have
doubled from the 5 or 10% of the late 1920s [5]. In non-
residential work, the proportion designed by architects was far
more. According to the *Architects' Journal* in 1939 it was about
85%. Consolidation of the profession may be seen in a near
quadrupling of RIBA membership between 1910, when it was
2,300, and 1940, when it exceeded 8,800, although the census
indicated only a small increase in total numbers of architects,
from 8,900 to 9,200. The RIBA absorbed the Society of
Architects in 1925, the year in which the Incorporated
Association of Architects and Surveyors, and the Faculty of
Architects and Surveyors were founded by those remaining
outside the RIBA. Registration Acts of 1931 and 1938
established a register of architects and protected their title,
thereby closing the profession [6]. It was the end of old-style
and loosely defined architects with strong links to the industry
and property development. Resulting gains in the esteem of
traditional clients were offset by losses in contact with practical
operations and project management.

Efforts to win higher standing in society were accompanied
by increasing professional responsibility and liability. Established trends continued to bring larger demands: bigger
projects, new materials, methods and specialisms required
fresh technical knowledge and management ability; new
legislation governing structural stability, fire precautions and
so on, protracted design times and negotiations. In 1919 the
profession could take some consolation for the passing of
earlier, simpler times, from the increase of fees by 1% of the
cost of the works, to a total of 6%. The 1938 Registration Act
perhaps represented the apotheosis of private architectural
practice, moving in a professional world like that portrayed in
the celebrated *Honeywood File* [7]. This described the pitfall-
strewn, but nevertheless agreeable path followed by a gentle-
manly architect putting up a country house for his wealthy
client. The rural builder was depicted as a reliable fund of
practical experience who knew his place in a working world
dominated by fine social class distinctions. An inkling of the
remoteness of non-fictional professional life from mainstream
society is seen in the archaism of titling architectural drawings

using the Latin 'V' instead of the English 'U', as in 'Proposed School at Bvshey, Hertfordshire.' Gentility was not always so much to the fore. Whitehand [8] has noted that among smaller town high street projects, local architects were losing work to their big-city brethren. This followed architects' proximity to promoters, who were becoming more concentrated in large centres. Another shift arising from change among promoters was the ascendance of salaried employee local authority architects. Official architects had existed in the 1920s and earlier, but their numbers had been too small and their prestige too low to rival private practitioners. This position was beginning to change by the late 1930s, with official architects becoming more powerful and numerous.

Allied professions and other bodies

What appeared to some as gentility, looked more like lethargy and inertia to others, at least when it came to technical innovation. According to Bowley [9], a climate of narrow conservatism among architects and their co-professionals was due in part to a lack of incentive for innovation, together with insufficient contact with the industry. Ideas already in existence languished for lack of stimulus to develop them. This was in part the price to be paid for casting the architectural

Figure 29 Joinery shop. High-quality contractor E. Turner & Sons, Cardiff premises, probably 1920s. Artificial lighting looks meagre for precision work. Working conditions contrast with stonemasons' yard. (Source: E. Turner & Sons, Cardiff.)

profession as 'client's friend' and directing it away from direct involvement in building production.

Like architects, structural engineers underwent professional consolidation, emerging in 1922 as a specialization in their own right, distinct from civil engineers, to form the Institution of Structural Engineers out of a transformed Concrete Institute [10]. Consolidation elsewhere included the founding of the Town Planning Institute in 1914, absorption of the Quantity Surveyors' Association by the Surveyors' Institution in 1922, and foundation of the Institute of Quantity Surveyors in 1938. Relations between the various professional groups was viewed rather more in terms of competition and demarcation than of shared experience. These professional bodies were joined by other new organizations in related fields, such as the Building Research Station (BRS) which originated under official guidance in the early 1920s for the investigation of new materials. Another example was the British Standards Institution which began as an Engineering Standards Committee in 1901, was incorporated by Royal Charter in 1929 and became the national organization for promulgation of standard terms, codes of practice and specifications of materials. Another body was the National House Builders' Registration Council,

Figure 30 Power stone sawing works. Turner's premises sometime before 1928. Stone is moved by heavy electric gantry crane and jib crane (left distance). Men work at shaping stone under open-sided lean-to (right). (Source: E. Turner & Sons, Cardiff.)

Figure 31 Undeveloped division of labour. Remote rural builder's yard, Lloyney, near Knighton, Welsh borders. Enterprise appears to combine wheelwrighting. In background is 'Builder's Arms' public house, perhaps another part of the concern. Locally grown timber is being sawn by steam. Proprietor Fred Jones is seated on sawbench, nearest engine. Date is 1929, but little seems to have changed for a half century or more. (Source: R. Hill & P. Stamper *Working Countryside 1862–1945*.)

founded in 1937 in an attempt to safeguard the quality of new private houses, some of which had been less than their proud owners had hoped. A growing number of associations such as the British Constructional Steelwork Association of 1929 and the Cement and Concrete Association of 1935 were set up to protect and advance sectional trade interests. Whether commercial, or disinterested like BRS, these bodies added to the sum total of technical and scientific information.

FIRMS

Range and size

Building firms maintained their own central bodies. Leading examples were the National Federation of Building Trades Employers (NFBTE), mainly to represent them in wage negotiations with the unions, and the Institute of Builders, increasingly engaged in education. The range of firms was broadly unchanged, but there were several novelties in addition to the established wide variety of size and specialism. At the largest scale were a few large general contractors, prepared to work anywhere in the country on both building and civil engineering. Smaller firms of contractors, speculative builders and specialist subcontractors continued to operate at regional and local levels, and jobbing builders and maintenance men worked close to home.

Newcomers to local authority work in the early 1920s were some direct labour organizations (there was one at West Ham as early as 1893). These were council employees competing with private contractors and usually directed by the local authority surveyor. As a form of public enterprise the performance, and very existence, of direct labour organizations (DLOs) was surrounded by heated debate about whether or not the competition with private firms was fair. The central government Office of Works was another minor house builder in the early 1920s, entirely overshadowed by private builders [11]. An even less auspicious appearance was made by Building Guilds, which were non-profit-making local associations of operatives. They built an insignificant number of houses before failing, apparently due to inexperience and lack of capital.

The size of most firms remained small, with 84% in 1930 employing not more than ten people. Slightly larger firms employing between 11 and 24 amounted to only 7% of all firms, while at the largest extreme less than 1% (317) of firms employed more than 200 people. The total number of firms increased slowly at first and then more quickly as the industry expanded. In 1930 there were 52,000 firms in Great Britain and Northern Ireland (to which the above figures also relate), over 2,000 more than in 1924. Five years later in 1935 the total was 72,000. The continued importance of very small firms was the reverse of the concentration in many other parts of the economy and may be attributed to two causes. Firstly, building still offered few economies of scale, so that most projects could be carried out as effectively and cheaply by quite small firms as by large (although it is likely that small firms were more vulnerable to adversity). Secondly, the industry was exceptionally easy to enter, since working capital was readily available and plant requirements small. Building attracted entrepreneurs, who were liable to find ease of entry matched only by ease of exit.

Contractors Opportunities for contractors were plentiful enough in the first few years of recovery from the First World War, but there were severe problems of shortages of labour, materials and working capital. When these obstacles eventually were overcome and a semblance of stability restored, small contracting firms still formed and broke up rather too quickly to make for a favourable public image. The performance of many firms attracted informed criticism on grounds of poor business planning and general inefficiency [12], and the reputation of many was not improved by questionable quality of products. Firms below the largest were less foot-loose in finding work than were promoters and architects. London promoters might well use London architects in, say, Leicester, but their contractors were likely to be local [13].

Caution and doubtful efficiency, often cloaked in stolid or complacent tradition, were common enough, particularly among smaller firms, but were not the whole picture. Among firms working on that minority of larger and non-residential contracts were some which were increasingly efficient in productivity, management and investment in equipment. Robinson [14] in 1939 thought that there had been very great changes in these fields over the previous 20 years. New firms of general contractors, he said, owed much to factories in their organization, and were mainly concerned to coordinate numbers of specialized subcontractors, rather than employ their skills directly. This last point was to prove prophetic for a great part of the industry.

Coad [15] has charted the rise of an exceptional major contractor, Laing. From early nineteenth century origins, the family firm had advanced to contracting (including civil engineering) around Carlisle with a turnover of £18,000 in 1913, rising to £29,000 the following year. The critical leap came in the First World War and by 1918 the firm was contracting nationally with 3–4,000 employees on northern and Scottish army camps and aerodromes. When limited company formation was adopted in 1920 turnover was £0.5 m., and the business was valued at over £40,000. Turnover continued to climb through the 1920s to around £0.75 m. as contracts were won from Plymouth to Aberdeen and from Anglesey to Brighton. Technically innovative 'Easi-form' concrete houses were built and a brickworks was opened in Carlisle. Impetus came from the dynamic John W. Laing (1879–1978), who strove for excellence of site management teams with sound tendering and costing systems, backed by control of labour productivity and materials use. The head-quarters moved to London in the mid-1920s and a property company was formed which acquired a substantial portfolio. Speculative house building followed in North London suburbs, carrying turnover above £1 m. in 1930. Mechanical plant was

introduced in the mid-1930s, when the firm had 15 large
excavators. At that time Laing was employing 3,000 men,
building about 1,000 houses a year, as well as eight large
contracts. With rearmament from the later 1930s the firm
benefited from further airfield contracts so that turnover
doubled between 1936 and 1939 and doubled again by 1942.
The main ingredients in this remarkable success story appear
to have been Laing's own entrepreneurial drive and his
emphasis on teamwork and management. This, and especially
project cost control, enabled the firm to take full advantage of
large defence contracts and the private housing boom.

Speculative builders

Laing straddled the divide between contractor and speculative
firms. Among speculative firms and jobbing builders the
chief exceptions to the rule of traditionalism were some larger
house builders mainly active in the 1930s in the London area.
As noted in the preceding chapter, many large concerns
engaged in all aspects of development, so that building was
only a part of their business. This vertical integration was often
accompanied by extensive subcontracting on site; the
vertically integrated firm was structured around decisions
about money and risk, with the technicalities of building
relegated to second place. Such firms raised capital by issuing
shares, whereas smaller speculative builders relied more on
bank overdrafts for current expenses and on credit from
builders' merchants (in turn indebted to materials producers).
Small builders also borrowed from developers, building
societies and private individuals, usually at an interest rate of
about 4%. Competition between speculative builders was
sometimes intense and profit margins of the order of 10%
were small compared with those which could be earned in
other fields outside building. When demand lagged, sales were
sustained by resort to publicity stunts such as firework
displays, floodlighting and free transport for house buyers
[16].

Sub-contractors

Much of the technically advanced work on site was executed
by subcontractors, most commissioned by main contractors
and some nominated by architects. Subcontractors were
employed extensively on non-residential building work,
where the size and complexity of construction tasks were
great. An increasing proportion of work was subcontracted
during the period [17], in turn increasing the number and
degree of specialization of subcontracting firms. As many as 30

might work on a single large project, many of them on site at the same time, including specialists in demolition, excavation, structural steelwork, concreting, masonry, joinery, central heating, lifts and other branches of services engineering, shopfitting, asphalting, floor tiling, fencing, plastering and painting. As the later nineteenth century was a time of proliferation of branded products, so this was a time of increase in the variety of firms working on site. The multiplication of subcontractors, creating new management responsibilities for main contractors, was one of the more far-reaching changes among interwar firms. It enabled the industry to handle new products and processes and to retain a necessary capacity for rapid change in operations and workload. The contrast between traditional subcontracting firms and progressive ones, say between deeply traditional craftsman masons and modern electrical engineers, was striking; in this was yet another contrast within the great entity of the building industry.

LABOUR

Conditions   Site operations, from foundation digging to roof tiling, continued to rely mainly on the services of men using manual skills and hand tools. Mechanization on site and fabrication of components off site advanced, but as a rule minor adaptations were more evident than thoroughgoing change. Construction mostly entailed fashioning materials on site at or near the point at which the finished product was required. This meant that large numbers of men worked on site, rather than in workshop or factory. They avoided some of the oppressive monotony of factory employment, but experienced poor general amenities and lacked weather protection. Permanent employment was more scarce than short-term employment, especially among small employers. Much of it was casual, being seasonal, by the week or even by the day for unskilled men, with little security. Tough working conditions taken for granted in a coarser nineteenth century world now began to look anachronistic alongside conditions in up-to-date factories outside the building industry. Yet perhaps this comparison was more likely to be made by middle class onlookers than by people on the sites: even the prospect of a waterlogged and chaotic site was a great deal better than the alternative of unemployment. Demand for building labour provided welcome job opportunities for men who otherwise faced the dole. Employment on sites was heavily concentrated in the prosperous South East and Midlands. In 1931 no less than 41% of employment in building was located in London and the South East, where only 23% of the population of Great Britain lived. The far more slender chance of a site job in the depressed regions was the unhappy reverse of this picture, although prospects were helped a little by maintenance work and some local authority activity. Regional imbalance was also eased by various materials-producing industries, some in depressed regions, which were stimulated by demand from prosperous ones. For instance, window glass needed in booming Middlesex housing estates made jobs in near-prostrate Lancashire.

Employment and unemployment

The ease, or lack of it, with which jobs could be found in building varied widely in time as well as place. During the First World War a great part of the labour force was enlisted in the armed services. In the unsettled aftermath of war in 1919, unskilled building labour was only two-thirds of its prewar numerical strength and skilled labour was even less. Those who survived the war to be demobilized did not attain prewar levels of output owing to disuse of their skills and lack of adequate training and experience. However, shortages gradually eased and the number of men at work increased year by year, but so did unemployment. In 1925, about 10.5% of building workers were without jobs, swelling to 30% at the worst point of the depression, in 1932. Some improvement followed that outstandingly bad year and by 1937 the proportion had fallen to 15%. Despite unemployment of these magnitudes, some shortages of skilled men developed in the late 1930s, due to a combination of heavy house building and growing rearmament work. Unemployment in building in the interwar years generally was higher than the national average. This peculiarity (in view of the prosperity of building) was due in part to the attraction of building to men forced out of work in other industries.

Size of trades

Roughly half of building labour was skilled or semi-skilled and the other half unskilled, although even nominally unskilled navvies certainly had skills not possessed by everyone. Among craftsmen the relative size of different trades shows evidence of continuity rather than rapid change. In 1924 the largest trade still was carpentry and joinery, with 19% of the employed people in building. Painters were the second largest trade, having risen to prominence since 1914 with 15% of employed people. There was then a gap before the bricklayers with 9%, followed in descending order by plumbers, masons (now well and truly eclipsed), plasterers and slaters. The position in the later 1930s was not very different, although bricklayers were closing the gap with the leaders.

Minor variations were to be found in the regions, suggesting that some distinctive local building practices lingered on. Masons declined least in the South West and Wales, and bricklayers were relatively numerous in the South East and Midlands. There were wide differences also in the proportions of trades engaged on different projects, with housing work probably requiring trades in proportions roughly typical of the industry as a whole. Large city-centre projects with many subcontractors, on the other hand, required the full range of newer skills and proportionately fewer traditional ones. Among the growing newer skills were steel erectors, reinforcement benders, and mechanical and electrical services engineers.

Wages

The movement of building wages was dramatic after the stagnation of Edwardian times. Increases which began just before the war in 1914 accelerated during it and reached an unprecedented peak in 1920. In that year average rates, like prices, were double or more than double their prewar levels, with unskilled men making the biggest gains. A typical rate in 1920 for the main craft trades was about 93p for a ten-hour day. In 1924, when the postwar peak had passed, the hourly rate in London for highly skilled stone carvers was about 8.75p, followed by the main trades at 8.1p. Slightly below this were the slaters and tilers, then glaziers and painters, followed by scaffolders and then labourers at 6.1p.

From the early 1920s wages began to be fixed on a nationwide basis related to the cost of living and graded according to place of work, although variations persisted due to payment of productivity bonuses. The fall from high wages and prices after 1920 was steep initially, though it soon moderated, and wages drifted down to a trough in 1933, near the time of greatest unemployment. They then recovered mildly to reach approximately the level prevailing in 1928 [18]. In 1937, the London hourly rate for most skilled trades was 8.3p, compared with 6p in the lower-paid country districts. The weekly hours worked, like the rates of pay, lacked national uniformity, although 46 hours seems to have been an average.

Comparison between the average annual earnings in building and in all industries show building, as before, in a moderately favourable light. The estimated figure in building in 1924 was £156 compared with £146 in all industries, despite slightly longer hours worked outside building. In 1938 the differential had narrowed somewhat, to £158 in building and £153 in all industries [19]. Building workers fortunate enough to retain their jobs between 1918 and 1939, like those in most other industries, experienced an increase in real earnings of the order of a third or a half.

Organization   Building trade unions experienced widely changing circumstances first in the war, when, in 1914, the largest union was the woodworkers' with 79,000 members. The next largest, the bricklayers' had less than half that membership [20]. Not much normal building work took place and, since the Munitions of War Act in 1915 made arbitration compulsory for any disputes, there were few strikes.

One growth point in an otherwise apparently quiet wartime scene was in unions with members in building for war purposes. The leading example was the labourers' union which experienced eight-fold membership growth to reach 65,000 by 1919. Elsewhere some influence, perhaps international events, was eroding earlier isolationism and narrowness of vision within the craft unions. This first became evident early in 1918 when the National Federation of Building Trade Operatives (NFBTO) was formed with powers to bring about uniformity of action among affiliated unions. Other divisions were healed when woodworking unions joined to form the Amalgamated Society of Woodworkers, and several 'trowel unions' combined to form the Amalgamated Union of Building Trade Operatives.

Heavy labour demand in 1919 and 1920 brought a new phase of union activity and membership growth [21]. Labour scarcity, difficulties in employing ex-servicemen, and housing shortage led the government to press dilution, the employment of men less than fully trained. This was resisted by the unions, more concerned with their members' prospects in the event of a future labour surplus than with the broader employment problems of ex-servicemen. Labour relations were aggravated further in 1922 and 1923 by the threat of lower wages and longer hours which accompanied falling prices and general depression. In 1924, the year of the first nationwide building strike, renewed labour shortages led the Minister of Health, Wheatley, to devise a 'gentleman's agreement' as part of his housing policy. In it the unions accepted a shorter training period than the customary five-year apprenticeship, in exchange for guarantees of more employment. Subsequently, although building was one of the 'front-line' industries in the 1926 general strike, disputes became fewer and smaller and in the later 1920s strength ebbed away.

There was no recovery until the worst of the depression was over and prosperity was returning in the later 1930s, when membership reached the levels of the early 1920s. New technology called for some adaptation: unskilled men increasingly undertook tasks formerly carried out by craftsmen; some on-site woodworkers continued to be displaced by pre-fabricated joinery; various crafts were displaced by the use of structural steelwork, concrete and artificial stone; plasterboard displaced some 'wet' plaster work, despite union opposition; plumbers continued to lose lead roofing to cheaper substitutes; and some labourers were ousted by mechanized plant. However, the impact of such developments was felt only gradually and no leading trade suffered decline on the scale experienced by masons before the First World War.

MATERIALS, COMPONENTS AND PROCESSES

Prices

The cost of building roughly doubled during the war and continued to increase steeply for the several difficult years following. Maiwald's index [22] shows that after the early 1920s prospects improved and it became progressively cheaper to build until 1933, when the lowest level was reached. Then costs began to rise slowly with the volume of building. In this pattern building approximately followed movements in general retail prices. The proportion of building cost made up by materials varied from one building to another, depending on design, and estimates differ as to relative importance. A rough guide was two-thirds of total cost for materials and the remaining third for labour, although no doubt a more equal balance often applied. Changes in the prices of materials overall were similar to those of total building costs, but some materials diverged from the typical. Timber and cement fell particularly steeply, while some kinds of brick did not fall at all. Overall, materials prices fell somewhat less than those of all industrial materials and manufactures taken together.

Supply

At first the supply of materials was dominated by the war, which disrupted timber imports, caused abandonment and flooding of claypits and conversion of plant to make other, non-building, goods. In their switch from ploughshares to swords, Crittalls went from metal windows to 4.5 inch shells. By the armistice most materials were in short supply, and brick and tile production was down to only one-third or less of their pre-1914 level. In 1919, the government released nearly all materials from wartime control and prices surged up, together with those of other goods. Some materials prices doubled within months and tripled by 1920. Supply difficulties were worsened by transport problems on the congested and run-down railways. Soon, however, this confusion began to clear and by 1921 bricks and cement production exceeded that of 1914, though timber and clay tiles took longer to regain 'normality'. Output of materials climbed to a peak in 1927 and, after faltering during the slump, went on to new heights in the late 1930s, when output was about double that of the troubled early 1920s.

Figure 32 Improved transport: early ready-mixed concrete delivery. This one worked from depot in Staines, Middlesex, apparently in 1930s. (Source: British Cement Association.)

Methods   One trend in the way in which materials were fashioned into completed buildings was further fabrication of components off site. They were then transported for incorporation in a ready-finished or near-finished state in the building. Provided costs were competitive (and this was by no means always so), the method had several advantages: specialized plant, skills and power could be used in the workshop, where productivity was higher and supervision easier; building time could be cut; shortages of skilled site labour were eased; and work was less dependent on the weather. Not all designers or builders were able or willing to grasp the advantages, but components which lent themselves to off-site fabrication and transport included steel columns and beams (some bearing the patriotic legend 'British Steel Only'); light sheet claddings, linings and panels (which eliminated time-consuming 'wet' operations); joinery such as cupboards, standard doors and window frames; and many minor items. Before the First World War many of the new branded goods had been quite small 'add on' parts of the building, like heating appliances and ironmongery. Now came larger sheet and board surfaces and finishes like plywood, and parts of the building carcass. By very slow degrees site operations were shifting from making to assembling.

The extreme development in off-site manufacture was the prefabricated houses of the 1920s. These came from various building and industrial concerns responding to official encouragement to overcome shortages and high prices afflicting traditional building. A highly publicized example was the steel plate and timber frame 'Weir' house; it met stiff opposition from traditionally inclined unions [23]. Other hopeful makers tried out an extraordinary variety of materials, including cast iron, pre-cast and in-situ concrete, and something called shredded wood and concrete. Novelty alone was not enough and most examples cost more than traditional building, required subsidy and sometimes performed poorly. Some types corroded, so that they required replacement after about 40 years. No more than 50,000 were built before enthusiasm waned and traditional methods reasserted dominance by about 1928. In all they helped to fuel the scepticism of technical innovation already strong in a conservative industry; traditional ways were shown to be cheaper and to perform better than the new.

One of the lessons of prefabrication was that traditional methods were seldom susceptible to radical alteration, being more open to gradual evolution. The further introduction of prefabricated joinery into traditional building was one example of evolution and another was the use of plant and power on sites. Such changes altered processes, but not end-products. This development probably was strongest in non-residential projects, although if road motor haulage is admitted in the definition of building plant, then even the most doggedly traditional house building was affected. The flexibility and cheapness of road transport compared with rail was particularly important for the industry, with its characteristic restless movement from site to site. A result was that scenes visible, for example at the LCC St Helier estate in 1929, where six locomotives puffed about an extensive temporary light railway system around the rising suburban terraces, became more scarce.

There was increasing mechanization also in the earlier stages of building operations to complement off-site fabrication in the later stages. Steam shovels were used more for large excavations, and other plant included heavy mechanical pile drivers, hydraulic and pneumatic riveters for jointing steelwork, spray guns for applying finishes, powered temporary hoists and concrete mixers. Artificial lighting and heating were increasingly applied to extend the working day and season. Another area in which progress was possible, though it left little mark on the finished product and required no plant, was in site organization. On the best-managed sites construction sequences were more likely than before to be arranged to give early roofing cover for the subsequent work (reducing bad weather delays). Similarly, materials deliveries would be arranged to avoid double-handling. Experiment with the new and departure from tried and tested methods probably was greatest on large industrial and commercial projects, where finished buildings often embodied most novelties, and where the scale of operations was largest and urgency greatest.

To build faster and more efficiently, the aim of most new methods, was not necessarily to build better. The effect of changes of technology on quality appears to have been more or less neutral. The best work probably was as durable and well executed as before, if more rare; the shoddiest jerry-building was largely curtailed by the by-laws, now universally applied. Of the middle range some observers were doubtful, believing that small speculative houses were more lightly built than before 1914.

Brick and masonry

Nearly every project, costly or cheap, embodied at least some brickwork, and on many it was the dominant material. Brick output in the UK doubled between the depressed year of 1912 (3,700 m. bricks) and 1937 (7,800 m.). The proportion of total materials cost represented by brick often appoached one-fifth in the case of houses, but obviously varied according to designs. In the early 1930s 225 mm brickwork with exterior distemper and interior plaster was estimated to cost 90p per sq.m, compared with £1.10 for a cavity wall of rustic Fletton brickwork. The substitution of red facing bricks added about 30p to the cost, but even this was cheaper than old-style 400 mm-thick rubble stone walling at about £1.50 [24].

The trend of brick prices was broadly similar to other materials, but with some detail differences. For example, between 1924 and 1937 Fletton prices fell from about £2.65 per thousand to about £2.30, while the price of the more costly second hard-stocks moved the other way. Fletton producers made one-third of all bricks produced in 1937 and their resounding commercial success in the south-eastern market was a striking feature of the time. Closure was forced upon many smaller makers unable to match the economies of scale of the newcomers dominated by the London Brick Company. By 1939 the number of brickyards was reduced to about a third of the 3,500 open at the beginning of the century.

The main alternatives to brick were stone and the more utilitarian blocks made from concrete, breeze, clinker and foamed slag. The variety of blocks and blockmakers, many of them small concerns, was wide and especially so early in the period, when alternative materials were scarce. Falling cement prices helped blocks to become ever cheaper, making them about the cheapest material for partitions.

Stone was confined by price mainly to prestige uses, with Hopton Wood material priced at £24.75 per cu.m in 1924, rising slightly by the late 1930s [25]. Occasional country work in local stone was cheapest, down to a mere sixth of the price of prestige ashlar work, but still it fell from use.

Timber

Timber and timber products held their position of importance in typical houses, amounting to about three-tenths of total materials costs. Where ground floors had once been solid, now they were likely to be suspended timber. In domestic and larger buildings new light timber-based sheet materials often replaced heavier frames and panels, and some structural timbers probably were lighter than formerly.

Timber imports were heavily cut during the First World War, being only one-fifth of prewar level in 1918. By 1924 the value of UK softwood imports, about 90% of softwood supplies (not all destined for building purposes) exceeded £32 m. and in addition there was £9 m. worth of hardwood and £5 m. worth of manufactured joinery [26]. At that time sawn softwood cost about £7.95 per cu.m in plates and lintels, compared with about £17.65 per cu.m for oak, a far cry from the days a century or more earlier when the two had been roughly competitive. Plywood, developed in the wartime aero-industry, by 1937 cost between 13p and 54p per sq.m, depending on thickness and quality. Various other novel sheet materials appeared, of which fibreboards were among the few survivors of the passing of postwar shortages.

Roof finishes The relative usage of competing roof finishes continued to change more frequently than most other major materials. Roofing materials costs accounted for well over 10% of total materials costs of typical houses, so shifts of preference affected large volumes of goods. One shift was the resurgence of clay tiles, UK output of which roughly doubled between 1912 and 1924, and more than tripled by 1935. Their success matched the rival concrete tiles which increased in output from a low level after the First World War to about a third of combined clay and concrete tile output in 1935. Slate production meanwhile declined by about a quarter between 1912 and 1924 and thereafter remained static in an expanding market. Underlying these changes of fortune was a complicated pattern of price competition in which slate prices fell least and concrete fell most of all [27].

Different qualities and haulage rates make generalization hazardous, but typical prices of materials laid in 1937, per 100 sq.ft (9.3 sq.m) were around £1.75 to £2.00 for pantiles and between £2.90 and £3.75 for slate (costly Westmoreland products were £5.50). Reed thatch at about £6.00 and Cotswold stone slates at £8.00 had now transferred decisively from humble vernacular to luxury usage. In sharp visual contrast to such rustic materials, there was strong growth in output of asbestos-cement tiles, costing between £2.25 and £3.50. Larger corrugated sheets at about £2.65 were slightly cheaper than corrugated steel sheets, which suffered accordingly. Compared with tiling and slating, costs of zinc and asphalt finishes were a little more. Lead was nearly double the cost of tiling and copper was more than double.

Cement, concrete and plaster

Cement and asbestos-cement sheet production increasingly passed by amalgamation to a small number of large capital-intensive manufacturers. Output almost tripled between 1912 and 1938 and prices fell more than those of any other domestically produced building material, about 30% between 1924 and 1938. This was due in part to fierce price competition, which was eventually curtailed by trading agreements between producers. Along with Fletton bricks and structural steelwork, the supply of cement-based goods became yet more independent of building. Processing of most bulky raw materials, once the responsibility of builders, was now handled by large, concentrated and quite separate industries; division of labour between firms had advanced.

Technical advantages and steep falls in price brought new and extended uses of cement: cement mortar instead of lime for bonding masonry; in-situ and pre-cast concrete for walls, floors, roofs and structural frames; concrete lintels and sills; fire-resisting cladding to steelwork; exterior rendering and paving; and concrete blocks. Some concrete was delivered to site ready mixed, much of it was mixed on site as required. About 8% of materials costs in typical houses were in cement and aggregates, no doubt more in some other building types, while very few new buildings indeed contained no cement products whatever. In the late 1930s reinforced concrete beam and column members (between £8 and £12 per cu.m) were rather more costly than steel for most applications, but reinforced concrete floors had few fireproof competitors.

The other major 'wet' material was gypsum plaster where, again, lime was largely superseded. Home production of plasterboard as a substitute for 'wet' plaster began in 1917 and, although opposed by organized labour and not yet fully reliable, it was gradually accepted. By 1939 there were four plasterboard producers, with a combined annual output of 26 million sq.m.

Services

Goods connected with building services continued to grow in number, variety and complexity. Large central heating installations could be solid fuel (some mechanically fired), gas or oil. Boilers for a 550 cu.m building cost of the order of £100, rising to £150 for a building of four times that volume. In addition an allowance of £8 to £12 was needed for each radiator. Medium-size electric traction lifts (hydraulic types were also available) were expected to cost of the order of £700 for a 12 m travel. Large country houses might have petrol- or diesel-powered electricity supply and there was a wide choice of types of electric heater. Where mains supply was to be had, the cost of electricity supply was around £2.50 per point (much reduced from Edwardian times); for gas it was only about £2. Cold water supply installation with two sinks, bath, three basins and two WCs cost about £22 for galvanized pipework, more for copper or lead; matching hot water system with small boiler, cylinder and pipework cost about £35, with another £5 for an auxiliary gas or electric water heater.

Other goods and plant

Very many goods remain to be mentioned, their existence supporting a growing network of builders' merchants. Such goods included ironmongery, ceramic tiles, paint and varnish, metal window frames, drainpipes, steelwork and glass. Concentration among glassmakers had reached duopoly; prices of sheet glass fell by over a quarter between 1924 and 1936 [28].

Structural steelwork usage increased greatly in high and long-span buildings. Rolled steel members often replaced timber beam and masonry arch alternatives because of performance advantages and faster building operations. Steel prices reached their lowest in 1932 when demand was at rock-bottom but by 1938 had risen above the level of 1924. Erection of heavy steelwork, and the excavation which preceded it, encouraged the use of heavy plant such as cranes and compressors. A 0.4 cu.m crawler-mounted mechanical excavator cost £25 a week to hire in 1939. Trenching machines cost £35 a week, three-ton steam cranes cost £5 a week, including driver, and a 0.14 cu.m capacity concrete mixer £2.50 a week. Such machinery remained largely the province of specialist firms.

Outside the combined building and civil engineering firms, most builders confined themselves to the use of small and simple plant. There were cradles (£1 a week to hire), pumps (75p to £1 a week), sheerlegs, new tubular steel scaffolding, tarpaulins, wheelbarrows (up to £1 to buy), handtools, carts, lorries and site huts. If a nightwatchman and lamp were required to safeguard the works, the cost was about 6.7p an hour. In case efforts were in vain, the 1937 cost of insuring the works for three months prior to handover was of the order of 3p per £100 value of building.

7

Building in crisis and reconstruction: 1940–1973

We do not want to waste a single penny, but we will spend every penny that is necessary for decency and health – yes, and comfort and beauty – for ourselves and our children.

(Association of Building Technicians (1946) *Houses for the People*)

DEMAND AND BUILDING PROMOTERS

Intensification, concentration and intervention

Building was convulsed by the Second World War and the political, social and economic changes which it brought about. First, normal building provision was suspended for over half a decade amid losses to stock from blitz and deferred maintenance. Then there was perhaps a quarter of a century of catching up with pent-up demand and adjustment to the building needs of society transformed by more wealth, more evenly distributed. Three powerful themes came to dominate the motives and behaviour of building promoters. The first, an increase in the scale and pace of building, is termed intensification. Activity advanced on a rising tide of economic growth which proceeded, despite setbacks, at a rate which compared well with that of the nineteenth century. Gross domestic product per head in the UK (at constant 1913 prices) doubled in the three decades after the mid-1930s, from £52 to £82 in the mid-1950s and on to £98 by the mid-1960s. At the same time the proportion of gross national product represented by building and construction increased from 4.1% in the mid-

1930s to 5.7% in the mid-1950s. New shapes and many of them, from shadow factories to tower blocks and from factory farms to multi-storey car parks, sprang up faster than ever before.

The second theme was concentration, the expansion and grouping of promoters into large organizations. Emergence of large public authorities and multinational firms was echoed by less obvious growth among smaller but more numerous organizations. Wherever power or capital was concentrated, promotion was further transformed from small, intermittent concern into continuous involvement, 'sophisticated' promoters replacing 'naive' ones [1].

The third theme among promoters was intervention, a greatly extended capacity of the State to influence decisions to build. Government came to more or less regulate the proportion of national resources available for building, influencing the proportions of different building types and controlling building location. Former private enterprises were brought under direct State control by nationalization, others were directed to a lesser or greater degree, and new quasi-autonomous agencies, such as the Housing Corporation,

Figure 33 Building in war. Precious steel being used on factory for Jas. Robertson, Fleetwood, Lancashire, 1943. Contractor Gregson's site hut graphics strike a period note. Site fencing is rudimentary.

Figure 34 Some of the 'poor remnant'. Scarce wartime labour on site in Fleetwood, Lancashire in 1943 has not been conscripted into armed services.

appeared. Motives which underlay government intervention arose from the exigencies of world war and, later, the redemption of electoral promises and manipulation of the national economy. Promoters were officially directed about what, where and whether they might build, for how much and in what form. Public promoters were controlled directly by government policy and decision while private promoters were influenced mostly by planning control, rates of interest, subsidies, loans and taxation. Adjustments to these much affected the cost of borrowing to build and the demand for the goods and services which a new building would help to provide. When governments helped to bring about a favourable financial climate, promoters were spurred into action;

when government policies led to an unfavourable climate, projects were deferred or abandoned. In all, government involvement appeared to increase the total amount of building activity, while reducing the freedom of action of many promoters. The earliest official intervention, the building by-laws, had affected how promoters might build. Now mature intervention affected very much more, from the very decision to build, right through (as will be shown) to the eventual lifespan of whole sections of the stock.

Public promoters

The rise of public promotion became dramatically evident when the government was suddenly forced into extreme action by the outbreak of war in 1939. Urgent demand for buildings of national strategic importance ('Action this day') poured from numerous branches of government, of which the Ministry of Works (formerly the Office of Works) under Lord Reith was prominent as coordinator. Departments such as the three armed services, Home Office, and Ministries of Aircraft Production, Supply and War Transport [2, 3] competed intensely for scarce resources. Planned balancing of demand and supply proved difficult; control of demand was incomplete and control of resources of materials and labour was insufficient [4]. Victory in 1945 profoundly changed the priorities held by the different departments, as the national economy was redirected towards revenue-earning exports and social provisions. Now it was the turn of the Ministries of Health (later succeeded in housing work by the Ministry of Housing and Local Government) and Education. Variations in the spending power and influence of departments followed successive transitions from wartime command economy to welfare state planned economy and then to a mixed economy. The effects of policy changes were visible in increased housing, education and health provision, in the advance of social services in leisure and recreation, and in specialized fields such as the Atomic Energy Authority.

Some public promotion came directly from central government departments, largely the Ministry of Works and its successors for building for defence. Responsibility for many other public buildings was decentralized to local authority level. The variety of local authorities ranged widely in size from the London County Council (LCC) serving a population of over 3 million, to district councils in some cases serving as few as 3,000 or so. There were over 50 county councils, rather more county boroughs, numerous non-county boroughs, urban and rural district councils, and the metropolitan boroughs and new town development corporations [5]. Authorities of different status had different powers of promotion and overlapping geographical areas which had accumulated haphazardly over many years. The picture was complicated, all the more so for increasing activity, and reorganizations such as that creating the Greater London Council (GLC) and London boroughs in 1965.

Equally complicated, because priorities changed almost continuously, were the relationships between the various branches of the public authorities. Houses, hospitals, fire stations, universities, law courts and post offices, for example, were promoted by a variety of local and central authorities, each with their own procedures, budgets and relations with one another. The main aim of central government regarding promotion was to scrutinize local authority proposals to ensure good value and fairness between authorities. Central government, often working through regional branches, influenced the size and standards of local authority programmes and checked project costs. Yet local authorities were more than instruments of central government, being popularly elected and legally independent bodies able to interpret building need in their own ways. The potential for independent action was considerable, although close relationships with central government mostly prevailed.

In early postwar years local authority promotion was restrained by central authority systems of allocation. These later gave way to rather more interventionist central government policies [6], aided at the level of building design by new techniques of project cost planning and control, and cost limits. House building was a responsibility of about 1,400 local authorities, of which only 250 were big enough to build more than 100 dwellings a year. The procedure was for elected members under the general guidance of the Ministry of Housing and Local Government (part of the Department of the Environment from 1970) to determine need. Priorities were settled, programmes agreed and financial resources were called up, enabling chief local authority officers to implement policy. Building costs usually were divided between local and central authorities, with the latter making an annual grant for a number of years towards repayment of capital borrowed by local authorities. The local contribution came partly from rents and partly through local rates and other income. Main sources of capital were the Public Works Loan Board, long- and short-term mortgages, public issues on the stock exchange, temporary loans and bank overdrafts [7].

Promotion of new schools by local authorities and the Ministry of Education (Department of Education and Science after 1964) differed in that the far smaller number of education authorities, fewer than 150, made for closer administrative relations. The Ministry of Education was regarded as one of the most enlightened government promoters, being helped by a nationally consensual view about the high priority of school building. Programmes were planned well in advance, unlike those of most other comparable building types, which were tied to the dictates of annual national budgeting [8]. This made non-education building programmes prone to damaging reversals in size of commitment from one year to the next. Responsibility for public promotion generally was difficult to pin down, lying as it did on a long bureaucratic chain stretching from Treasury and central government departments at one extreme, to chief officers and politicians of district councils at the other. In extent and complexity, public promotion rapidly developed well beyond anything that had existed previously.

Private promoters
Private promotion differed from public because activity was relatively light for some of the time, and methods more direct, as well as less accessible to public view. Until the early 1950s private promotion was displaced from its former pre-eminence by State intervention. Later, private promotion regained importance when industrial and commercial building gathered pace and private house-building was fully resumed. Compared with prewar conditions, individual private promoters were more rare and committee promoters more common. Growth of promoter organizations made responsibility for decisions to build in the private sector, like the public, more attenuated.

The most visible of private promoters were developers who first set to rebuilding bombed sites. When these were filled it was wryly observed that developers resumed demolition where Hitler had left off. They did so in response to apparently insatiable demand for central urban commercial accommodation. Developers of great entrepreneurial zeal, working with local authorities seeking prestige and gain, soon produced striking results. A few risk-taking developers, such as Jack Cotton, made immense profits (and attracted matching publicity) from speculative offices and shops. Later, colourful

individuals were supplanted by more impersonal depart-
mentalized property development companies engaged on
comprehensive central area redevelopment. Their initial
approach was by raising short-term loans of up to three years
from clearing banks and, particularly later, merchant and
secondary banks, the issue of stocks and shares, and use of
income from earlier projects. The sums required in purchase of
a jig-saw of existing old property ownerships, legal and design
work, demolition and rebuilding were very large. In the longer
term, capital from insurance companies, pension funds and
property unit trusts was frequently involved. The credit
market became progressively more sophisticated, at times
involving sale and leaseback [9] and networks of consortia,
nominees, subsidiary companies and agents. The financial
success of developers encouraged local authorities and
institutes working jointly with developers to press ever harder
partnership terms in order to share the large gains to be had in
a mostly sellers' market. Traditional roles of developer, short-
term financier and long-term financier merged as they adapted
in a fast-moving field to pressures of inflation and desire to
secure better yields [10].

Private promoters were active also in suburban speculative
housing estates, factories, warehouses, hotels and so on. The
open market for accommodation expanded, so it would appear
that occupiers increasingly sought to buy or rent 'off-the-peg',
rather than purpose-built, premises. It was estimated [11] that
by the late 1960s not more than one-fifth of new offices were
built by their intending occupiers, the remainder being
supplied by developers through the open market. Here was a
growing trend for private sector promoters to be concerned
with the exchange-value of their buildings, rather than use-
value (public sector concern was more with use-value). Here
also was evidence of the move away from 'naive' promoters
occasionally commissioning their own premises, towards
'sophisticated' promoters building speculatively for the market,
as had long been common in lower-cost housing. Frequently
the benefits of speculative and custom building were combined
in a hybrid when a basic building shell was erected speculatively, for subsequent fitting out when the identity and needs of
the occupier were known. An example was shops initially
consisting of a basic shell, for later addition of bespoke internal
surface finishes, services and shop front. Many factories were
provided in a similar way. This enabled the advantages of an
open market in accommodation, such as sensitivity and

rapidity in response to demand, economies of scale, and specialization of those who provided the buildings, to be combined with the advantages of meeting the bespoke wants of occupiers.

Mobility and planning

The location of new buildings was affected profoundly by the countervailing forces of planning policy and increased mobility. While greater mobility widened the choice of potential sites, planning policy restricted and directed that choice. Greater mobility came from an immense increase in numbers of motor vehicles (nearly four-fold between 1948 and 1968), although offset partly by an associated decline in public transport and cycling. Old constraints favouring central urban sites diminished and suburban and rural locations became more attractive. Decentralization, begun well over half a century before by railways and tramways, was greatly intensified by motor transport. Settlement patterns belatedly began in places to follow a low-density and car-dependent North American pattern.

The development of town and country planning, from a rudimentary influence between the wars, to a very strong one, began with a wartime transformation of attitudes. This found expression in the early postwar years, when long-debated planning measures formed part of an attempt to make far-reaching changes for the improvement of society. Attempts were made to promote efficiency and prosperity, relieve unemployment and congestion and preserve amenity, largely by means of planned building location. Comprehensive planning control was established by the Town and Country Planning Act of 1947, derived from the findings of the Barlow, Scott and Uthwatt Reports. The new system was based on land use plans compiled by the local authorities which also dealt with applications for permission to build. Further legislation later adjusted and elaborated the system in the light of experience, and official commitment remained unwavering. The scope of planning in its national, regional and local aspects was extensive [12], and included financial incentives for development in poorer regions, Board of Trade control of industrial development, and dramatically sudden interventions like the 1964 'Brown ban' imposed on office building, mainly in London. By such means choice of building site and form, so long determined only by promoters' internal economies and preferences, were subjugated by broader societal interests.

Regional planning policy introduced new factories in formerly depressed heavy industrial areas such as the North East and South Wales. Planning policy in the South East was the opposite, being intended to deal with congestion and the threatened breakdown of overstretched public services stemming from growth. Ailing regional economies were strengthened and overheated ones cooled by designation of new towns such as Peterlee and planned town expansion schemes such as Basingstoke. Yet such schemes were insignificant in total compared with the sum of new building on cleared sites and at the edges of existing towns. Outward expansion of major towns was constrained by green belts so that growth, where it was permitted, was more orderly than hitherto. Infilling and carefully considered urban extensions were the aims although, where pressure for new development was intense, there were problems such as the leapfrogging of green belts.

Urban renewal

Many forces gathered to favour urban renewal. They included the effects of economic growth in raising consumer spending and white collar employment, hence demand for shops and offices; rising expectations about the efficiency, convenience and appearance of buildings; desire for civic improvement, among elected representatives and local authority officials; advancing age of the building stock; increased traffic requiring more road access; government slum clearance policies; greatly increased land values, especially in business districts, inviting replacement with larger buildings; and finally, the easing in the 1950s of acute accommodation shortage, making replacement feasible for the first time for 15 years. Piecemeal redevelopment of sites proceeded, but was increasingly overshadowed by comprehensive schemes in which developers' capital and expertise were linked with the compulsory purchase and land use zoning powers of local authorities. Activity spread from central London by stages to smaller town centres, in some cases giving rise to symbols of municipal status and prosperity, but in others leading to over-provision. Renewal was not confined to commercial buildings, for great tracts of old housing also fell through an onslaught on the slums, releasing land for rebuilding purposes at a rate sometimes exceeding the promoters' capacity to reuse it [13]. Many other old houses were improved, with nearly half a million dwellings the subject of local authority improvement grants, worth over £50 m. between 1965 and 1968. The amount of private time and money lavished in such ways is not recorded.

Rural activity   Rural building activity was small compared with the immensity of that in and around the towns. The only major exception was during a few war years, when there were frantic efforts deep in the countryside to provide camps, depots, stores and well over 400 airfields. This activity soon died away, leaving mainly agricultural provision, village expansion near big towns and some scattered houses elsewhere.

Quantity of building   Attempts to understand building quantity in postwar years, more than earlier ones, are beset by two problems. One is the diminishing value of money and the other is the changing nature of buildings. Effects of inflation are familiar enough, but further explanation of the problem of comparability is needed, since there is no recognized unit volume of output in building. This is apparent from contrasting a typical house of, say, 1946 with one of 1973, with differences of floor area, services, garage and so on which affect quality and cost, making direct comparison difficult. Similarly, typical factories, offices, and other building types changed in allied ways. Being mindful of the changes among buildings of like purpose, the

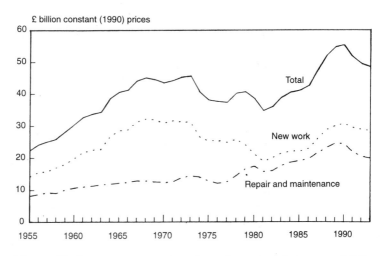

Figure 35 Output: new work and repairs and maintenance, 1955–1993 (£bn. at constant 1990 prices). (Crown copyright. Reproduced with the permission of the controller of HMSO. *Housing and Construction Statistics 1983–1993* Department of the Environment.)

trend in total volume of building activity may be examined, as expressed in price of building output.

Between 1954, when wartime disruption had receded, and 1970 the total price of UK construction output, at constant prices, more than doubled, from an index of 64 to one of 132 (1963 = 100). A further indication of growth over the same interval was that construction output at *current* prices increased from 5.7% of gross domestic output to 6.3%. At the same time, however, construction output at *constant* prices, as a percentage of gross domestic product, showed a slight fall, from 5.5 to 5.3. This discrepancy, Sugden [14] has pointed out, was caused by a relatively faster rate of price increase in construction than in other industrial fields. The effect was of a price rise in construction, relative to the rate of price increase for all goods and services, of about 16%, accompanied by a relative fall of about 3% in the volume of construction output. Promoters were having to pay progressively more for buildings than for other categories of expenditure. This appeared to slightly diminish the volume of building relative to other aspects of the growing national economy. The higher cost of buildings was attributable in part to higher-quality products, particularly in respect of services. Also there was a tendency for productivity in building to lag behind that in other industries. A result was that larger cost reductions, or at least slower price rises, occurred outside building than in it, hence there were widening price differentials between the building and non-building fields.

Some of the various influences on levels of building activity are already familiar, but others took new forms. Economic growth raised real incomes, thereby stimulating demand for a growing range and quantity of buildings. The birth rate was higher than before the war (although well below nineteenth-century levels), lifting the population of England and Wales by 5 m. between 1951 and 1971. More significant for housing need was an increase in the number of separate households, which was proportionately greater than the population growth. Regional and local migration also continued to play a part with the drift to the South East and loss of people from old town centres to new suburbs continuing prewar trends, though often at a faster pace. Replacement of outworn or unsuitable buildings, as requirements changed and fabrics ceased to be capable of repair, stimulated replacement demand to new levels. A much enlarged source of investment demand came from domestic owner-occupiers borrowing from building societies, insurance companies and local authorities. Owner-occupation increased from about a quarter of all dwellings in 1945 to over half by 1973, while private landlords escaped in growing numbers from a less and less attractive form of investment, due to rent and other controls. Further investment demand stemmed from institutions such as insurance companies channelling money into large commercial buildings, usually in exchange for income.

Many of these influences on building activity themselves were affected by government policy, exerted in two ways, the first being direct promotion of building. The second was through side-effects of policy, developing late in the period into explicit government use of building as an instrument for manipulating investment in the economy as a whole, to promote general stability and growth. Intended and unintended impacts of government policy on building activity were crucially important, at times (perhaps all times) being the strongest single influence of all.

Fluctuations There were four phases in demand for new buildings, beginning with wartime control over civilian building, initially unsure, but effectively asserted in 1940. A licensing system for work exceeding £500 (later much less) was enforced [15] to prohibit non-essential work. There seems to have been a good deal of evasion in an industry never the easiest to comprehend, let alone control. Systems of allocation and priority were hastily improvised by government in order to prevent the industry being overwhelmed by crushing demand for war work. Trial and error led by 1943 to a building programme which was centrally planned and coordinated far beyond any other in this country, before or since. By that time the gross value of building and civil engineering work, which had exceeded 1938 levels in 1941, was already falling and plans were being drawn up in anticipation of peace.

Victory brought the second phase of activity, in which demand changed in nature rather than intensity. Resources remained strained to the utmost and, amid deepening concern with costs, government retained rigid control over the amount and type of new buildings. Priority was given to blitz repairs, local authority housing and schools. The few private promoters permitted to proceed, such as industrialists in development areas, were helped by the low cost of borrowing. Gradually the austere economic climate moderated, bringing the third phase in the early 1950s. It was of brightening prospects, shorter and less severe business cycles, full employment, a more diversified economy and expanded social and welfare provisions. Building restrictions were relaxed in 1953 and abolished the following year, activity expanded, a free market in the provision, if not location, of buildings was re-established and accumulated arrears of demand were tackled. Keynesian economic policies brought prosperity, at least of a superficial kind, with a cycle of alternating boom and credit squeeze. Building was affected by these 'stop-go' sequences, being vulnerable to credit restrictions which cut more deeply into capital than current expenditure. Some building types, such as factories for consumer goods manufacture, were especially prone while others, such as local authority housing, enjoyed some immunity.

The fourth phase of activity was a hectic time of property boom, accelerating inflation and uncertainty with which the period ended in the early 1970s. Deep-seated economic problems, increasingly evident from unfavourable international comparisons and worsened by the OPEC oil crisis, brought the outlook for building and the economy as a whole to a very unsettled position. Expansion had been such that, from an output of over £6,500 m. (at 1975 prices) in 1955, the total for 1973 had more than doubled to reach £13,500 m.

ADDITIONS TO BUILDING STOCK

Housing

Housing remained, by a shrinking margin, the largest single building type. Housing output represented slightly over 30% of the value of all building and construction in the later 1950s, falling a little by the early 1970s [16]. About 7.4 m. dwellings were built between 1940 and 1973, split evenly between public and private sectors. In wartime only a trickle of 5–10,000 dwellings a year were built, mostly to serve new camps and factories, but as clearly as 1941 preparatory discussions began on future plans.

With peace, housing received the same high priority as it had in similar circumstances in 1919. The Housing (Financial and Miscellaneous Provisions) Act of 1946 granted a treasury subsidy of £16.50 a house for 60 years, subject to local authority contribution of a much smaller sum. Eleven major Acts followed in the next 25 years, some reflecting political reversals. Tightly stretched house building resources after 1945 were channelled mainly through the local authorities. Their housing expenditure in the late 1940s was more than five times that on all other local authority buildings combined. House completions exceeded 200,000 a year by 1948, at which time private house building was restricted to a maximum of one-fifth of local authority allocation. This was soon eased and then freed entirely in 1954 [17]. Meanwhile the level of subsidies to 'housing crusader' public authorities was raised and two years later their provision began to be shifted from general housing needs to slum replacement. Annual output reached a new postwar peak of over 300,000 in 1954, and in the ensuing fall to about 240,000 in 1958 private completions passed those of local authorities for the first time since the war. They took the leading position thereafter.

Housing measures of the 1960s included an over-ambitious (and unattained) output target, and an alteration of the basis of Exchequer grants to that of low interest loans in 1967. House completions [18] picked up gradually from the early 1960s to an all-time peak of 372,000 in 1968, though still not so very far above the prewar peak. By 1973 completions had fallen to 264,000, of which 174,000 were private, 72,000 were local authority and fewer than 10,000 each were by new town corporations and housing associations [19, 20]. Set against this decline in new work there was growth in rehabilitation.

The range of quality and cost of new houses in the 1940s narrowed, with the disappearance of high-quality examples and improvement in the lowest standards. New permanent houses, having an average floor area in 1947 of 96 sq.m, were larger than most prewar equivalents. Quality improvement came from recommendations in the Dudley Report [21] and the ensuing *Housing Manual 1944* [22], which suggested an area of 84 sq.m for five-person three-bedroom houses. This size was often exceeded in early years, but from the late 1940s economies brought reductions. Average floor areas were squeezed from a peak of 98 sq.m in 1949 to 83 sq.m ten years later. The fall in quality was accompanied first by large numbers of completions (more meant worse) and then by the shift to slum replacement.

Lower standards for new suburban local authority terraces were balanced partly by greater effort on schemes with high flats. Early postwar flats were few, but from the early 1950s 'mixed development' gained acceptance. Flats sited among family houses gave fairly high densities, as propounded in the 1943 *County of London Plan* [23]. Novel blocks of flats and maisonettes were not cheap, yet their extra cost, incurred by

Figure 36 Industrialized building. An 11-storey block of 44 local authority flats rising in Kidderminster in 1963. Concrete panels were cast by system proprietor Bison in Wolverhampton, transported by road and erected by tower crane of main contractor Bryant.

complexity of structure, services and building operations, did not retard their advance. Here was a triumph of fashion over economic rationality.

The private sector, by contrast, relied on a well-tried range of low- and medium-density single- and two-storey detached, semi-detached and occasional short terraced houses. In this field little fundamental change took place except for (as rueful mortgagees reflected) the price, although there were superficial changes. Resumption of large-scale private house building is typified by examples built by Taylor Woodrow, of which three-bedroom types of 85 sq.m area put up in Kidlington in 1953 were priced at £1,655 each (including land). Similar houses at Old Windsor were priced at £1,950 and superior versions were offered at £2,750 [24].

Private speculative houses appeared in large numbers in the 1960s, but it was local authority high-rise flats which attained

Figure 37 Placing a prefabricated floor slab. Four erectors at work towering over Kidderminster. Joints of wall panels, complete with glazing from the factory, are visible.

greater prominence. They reached a peak in 1966 when one-quarter of all new local authority dwellings were in blocks of five or more storeys. Soaring and potentially cloud-capped towers, it was noted, might confer prestige, catch votes and be a visible sign that the council was doing its job. An architectural ideal was taken up by various public interests and the proprietors of building systems. Before long, however, social shortcomings began to be recognized and were reinforced by economic arguments that land savings failed to compensate for inherently high building costs. In 1966 the average cost of flats in blocks of five or more storeys exceeded £54 per sq.m, compared with less than £32.30 per sq.m for houses. Government enthusiasm waned and a disastrous collapse at Ronan Point in the East End in 1968 merely underlined what was already obvious (if not always to the news media), that in future high-density housing was more likely to be low-rise than high. Elsewhere, under the recommendations of the 1961 Parker Morris Report [25], housing standards were improving

Figure 38 Small speculative housing. Local builder erects terraces in planned expansion of Basingstoke, Hants, January 1966. Joinery and other materials languish in the mud. (Source: L.A. Wilkins.)

with better heating and minimum floor areas of 89 sq.m for a five-person house (83.4 sq.m was the current average). Although hardly a transformation since the heady, but short-lived, days of Tudor Walters 40 years earlier, it was an improvement on the 1930s and 1950s.

Standards of private housing did not differ greatly from public, although the range was wider. The cheapest private examples appear to have been inferior to local authority equivalents, but the most costly private houses had no public rivals. Most private provision was between 70 and 93 sq.m, limits which included almost two-thirds of new houses mortgaged in 1962 by the Co-operative Building Society. Only about 3% of that sample exceeded 140 sq.m. The most expensive houses are likely to have been fewer in number, size for size, than before the war. A suggestion of relative leanness in quality of private provision was that in the early 1970s only about one in five new private houses exceeded local authority Parker Morris standards [26]. By then about a quarter of all building work by value was private housing and a seventh was public authority housing.

Public and social buildings

Public and social building activity increased from negligible levels in wartime to about one-fifth of all building activity in 1957 and over a quarter by 1972. Schools formed a sizeable

part of this category, beginning with some classroom extensions and provision for school meals during the war. A severe
accommodation shortage developed from the outcome of the
1944 Education Act, bomb damage, insufficient wartime
building, population growth and the construction of new
estates requiring new facilities. Education buildings as a
proportion of all local authority building increased fairly
steadily from about a twelfth in 1948 to well over a quarter in
1958. Nearly 600 new schools were completed in that year,
about the same figure as in 1970 [27], although there were
intervening fluctuations. Private school building was light in
comparison with public, about one-fifth measured by value
of new orders in 1973. School design developed and new
methods of construction were tried.

Consortia of local authorities which combined the functions
of promotion, design and component procurement devised
systems such as CLASP. This set out to reap benefits from low-
price bulk purchase agreements, pooled experience and shared
development costs. The value for money believed to come
from schools was largely attributable to the Ministry of
Education development group and one or two pioneering local
authorities, notably Hertfordshire and Nottinghamshire [28].
An indication of the variety of schools in the late 1960s comes
from a sample of seven discussed by Ward [29] which ranged
from 930 sq.m each costing £62,000 upwards to 12 times that
cost and area.

Building for higher education started with far lower priority
than school building, but growth came eventually, in keeping
with other aspects of public spending. By the mid-1950s the
number of full-time students in higher education in Great
Britain reached 122,000 (compared with 69,000 in 1938–39).
Colleges of Advanced Technology were designated in the later
1950s and new universities followed in the 1960s in response
to population pressure, desire for local and national prestige,
and the wish of more and more school leavers to go on to
higher education. Impetus for expansion reached a peak in
1963 with the publication of the Robbins Report, by which
time seven new universities were already in hand. The
University of Sussex, for example, planned about 33,000 sq.m
of accommodation worth £2.8 m. in its first four years.
Between 1960 and 1970 the number of all university students
more than doubled to reach 220,000. Many non-university
institutions were re-ordered in name and status, so that by
1971 there were 30 polytechnics and over 600 art, agricultural

and other major further education establishments. In 1969
typical arts buildings cost slightly more than secondary
schools, at about £73 per sq.m, and laboratories cost about £20
more.

As with higher education, so with health provision, where
early activity was light, but expanded later with attempts to
catch up arrears. The founding of the National Health Service
in 1948 did not bring a heavy building programme, and
hospital building, which was the concern of Regional Boards,
remained below prewar levels. Annual capital expenditure on
hospitals in 1949–50 was £9 m., and local authority expenditure on clinics, ambulance stations, provision for the handi-
capped and so on remained below a third of that figure.
Awakening came in the 1960s with efforts to modernize a
decidedly elderly hospital stock. Annual expenditure of £26 m.
in 1960–61 almost quadrupled by 1967–68. Typical buildings
were costly and, at about £100 per sq.m in 1969, equivalent to
about two-and-a-half times the unit cost of houses. The
difference was explained by the exceeding complication of
hospitals, from the time taken to formulate design briefs, to
their deeply involved plans, structures and services.

Library building followed the general pattern of public and
social buildings with an apparently light programme in the
1940s, picking up in the early 1950s and, with growing
prosperity, well sustained in the following years. Projects in
1969 typically cost £90 per sq. m and ranged from about the
size of a house up to 5,000 sq.m or so [30]. Accommodation
for defence purposes, and law, order and public safety, was
dominated by wartime provision of 18,000 concrete pillboxes,
tens of thousands of gun emplacements, hundreds of airfields,
camps and training establishments which exceeded £120 m.
value each year from 1940 to 1943. Peacetime spending was
more moderate, with activity being carried on by the Ministry
of Public Building and Works and its successor the Department
of the Environment. On the civilian side, building for police
and fire services commonly was less than one-tenth of
wartime military spending. In the 1960s there was limited
activity in the field of town halls, museums and art galleries,
the quality summit of public prestige building. Costs were at an
appropriate level, with civic suites (about £135 per sq.m in
1969) being triple that of low-cost houses, although depart-
mental offices cost about the same as good quality private
offices. Places of worship [31] were often associated with
community centres, in physical proximity if not necessarily in

source of funds. The cost per sq.m. of churches in 1969 was about £90 and chapels were rather less, but both were comfortably below specialized secular buildings. Public authorities (not so many voluntary agencies as in the past) provided small numbers of other buildings across a remarkable range of types. They serve to remind of the richness of human activities, as well as of the ambitions of the unfolding welfare state: leisure and sports facilities, markets, depots, wartime ARP shelters, bathing huts, nurseries, youth centres, old people's accommodation and, finally, crematoria.

Industrial building

The wealth to fund the swelling welfare state came ultimately from industrial buildings. They formed the next largest category and one more architecturally uniform than the last. During the war there was a struggle to expand strategically important industries and after it there was diversification in consumer goods manufacture. In the late 1950s the value of new industrial work was about 15% of building and construction output. The industries with highest capital expenditure on new buildings were, in descending order, chemicals and allied industries, engineering and electrical goods, food, drink and tobacco, and metal manufacture. Other prominent industries were vehicles and aircraft, paper, printing and publishing, shipbuilding and textiles. Despite an upward trend, by 1972 the value of industrial building had slipped relatively to nearly 10% of building and construction output, below the level of commercial building.

Factory and warehouse building ranged from vast utilitarian sheds, such as Ministry of Supply stores, to small groups of rented municipal 'nursery' workshop units, each about the size of a pair of houses. Again, there were large developments including on one site facilities for processing, producing, storing and despatching, as well as researching and administering every aspect of whole groups of products, such as pharmaceuticals. Agricultural buildings, for an industry revived by the war and remaining prosperous after it, increasingly converged in design with cheap manufacturing accommodation. Various standard buildings appeared, in their most extreme form stark and repetitive factory farm installations for poultry and pigs [32].

Despite a patchy national record of manufacturing performance, some building groups were large: in 1964 £383 m. invested in new work for private industry produced 1,200 buildings with a total floor area of 3 million sq.m. Here was a field where unit costs of large projects were lower than those of small projects. Costs varied depending on the particular industry so that in the late 1940s, when heavy factories of several storeys cost about the same as cheap houses per unit of floor area, light sheds cost only half that amount. Light single-storey factories of the type often built speculatively and which probably made up the bulk of industrial floorspace, cost something midway between the foregoing extremes. In the late 1960s similar accommodation, together with an allowance for some associated office space, cost about £73 per sq.m. This was much the same as warehouses, but heavy industrial buildings with long spans or bearing heavy loads could cost half as much again.

Commercial buildings   New commercial buildings were quite scarce until relaxation of official controls and growth of consumer spending from around the mid-1950s. Expanding white-collar activities of managing and administering required new offices. Less routine activities sprang up in new research centres, laboratories and studios. Retail trading expanded with new products and services into new shops, stores and supermarkets. Much leisure and entertainment migrated from private houses to specialized commercial surroundings of hotels, public houses, halls and clubs. Concentration of ownership and building promoters was at its most evident in retailing, where national chains expanded, but similar forces also existed in financial services and elsewhere. In the late 1950s commercial building amounted to one-tenth of the total value of building and construction output, advancing several per cent further by 1972. In that year offices were by far the most important commercial building type, followed by shops (worth about half their value) and entertainment buildings (worth about one-third).

Office building began to spread after early impact from about 1954 in central London. In Croydon, probably the most imposing manifestation outside the City, 500,000 sq.m of floor space was built or approved between 1957 and 1964. Other speculatively led developments were also getting under way in major cities, and in central London the pace accelerated to a peak in 1962. Planning restrictions were imposed then, but demand for space had already begun to slacken, not to return to former levels for a decade. By 1973 activity was again fuelled by spiralling office rents and recovered so strongly that further restrictions were thought necessary. During the 1960s peak the average size of office buildings in central London appears to have been approaching 4,000 sq.m, often subdivided for rental into units of about a quarter of that size [33]. Costs per sq.m in the late 1960s ranged from about £65 up to £80 for higher-quality owner-occupied premises.

Many comprehensive redevelopment schemes incorporated shops beneath offices, while in suburbs and small towns, new shops replaced many older high street buildings. Early postwar shop building activity was light, being mostly confined to bomb damage replacements and bringing essential amenities to new estates. Activity accelerated during the later 1950s and intensified around the mid-1960s, when large developers intervened in many town centres as retail competition sharpened. Multiple retailers increased their market share, largely at the expense of independent owners and co-operative societies. A leading example, Marks and Spencer, built 140,000 sq.m of new floor space between 1954 and 1968, quite apart from rebuildings. Leisure and entertainment building included hotel provision from the 1960s, stimulated by increasing tourism and a government subsidy late in the period, as well as rising business demand. In 1969 banks were one of the most costly commercial building types per sq. m at £120 (but still cheaper than a small number of projects such as theatres) while department stores were £78, public houses £73 and, among the cheapest commercial buildings, service stations with showrooms were £54 and simple shops with flats above them £43.

LOSSES FROM STOCK

It was an energetic period in many ways, including destruction. Losses from stock were far greater than hitherto and the economic life of many building types may have begun to shorten. Even so, houses were said, in the 1960s, to be subject to clearance at an annual rate of only something less than half, and probably less than a quarter, of 1% of stock. This was probably slower than the rate for industrial and commercial buildings. The most effective agents of demolition were large urban local authorities keen to eliminate houses built before about the last quarter of the nineteenth century. Other agents were private interests, and some public ones unconnected with slum clearance, which perceived that the values of some sites were higher than the values of the old buildings standing on them. Potential benefits of rebuilding were mainly financial gain, but also improved service to customers, enhanced reputation and heightened satisfaction to owners. Changes in technology, taste and fashion condemned many buildings as diverse as cinemas (of 4,800 in 1939, fewer than half were open by 1966), country houses (well over 400 destroyed between 1940 and 1973), gasworks and churches. The origins of obsolescence were almost always less physical than economic and social.

Building loss in the period opened with violently intense, though mostly arbitrary, devastation by the *Luftwaffe*. In London about 5.4 million sq.m of commercial and industrial floor space, including over one-tenth of all office space, was destroyed or damaged. The number of houses in England and Wales destroyed by bombing was 475,000. A long respite followed while losses were replaced and pent-up demand was met before slum clearance was resumed in the mid-1950s. It proceeded at about 20,000 to 35,000 dwellings a year, accelerating to about 65,000 in the 1960s. Far smaller losses were due to commercial expansion, natural calamities like fire and flood, or artificial calamities (in the views of many occupiers) like road widening. Among other building types were corner shops, halls and workshops which obstructed comprehensive redevelopment, and redundant specialized buildings such as railway installations after the Beeching closures.

Demolition was almost inevitably heavy in a stock of buildings larger than ever and belonging to a society which boasted its affluence. Attitudes towards clearance began favourably associated with the idea of progress, but were gradually redefined towards hostility. The case for conservation and reuse rather than destruction, even of the commonplace, was pressed more and more by individuals and amenity groups, and eventually taken up late in the period by local authorities. The initial swing to conservation may be attributed more to lay public opinion than to building promoters, whose views generally appeared to lag in this respect.

BUILDING FORM

Grouping of buildings

The grouping and form of buildings developed partly along lines which emerged before the war and partly in novel directions. The size of the largest projects continued to increase in volume and height (overwhelmingly so among some office and flat towers). Elsewhere suburban medium-density development found greater favour than ever. A novelty was rigid segregation of building types of like function according to planning policy – here an industrial area, there a housing estate and elsewhere a shopping zone. This was seen most clearly in the new towns, very many of them in the South East. The antithesis of this land use pattern appeared very occasionally as 'megastructure' complexes tightly combining a mixture of building types. Town centre examples combined shops, offices, multi-storey car parks and perhaps a library or public house, while some new universities brought together teaching and laboratory space, lecture halls, shops and a bank. This was a way of using sites intensively, a practice encouraged by escalating land values which stemmed in part from restriction of supply through planning policies. Agricultural land was said to have increased from an average of £62 per hectare in 1939 to £1,600 in 1972 [34]; in Greater London some sites increased over 200-fold in a similar period.

**Standardiz-
ation**

Many buildings were more repetitive in their general layout than hitherto (most mass housing always had been), and more standardized in their component parts. Repetition and standardization applied in many different ways, for example: interchangeable components of system-built schools; repetitive bays of industrial and commercial blocks; 'off-the-peg' home extensions, industrial and agricultural buildings, system-built high flats and demountable 'instant' accommodation. During the war economies in design and production, possible through standardization, were exploited fully. Standard ordnance factory units, stores and other buildings were rushed up and development work was undertaken at all levels from construction details and specifications to the design of whole buildings. Prefabrication went hand in hand with standardization and was officially fostered at times when traditional resources for building were most stretched. The main purposes of standardization were economy of costs, labour and materials by variety reduction through elimination of trivial differences among components. There also seemed to be a sense of fashion in keeping abreast of leading practice in other fields [35]. This borrowing of ideas developed outside building, for use in the industry, was pressed by manufacturers (as with housing systems from aero and ship building industries) and by promoters (as with components from school building consortia).

Convergence A probable effect of more repetition and standardization was less variety in appearances. This outcome was also encouraged at the district level by rationalization and consolidation of building codes. A leading measure was the publication of the *Building Regulations 1965* [36] which advanced universal practices over local ones. Convergence seemed to be taking place in the appearance of certain categories of buildings such as primary schools and branch libraries; supermarkets and warehouses, and private and local authority houses. If visual uniformity was growing, its origins appeared to lie among designers' intentions, economics of production, and the growing preponderance of corporate over individual promoters, leading to reduced individuality. It is possible that the differences between some types of buildings, based on function and symbolism, were beginning to follow extinct regional differences based on materials, down the path of decline.

Modern movement After slow interwar progress, acceptance of many superficial characteristics of the modern movement in architecture was rapid, reaching a prominent position by the time of the 1951 Festival of Britain. This acceptance was balanced by rejection of much that was traditional, especially in buildings above the scale of housing: applied ornament was widely abandoned; framed structures often superseded load-bearing walls, even for quite small buildings such as primary schools; light wall claddings and large windows replaced heavy masonry walls with small openings; pitched roofs were replaced by flat ones. The latter made deeper and more complicated plans possible, with projecting wings, recesses and courtyards. Another change seems to have been further reduction in the bulk of building fabric per unit of floor area. This advance towards lightness was in part possible through increasing use of synthetic and processed materials such as plate glass, concrete, plastics and aluminium. Most interiors held many reminders of rising material standards in the shape of more fittings, heating and lighting.

Lighter, brighter buildings were accompanied by several developments unforeseen by early protagonists of the modern movement. One was promoters' growing concern with value for money from their buildings. This took the form of pressure to cut costs by eliminating all spaces and features which were not demonstrably functional. In some cases such as schools, avoidance of redundant space in the interests of economy was said to be entirely beneficial, and elsewhere it might be only designers' flights of fancy which suffered. However, in some other cases undue zeal in cost-cutting led to duller if not worse buildings: one example was officially declared minimum standards, such as Parker Morris, observed in practice as maxima; other examples were rooms in which ceiling heights were brought down to a uniform minimum, and in which circulation spaces were cut to make oppressive narrow corridors. Some such cases drew attention to conflict between different levels in the promoters' extended management hierarchies, such that the capital saving of one department reappeared as the increased running costs of another. Not that cost limits and their inhibiting effects were new; rather it was the extension of limits to nearly all higher-quality, as well as cheaper, buildings.

Another development was increased provision of complicated services and reliance upon active systems under the control of complicated instrumentation. This, rather than simpler passive systems of heating and ventilation aided by heavy-mass building fabrics. Promoters' money, guarded jealously in respect of floor areas and specification, seems to have been more readily tapped for building services. This suggested promoters' changing preferences from spending on building volume to environmental performance. In extreme cases there were artificially controlled interior environments, with very deep rooms relying on artificial lighting, windowless rooms dependent on mechanical ventilation, and air-conditioned buildings. Some of these features appeared in high-density housing from the 1950s, and others were used increasingly to meet the needs of complicated planning, prestige and high performance, for example in computer rooms and auditoria. Reliance on heavy energy consumption made it possible to provide accommodation of standards, and in places, which were otherwise impossible. Services also conveyed a progressive image of technological confidence. In 1973, difficult questions about energy costs posed by the oil crisis and ensuing recession, had barely begun to be asked.

8

The industry fights for freedom and growth: 1940–1973

Please inform me what safeguards you have to ensure–
(a) that new factories or building undertakings are really essential;
(b) that the plans and designs for such undertakings are of the most economical character;
(c) that building labour is used to the best advantage.

(Winston Churchill, Minute, 26 August 1941)

CHARACTER AND INFLUENCES

Demand and capacity
The period was a unique interlude in which demand generally matched or ran ahead of the capacity of the industry. Capacity was reduced in the transformation from peacetime work to that for defence and armaments. Resource problems of materials and labour supply arose (as well as some business opportunities). The coming of peace and Keynesian national economic management brought with it heavy public building programmes, commercial developments and the rest. Concern within the industry moved from the age-old bugbear of whether future workload would match capacity. Instead there was concern over resources, about matching capacity to rising demand. It was a less burdened period for the industry, with a rare freedom from workload uncertainty; from 'Where is the work?' to 'How shall we cope?'

At the same time the productivity performance of the industry was poor. Matthews *et al.* [1] noted a substantial fall in productivity between 1937 and 1951. It was so great that the absolute level of productivity prevailing before the war was not regained until the end of the 1960s. The annual growth rate in total factor productivity in construction 1937–51, was −2.5% (recovering to 1.8% in 1951–64 and 1.6% in 1964–73). They also noted that not only was this fall unparalleled in other sectors of the economy, but advances in building materials and methods were more rapid than ever before. Official anxiety about low productivity found expression in Anglo-American comparative studies and working party reports [2]. Matthews attributed the fall to full employment: people were now paid to wait for weather improvements and late deliveries, rather than being laid off; poor labour who would formerly have been unemployed were now attracted to construction; and there was a lack of disincentives without the threat of unemployment. Also hold-ups were more frequent when pressure of demand was higher.

With problems of overheating, rather than fear of slackness, there was some resentment towards official direction and policy changes. The industry felt the effects of government direction most during the war, when unprecedented official planning powers were assumed. Buildings were required with greatest urgency, often without regard to costs, from an industry harnessed by such measures as compulsory registration of firms, control of materials and licensing of work [3, 4]. Controls were maintained for six or more years after the war, while problems of overloading, inefficiency and low productivity persisted [5]. After a false dawn when licensing restrictions were eased only to be reimposed, lasting relaxation came in the early 1950s and was followed by expansion of activity. Nevertheless complaints continued through the 1960s and after that successive governments failed to take account of the disruptive consequences of their policies [6]. When cuts were imposed or lifted there were long lags before change was evident, because new orders, rather than work in hand, were affected. By that time the reverse influence could be what was required. Yet the building industry was not unique in facing problems of 'stop-go' which were a characteristic of the whole national economy. Complaints from building were exaggerated, for it was not until 1969 that 'stop-go' policy caused an absolute, rather than a merely relative, fall in building output. The building industry had found, in the shape of government, a scapegoat for one of its major (and time-honoured) problems.

Internal relations

Relations between the diversity of constituent parts, or interest groups, making up the industry were fragmented. Relations were still hierarchical (if less so than before the war) and, if anything, views were sustained by prewar success and prosperity coupled with enjoyment of heavy demand. This was a mix likely to addict people to the security of what was familiar. Traditional methods had worked before the war when the tempo was slower and, anyway, now everyone was too busy to look for ways to improve. Yet times had changed and adaptations would have been timely: high labour costs were making new demands on managerial skills; promoters' urgency was putting strains on the capacity of firms to deliver on time; new technologies and products were arising; and above all, demand was heavy. Where change in the industry did occur it was likely to be within a constituent part, affecting a discrete interest group, rather than across boundaries. One part of the industry would adapt without much reference to other parts – here the consultants, there the contractors, and so on: overall procedures and relations were left more or less untouched. For example, there was persistence of the division

Figure 39 Steelwork in the wet. Light frame for industrial building rising from site slab in later 1950s. Contractor E. Turner & Sons have hired the crane. (Source: E. Turner & Sons, Cardiff.)

Figure 40 High rise. Riverfront-sited Viking Hotel, York in 1960s built by Shepherd Construction Limited. In the foreground are paraphernalia of wet construction: blocks, bricks, slabs, sand, cement bags and mixers – and the inevitable site hut. (Courtesy of Shepherd Construction Limited.)

of responsibility between design and production already noted [7]. This was said to damagingly isolate the two sides and lead to failures of understanding. Again, communications were claimed to be poor in a field where there was independence of the parts hazardously mixed with uncertainty [8]. Firms were forced to accept independent, but ill-defined responsibility for their work, despite dependence on others for information. The uncertainty which arose over timing and quality of information created a fertile breeding ground for dispute, delay and financial claims.

External relations

Many of the problems centred on the means by which demand was brought in touch with agencies of supply, in other words the methods of tendering and placing contracts for non-speculative work. In debate about the relative merits of different ways of selecting contractors, traditional open tendering lost favour. Although it upheld competition by being open to any firm to submit a price, it disadvantageously wasted unsuccessful tenderers' time and sometimes led to inadequate contractors winning projects. Selective tendering, in which only an approved list of contractors were invited to compete, reduced these problems and was successfully advocated by many, including the authors of the 1964 Banwell Report on the placing and management of contracts [9]. This followed an earlier official study on contracts, the Simon Report in 1944 [10]. Negotiated contracts also found favour through opportunities to save time and allow firms to offer their own constructional systems. This approach could be used both when promoters initially commissioned consultant designers in the customary way and also when promoters initially commissioned building firms which then employed their own designers. The latter case of a package deal, or design and construct, in which building firms provided both design and production services, earned a fair record for completion on time. On the other hand, without independent specialist supervision, the reputation for rectifying faults and keeping to cost estimates was poor [11]. For most non-speculative projects an independent design team continued to be commissioned initially by the promoter, or was already in their direct employment. By the close of the period package deals were used for about one-third of all new factories, rather fewer offices and nearly a tenth of local authority housing contracts.

All in all, the industry portrayed a mixed image. The war had heightened awareness of what could be achieved by application of science and technology, mass production and mobilization of mass resources; beside this, building looked old-fashioned and (literally) stick-in-the-mud. Fine, lasting traditions became redefined as unprogressiveness. Performance and quality of service was subject to criticism on various grounds. The casual observer saw sites which, compared with most other industries looked technically backward and with poor working conditions. Some users of new products (such as the occupiers of Ronan Point) had questions about the quality of products. Direct engagement with the industry at the higher levels could be dauntingly complicated for promoters. At lower levels, among jobbing and maintenance firms, uncertainty was a common complaint. In mitigation, the industry was hamstrung by division into parts (a barrier to fruitful cooperation as well as effective parliamentary lobbying), old management skills facing new challenges of pace and complexity, low research and devlopment effort, and the high cost of substitutes for traditional technology. As always it was necessary to remember just how large the industry was – large enough to embrace high-flying entrepreneur, skilled craftsman and reliable family firm, as well as all the others. Meanwhile, while demand remained high and rising, there was limited incentive for far-reaching change; generations of bitter experience of workload fluctuations had taught that there was challenge enough, and more, within short-term horizons. And the industry was able to point out that many promoters had unrealistic expectations about the time-scale of building and no grasp of the disruption to programmes and impact on costs caused by inadequate and irresolute project briefing.

PROFESSIONS

Architects　　Moving to one of the major entities of which the fragmented industry was composed, the architectural profession began to have relatively more salaried and fewer self-employed members than formerly. In the early 1970s the 3,600 private practices in the UK between them employed about half of the profession, the same proportion as they had done a decade or more previously. A survey [12] of 1962 showed that 13% of private practices had more than ten staff (and carried out over half of all work certified, including most big projects), while 69% of practices had fewer than six staff. Local government architects made a notable climb to positions of power in the 1940s and 1950s, with the number of RIBA members in local authorities up by a quarter between 1939 and 1948. There were 135 local authority architects' departments by 1957, many quite large, employing over a quarter of RIBA membership. Many local authorities with their own architects' departments placed some commissions with private consultants in order to draw on special experience for important projects, meet peaks in workload and give stimulus.

Architects also obtained salaried employment in government departments, hospital boards and nationalized industries, where altogether about 10% of RIBA membership was employed in 1957. A further 6% were employed directly by industrial and commercial firms, including contractors, where a strict code of professional conduct barred architects from top-level management. The highest and lowest earners in the profession were principals in private practice, while local authority architects received middle-range incomes. Overall, the earnings of the profession were not as high as those of leading professions outside building, although a few architects with the very highest earnings seem to have done very well.

Professional leadership, mainly through the RIBA (to which a majority belonged) soon reflected the rise of public sector architects. A spell of fervour for reform in the 1960s faded in the 1970s, when the profession found itself in an uncomfortable position between the upper and nether millstones of client and contractor, not an easy place in which to uphold the values of the community. Architectural staff were scarce, leading to rapid turnover and difficulty in meeting commitments on time. Growing numbers of technicians and unqualified assistants were taken on and the Society of Architectural and Associated Technicians was set up in 1965 (known as the British Institute of Architectural Technologists from 1986). A less tangible problem than staffing was the view, increasingly questioned later, that the artistic side of architectural skills had become obsolescent in a scientific age [13] and that new functional skills were needed. This view originated in the demands of technology and criticism from builders that lack of progress was due to the 'inefficiency and folly' of architects. Their practical understanding was compared unfavourably with that of engineers, and the lack of incentive for economy in design implicit in the fee structure was pointed out [14]. If architects sometimes appeared under pressure from events [15] it was equally true that the work of a minority, at least, gained the highest international acclaim, and that some led the industry in the field of technical developments. It was also true that measures were taken to tackle shortcomings as they arose, for example in management.

Quantity surveyors

Quantity surveyors numbered fewer than a third (6,000) of the number of architects in the mid-1960s, most in the 700 practices in the UK, but some employed in public authorities. Many quantity surveyors engaged on the design side of the industry were members of the Royal Institution of Chartered Surveyors (proclaimed a Royal Institution in 1946), while many others employed by builders belonged to the Institute of

Quantity Surveyors, which was about 2,000 strong in the mid-1960s.

Traditional quantity surveying skills were close to practical aspects of building and the profession hitherto had not sought much involvement in early design decisions. It main functions had been to compile bills of quantities, price and agree the progress of works, and settle final accounts. More experienced promoters with higher cost consciousness caused new functions to be added gradually: preliminary estimates to advise on costs from an early stage of design; cost planning and cost control to obtain balanced spending in design and during construction, and to find among alternatives the one giving best value for money. New concern with predicting as well as accounting for costs, together with direct appointment of quantity surveyors by promoters (rather than through architects), brought the profession closer to initial decisions about projects. In doing so, professional influence was enhanced.

Engineers Structural engineers, slightly fewer in number than the quantity surveyors, continued to be engaged for large projects and many smaller ones. They either acted as consultants nominated by the architect and paid by the promoter, or were employed direct by firms of contractors or manufacturers. A small minority, along with architects and others, joined forces to form multi-disciplinary practices offering all necessary services for the design of large schemes. Engineers' skills were employed mainly in designing foundations and frames, where strong links with technology and the industry were retained.

A growing number and variety of engineers possessed other design responsibilities which were essential to large projects, namely mechanical, electrical and other services work. Again, some acted as consultants while others were employed by engineering firms supplying goods to the sites. The Institute of Heating and Ventilating Engineers, founded in 1897, began to play a more prominent role. The pace of technical change in some building services and pressure of demand sometimes appeared to outrun the capacity to provide advice to the remainder of the design team.

FIRMS

Size and number The number of building firms remained large throughout, but fell somewhat during the war, recovered, and then declined gradually from the late 1940s to a total of over 90,000 in Great Britain in 1973. Very small firms survived in large though declining numbers, with the proportion of one-man businesses falling from over a third of all firms in 1943 to about a quarter in 1973. In that year about 90% of all firms employed fewer than 25 people and rather under 2% of firms employed 115 or more. The time-honoured pattern of easy entry and short life for many firms persisted, due, as ever, to easily available credit and an unwavering supply of hopefuls keen to found their own businesses. The efficiency of firms varied widely so that there were heavy casualties among a postwar glut of small firms. Failures in building continued to be numerous through the period. Equally, firms were very numerous and statistical presentation often conveyed a misleading impression of high failure rate. Profits in the late 1950s were said to be somewhat below the average for industry as a whole, and in the bouyant 1960s typically reached 8.5 to 9% which was similar to, or higher than, manufacturing industry, but less than non-manufacturing industry [16].

Large firms   National contracting firms attained stronger and more influential positions. They brought with them greater anonymity with their company formation, consciousness of profit and loss, and propensity for litigation. Their emerging dominance amid persistence of many small firms is seen in a comparison between the amounts of work carried out by each group in the early 1970s. The largest 0.1% of firms carried out the same proportion of work, almost a quarter, as that carried out by the smallest 90% of firms. Yet large firms appear still not to have benefited overwhelmingly from the economies of scale which more and more came their way. Among them were superior ability to raise finance, attract high-quality staff, spread risks of loss-making projects, procure goods in bulk at cheap rates, make full use of indivisible resources such as specialist manpower, and survive extremes of workload. Some of these advantages helped to give large firms higher output per man than smaller firms, but this also in part was because they avoided much labour-intensive maintenance work.

Two disadvantages of large firms had the effect, in the short term at least, of allowing smaller firms to compete on equal terms, despite their lower resistance to misfortune. The first handicap of large firms was a danger of outgrowing their management capacity, and the second was their higher overheads. The latter were such that the proportion of office workers relative to site workers increased with time and size of firm. About a fifth of large firm employees held administrative, professional technical and clerical (APTC) jobs but, despite wide variations, most small firms had a much smaller proportion. The firm of Wimpey, latterly with a staff of 9,000, illustrates a general trend in which overheads crept up, in that case from 4% of turnover in 1944 to 5.5% in 1969. The structure of such firms was complicated, often with associated property, materials-producing and subcontracting companies. Typical larger firms had sections devoted to plant and transport, joinery making, planning, work study, design services, bonus surveying and site safety [17]. Key figures below top management included estimators, buyers, planning engineers, contracts managers and surveyors, and on site on the largest projects were project manager, site manager, site agent, section foremen and general foremen. Smooth running

Figure 41 Scaffolders' delight. Brickwork is rising six storeys on St James Hospital, Leeds in the 1960s. Two concrete mixers are fed (lower left) while truck delivers concrete blocks. Tower crane is in use. (Courtesy of Shepherd Construction Limited.)

of projects depended on them, but people with the right knowledge and skills were scarce.

Typical development of the largest firms began with wartime transfer from speculative house building to large contracts, including civil engineering. This freed them from problems of dispersed management and from having capital tied up in land stocks. Two firms which used their wartime experience to good effect were John Laing and Harry Neal Ltd [18]. In the 1950s and 1960s many firms moved into property development. Among them were Laing which formed, in 1954, the first of a series of over 50 companies for that purpose. The largest firms expanded strongly during the 1960s when, for example, the same firm tripled its turnover in seven years. In 1970 the 'big six' were Wimpey, with a turnover of £225 m., Laing, Sir Robert McAlpine and Sons, and Richard Costain, all with turnovers exceeding £100 m., and slightly smaller, Taylor Woodrow and Wates [19].

Figure 42 Winter working. Academic building rises from mud and snow in Hull in 1960s. Productivity will have been helped by repetitive design of building. (Courtesy of Shepherd Construction Limited.)

Medium and small firms

Medium-sized regional and local firms, many with a family controlling interest and reputation for good quality work, were the most vulnerable to new conditions. They were too large to survive on maintenance work alone, but too small for the biggest contracts which would have smoothed out troughs in their workload. Another handicap was the proneness to recession of speculative house building, to which many were heavily committed. Small firms, such as that portrayed by Foster [20], shared some of these problems when engaged in speculative building, small contracts and conversion jobs. The very smallest firms continued to be simple partnerships or one-man businesses, rather than limited liability companies, active with light repairs and maintenance, in extreme cases en-livened with window cleaning. Small firms were represented at the national level by the Federation of Master Builders, while the NFBTE continued to represent larger firms. Increasing awareness of public image could be seen in promotion of professionalism by the Institute of Builders (Institute of Building from 1965).

Direct labour

Much maintenance and a minority of projects were carried out by building departments attached directly to local authorities, public utilities and some large private organizations. Much support for such direct labour departments came from some large urban local authorities around London, which became active after the war. In the mid-1950s about 4% of new work, mostly housing, was handled by direct labour organizations (d.l.o.s), but the proportion fell later [21]. In the 1960s about 15% of local authorities carried out at least some new work by direct labour [22], a few entirely so, and virtually all carried out maintenance that way. Political controversy still shrouded the subject and made comparisons with private contractors difficult, but on balance direct labour quality appears to have been quite high, while operations sometimes were planned poorly and suffered from weak incentive to control costs.

Sub-contractors

Within the labyrinthine complexity of the untidy and shambling giant which was the building industry, the number of subcontracting firms multiplied. More firms, a greater proportion of work undertaken by them, and higher degree of specialization, were all continuations of trends which were evident before the war. By the early 1970s more than half of the firms in the construction census were specialists of one sort or another, whether (in order of descending magnitude) painters, plumbers, joiners and carpenters, electricians, plasterers, heating and ventilating engineers, plant hirers or roofers. The list was extended by smaller numbers of specialists in suspended ceilings, insulation, flooring, reinforced concreting and many other fields. About one-third of all work in a typical project was subcontracted, but on some large schemes a total of over 50 subcontracting firms might account for as much as 70% of the work. Many larger subcontractors obtained their work by tendering, while smaller firms relied more on architects' nominations. In more technically advanced fields, such as mechanical services, subcontracting firms contributed also to design.

Specialization boosted productivity, so that subcontractors compared well in this way with general contractors, although firm size was usually smaller. Apart from productivity, there were other reasons for the growth of subcontracting, including increased technical complexity and the inability of contractors to find continuous employment for specialists in slack times. One consequence of increased subcontracting was a heavier burden of management and coordination on general contractors, which sometimes led to stress. Another consequence was the growth of controversy surrounding the 'lump', otherwise known as labour-only subcontractors. They were gangs of self-employed operatives engaged as sub-contractors for their labour (but not materials or much equipment), mainly on private house building in the South, particularly after the 1966 imposition of Selective Employment Tax (SET), and often at high rates of pay for piece-work. Self-employment opened the way for tax evasion by these workers and saved the general contractor SET, holiday pay and so on. High general labour turnover and some site management of doubtful quality, were thought to have helped the growth of the 'lump' to something approaching 200,000 men by the late 1960s [23].

Builders'
merchants

Builders' merchants continued to provide the necessary link between sites and producers of goods. Merchants maintained stocks, absorbed shocks when demand fluctuated, collected and delivered goods, helped manufacturers by dealing in small lots when necessary, possessed knowledge of sources of supply, and provided technical advice and credit. There were about 4,000 merchants in Great Britain, with a trend among them towards concentration. They handled the majority of all materials and components, with the exception of goods, such as bricks, which some large builders preferred to buy direct from the makers. Merchants varied widely in size, with some of the larger supplying the smaller, and some specialization between firms handling heavy goods and light, and the retail do-it-yourself market.

Research and development

Various bodies concerned with research, development and dissemination guided building design and operations through a growing mass of regulations and recommendations [24, 25]. Research activities roughly reflected the economic and social priorities of the times (just as building did), in the way in which directions changed and activities rose and fell. In wartime there were government attempts to speed construction, economize on manpower and materials and substitute new resources for scarce traditional ones. New Directorates of Post-War Building, and Building Materials were created under the Minister of Works and studies were pressed forward on Codes of Practice, standardization and non-traditional construction [26]. After the war, efforts continued to be made to introduce more efficient methods and the Building Research Station alone employed well over 300 people in 1947. Growth appears to have slackened in the 1950s, although work quietly proceeded in public bodies such as the Forest Products Research Laboratory (later Princes Risborough Laboratory) and Fire Research Station. In comparison with other large industries, privately conducted research and development remained what it always had been, conspicuously light.

Some expansion, mainly publicly funded, came in the 1960s, when research in construction stood at only about one-tenth of that in all industries, relative to value of output. Increasing efforts to disseminate information were made through the technical press, Building Centres and other channels. A Directorate of Research and Development was set up in the reorganized Ministry of Public Building and Works and there was growing activity in other ministry development groups. A National Building Agency was established in 1964 to promote mainly housing development. Two years later the Agrément Board was created to assess new building products. Elsewhere an increasing quantity of research was promoted by such bodies as the Timber Research and Development Association (TRADA), Construction Industry Research and Information Association (CIRIA), institutes of higher education and trade associations.

Do-it-yourself

The amateur contribution to building has so far been neglected. Yet it had long existed, as recorded by Samuel Pepys in his diary for 7 February 1666, and as when Charles Pooter made his brave (but streaky) showing with red paint in 1890s Holloway [27]. Hobbs' decidedly more earnest guide of 1926 [28] 'for the householder and amateur craftsman' included an ambitious range of skills, from preparation and storage of lime to laying bituminous felt roofing and casting concrete fence posts. Increased leisure time and rising real costs of employing builders must have stimulated growth. Home maintenance and decoration cannot easily be quantified, but growing popularity (or at any rate volume) may be traced through the rise of publications serving the do-it-yourself market. In 1951, the monthly *Popular Handicrafts* began to include a do-it-yourself section and three years later *Handyman* appeared, followed in 1957 by *Do-It-Yourself* magazine [29]. The appeal of the pastime, helped by television coverage, broadened into a mass one (annual wallpaper sales tripled in the decade before 1958) and deepened, so that high street retailers multiplied. Interior painting and decorating skills were acquired (more or less) in nearly every household, while a dedicated minority learned to deal with services and building new extensions.

A 1973 survey [30] found that do-it-yourself ranked fourth in estimated frequency of participation, behind gardening, needlework and knitting, and games of skill. Here were growing numbers of people who, as promoters, designers, contractors and operatives all rolled into one, were a species of economic anachronism, reversing the march of division of labour. Growth was further stimulated by greater spending power, new goods and a growing desire to combat anonymity by 'personalizing' the home. Much work was undertaken because building industry wages in effect had priced the industry out of the small jobs market. What firm could compete with householders whose labour costs were free and who derived great personal satisfaction from their efforts? The pinnacle of do-it-yourself was in self-build housing, where enterprising individuals singly or in small groups built their own houses.

LABOUR

Size of labour force

From the unpaid we turn to those who worked on site for their livelihoods. Wartime conscription quickly reduced the large labour force hitherto inured to endemic unemployment, and the remaining 'poor remnant' got as much to do as they could manage, and more. Official plans were drawn up early to meet the anticipated return of ex-servicemen to the industry and after initial shortages the labour force approached its prewar size by 1948. In that year manpower in building and contracting in Great Britain was 1.45 m., fluctuating thereffter to reach 1.8 m. in 1968, and declining to about 1.6 m. in 1973. By that time employment in construction amounted to over 7% of the national labour force, of whom about 907,000 were employed by private contractors and 242,000 by public authorities. In addition, there were estimated to be 117,000 working proprietors who were self-employed owners, managers and partners, and 367,000 administrative, technical and clerical staff, few of whom worked on sites. With a very approximate allowance for the statistically elusive self-employed workers, and also certain small categories not covered above, the grand total for the industry was said to amount to some 1.9 m. [31].

Full employment

The transformation from prewar insecurity to postwar security through near-full employment was probably the largest improvement in operatives' experience since the early nine-teenth century. Full employment was sustained more or less continuously after the war by government policy, to the extent of severe and sometimes desperate shortages of some crafts-men, as in the early 1970s. At the same time it was true that unemployment in building was higher than the national average, partly because out-of-work men from other industries registered as building labour, just as they had before the war. Another reason for this higher unemployment was the casual and transitory nature of the work, with jobs appearing and disappearing as projects started and finished. Labour turnover was particularly high among younger men (they were relatively numerous in building), and among the unskilled and those employed by larger firms; one-fifth of a 1965 sample of operatives had been employed by their current firm for less than a year [32]. The consequences of full employment, and the associated stronger bargaining position of labour, included better wages and general conditions as well as lifting of insecurity. Men were spared the need to drive themselves as hard as they once had for fear of losing their jobs.

Recruitment, training and conditions

Almost all operatives were recruited to the industry direct from school at 15 or 16 years of age and educationally were similar to other manual workers. Doubts about their performance were expressed from time to time, perhaps because an unattractive public image of building deterred many of the more able school leavers. Recruits increasingly were trained through apprenticeships and systems of day release to technical colleges, but this was by no means universal. About half of a sample taken in the 1960s had never begun an apprenticeship, nearly one-third had completed one, and the remainder were serving one or had begun but not completed one. In about 1963 the length of apprenticeships was reduced from five years to four and shortly afterwards the Construction Industry Training Board began to make levies on firms in order to pass on grants for approved training courses. At that time about two-fifths of all operatives worked in smaller firms employing less than 50, where a relatively high proportion were skilled. Over a third of operatives worked in larger firms employing between 50 and 500, and the remainder were in the largest firms each employing over 500. A decade or more earlier it was noted [33] that typical labourers followed the employment patterns of their fathers and led semi-nomadic lives, moving from site to site and town to town. They were said to owe more loyalty to their foremen than their employers and to appreciate working on varied, lightly supervised and outdoor tasks. Later the scene did not change very much and job satisfaction remained reasonably high, probably helped by improved site amenities to soften the effects of bad weather and the rough nature of much of the work. A dark side of site work was the continuing poor safety record, with over 250 fatalities a year and innumerable less serious accidents at times in the 1960s.

Size of trades　　The importance of traditional craft trades gradually faded relative to new skills (but seldom absolutely), such as those of frame erectors, fixings specialists and plant operators. Fluidity between the tasks of skilled and unskilled men increased in wartime and old boundaries between the crafts generally became less distinct [34]. By the late 1960s slightly over half of all adult male operatives were craftsmen, one-fifth were general labourers and the remainder roughly equal proportions of foremen and miscellaneous grades [35]. The expanding trades of the late 1950s and early 1960s were carpenters and joiners, electricians and, most of all, heating and ventilating engineers. Those which lost strength, but not by much, were bricklayers, plasterers and painters. In 1973 the largest trade group (excluding the self-employed), with 13% of all operatives, was carpenters and joiners ('chippies'), just as it had been before the war. Painters, with 9%, and bricklayers with 7% followed, and then electricians, plumbers and gas fitters, and plant operators, each with over 5%, and finally the other crafts, none of which exceeded 3%.

Wages and hours

The income of operatives began to increase in real terms during the war, when wages generally went up by almost half, and earnings even more, while the cost of living rose by 29%. Building craftsmen's rates increased rather less than those of labourers, to begin a narrowing of skill differentials which continued in peacetime. War conditions also brought holidays with pay from 1943, and extended notice of dismissal. From 1945 employers guaranteed half-pay for time lost due to bad weather, with a minimum guaranteed payment for the week, later extended to cover stoppages arising from other causes. In 1947, incentive payments for a minority of operatives were formally introduced, in the face of opposition. These, together with other bonus payments and overtime, increased most earnings well above rates agreed in the National Joint Council for the Building Industry. Various payments in addition to basic rates continud to be made widely, especially to younger men and employees of the largest firms, in order to stimulate recruitment and productivity.

As actual earnings exceeded basic pay, so actual hours worked usually exceeded hours agreed nationally between employers and operatives. In 1948 the average weekly earnings (as distinct from wage rates) for a 46.6 hour week were £6.44, almost exactly double that of 1938, when average hours worked were fractionally less. By 1958 averages had reached about £12.07 for 48.2 hours. Thre were some differences between trades, despite theoretical parity, but far more significant were changes in the cost of living. From an index of 100 in 1937, this moved to 170 in 1948, and 265 in 1958. Overtime payments enabled operatives, whose basic rates were several pence an hour less than the average for manufacturing and other industries, to bring up their earnings to the national average. In 1968, when the cost of living index was 357, the basic weekly pay of craftsmen was £16.90 for a 40 hour week, made up by overtime and other extras to £22.73. This was just ahead of labourers' earnings of £20.64. Rising inflation carried average annual retail price increases of 3.3% between 1953 and 1969 up to 6.4% in 1970. In 1973, retail prices increased 9.2% cent and average weekly earnings of adult manual workers in construction were £41.41, which was 11 p less than those in manufacturing industry [36, 37].

Organization   Trade unions found conditions early in the period in their favour. Wartime internal reorganization accompanied increasing membership and greater recognition by government, in exchange for relaxation of working rules inhibiting efficiency. Decline followed in the 1950s and 1960s when membership tailed away to about one-third of all those in the industry. In the mid-1960s the larger of the 20 unions affiliated to the NFBTO were the woodworkers, with 122,000 members, the Amalgamated Union of Building Trade Workers with 80,000, the painters and decorators and the Transport and General Workers, each with about 60,000. Other unions with sizeable memberships included those of plumbers, general and municipal workers, and plasterers. These, with the remainder, brought total membership of affiliated unions to over 400,000 although many unions (for example the T&GWU) had other members outside building who were not affiliated. Union mergers took place in the 1960s, such as that between electricians and plumbers, and the Union of Construction, Allied Trades and Technicians (UCATT) emerged in 1968. Union membership was highest among larger firms and direct labour organizations, but low compared with manufacturing industry. Some restrictive practices hindered innovations in production and wasted resources [38], but they appear not to have been unduly widespread. Negotiations between employers and operatives were generally amicable and there was no great loss of working days through disputes: the largest was in 1963 (356,000 working days lost) and 1972, when heavy demand exposed some large projects to disruption. Most strikes were unofficial and negotiating machinery was adequate, if slow-moving.

MATERIALS, COMPONENTS AND PROCESSES

Prices   Building costs, like wage levels, were profoundly affected by the changing value of money. A general understanding of trends is also complicated, as ever, by changing standards and quality of building. Materials prices probably increased by about two-thirds between 1938 and 1946, and again by about the same amount between 1946 and 1955. From 1938 to 1955 the nominal price of labour seems not to have risen more than that of materials. From the late 1950s the official index of new construction costs (1970 = 100) went up from 70 in 1958 to 88 in 1968, almost the same increase as that of the retail price index. By 1973 the construction cost index had reached 147, having increased rather more than retail prices. The overall trend, if anything, was for materials prices to rise less quickly than labour, although increases in world commodity prices sometimes worked in the opposite direction for imported materials such as timber. Near the close of the period a typical project was likely to embody labour costs of more than half, and materials costs of less than half, of the total cost.

Building methods

The relative proportions of cost of labour and materials in a project were determined by the methods of construction chosen by designers usually in advance of contractors' involvement. When an architect or engineer decided at the design stage on, say, precast concrete floors, it was unusual for the contractor, once appointed, to propose an alternative, even where it would have suited them to do so. Contractors' freedom over building method generally was limited to minor product specification and alterations agreed in the light of changing circumstances as the project went ahead. Occasionally contractors decided what methods to use before winning a contract, but this was limited mostly to package deals and industrialized system building. For the most part, professional designers decided *what* to build and contractors *how* to build it.

The evolution of building technology, historically slow, mildly accelerated. New methods, materials and components were introduced by designers, builders and manufacturers at a rather faster rate than hitherto. Once introduced they probably diffused through the industry rather less slowly and erratically than hitherto. Experience elsewhere suggests that the progress of a successful innovation followed an elongated S-shaped curve. Initial take-up among the pioneers was slow, but accelerated as acceptance by the majority increased, with final deceleration as the most resistant minority finally were won over. As innovations arose a little more quickly, obsolescence of some traditional methods and materials also probably accelerated. Innovations were encouraged by a new-found faith in postwar society in modernization and the efficacy of scientific problem-solving. Among the promises held out by advocates of change in building (and after the war they were quite numerous) were cost savings and higher-performance buildings. It was argued that these qualities would spring from greater mechanization, specialization and economies of scale, probably involving transfer of more site operations to the factory. There, controlled conditions would avoid delays due to bad weather, and increased productivity would follow mass production methods. Site operations would be reduced to rapid assembly of ready-finished precision components. Had not materials suppliers such as cement and glass makers, as well as non-building industries, already benefited enormously from similar changes?

Such ideals were not novel when the government took them up in an 'immense but rather heterogeneous effort' [39] to meet wartime scarcity and heavy demand. Part of that effort took the form of EFM (Emergency Factory Made) temporary bungalows. About 160,000 were made, largely by the aero-industry attempting to diversify out of wartime production, between 1945 when they cost £600 each and 1948 when they had reached £1,300. The effort foundered on over-optimism, especially over costs, while traditional builders looked on with characteristic scepticism (although many of the bungalows still survive) [40, 41]. A related government drive involving less novel products was the construction of various permanent non-traditional house types, which amounted to 16% of all new dwellings between 1945 and 1955. Better-known proprietary systems were Airey, Cornish Unit and Wates (all pre-cast concrete examples), Laing Easiform and Wimpey No-Fines (both in-situ concrete), and BISF and Unity (both steel frame). Most of these systems failed to compete with traditional construction on cost and once official support ceased they were quietly dropped. In the far smaller programme of school building the position of progressive methods was better sustained with 'closed' proprietary systems (such as one of aluminium) later giving ground to more 'open' ones devised by public authorities [42].

Impetus for change in house building methods returned in the 1960s, with fears that the traditional industry would be swamped by demand, particularly with insufficient skilled labour. Again private building firms were stimulated by demand and government to take up the challenge of industrialization by developing and adapting numerous systems, some from Scandinavia and France. Concrete wall panel construction was favoured for high-rise flats and, in smaller numbers, timber frames for houses, although many other alternatives were tried. The proportion of public sector housing starts by industrialized methods doubled between

1964 and 1967, when it reached 40% (the same proportion as for schools); as output climbed, so prices fell. But all was to little avail, for deep cuts in high-rise and other building programmes soon returned system house building and its proponents to the doldrums. Subsequent social and technical events have cast a shadow on many of the products [43].

Problems of industrialized methods

The circumstances of the second failure of industrialized methods (the first was after the 1914–18 war) throw light on the technical conservatism of the industry. Perhaps the most intractable problem was the familiar one of fluctuations in demand. Heavy capital investment in factory and plant for making prefabricated buildings meant high fixed costs and hence economical operation only when production was near full capacity. For example, one firm which invested £300,000 in a factory in the 1960s needed a yearly output of 2,500 dwellings to justify their enterprise. Large sustained markets were essential and when public sector orders faltered, plants lost money and were closed. Other problems included the coordination of large numbers of small conracts; the geographical limit placed on markets by heavy transport costs; high overheads of factory work compared with site work, giving severe cost competition from traditional methods; and a mixed response from design professions concerned with the quality of finished products, amply vindicated by the Ronan Point collapse. Additionally there were difficulties in standardizing products in order to secure long unbroken production runs, due to the variety of controls on building and lack of dimensional coordination, both of which eventually received official attention.

Underlying many of these problems was a lack of unity of decision by promoters, designers and producers in agreeing the aims and nature of the innovations. In all, resort was made to industrialized methods only when demand was high; they were dropped when demand fell. Only the caravan and mobile home makers (outside our scope here) were able to provide some sort of accommodation from the factory, at a price people were prepared to pay, and cope successfully with fluctuations in demand.

Traditional methods

Among traditional methods were small evolutionary changes due in part to the efforts of progressives elsewhere. Innovations, though not always lastingly successful, helped to put traditional methods in new perspective, by giving a basis of

LEEDS COLLEGE OF BUILDING

Figure 43 Mobile plant. Period crane at work in Hull in 1960s. In background large in-situ concrete frame has reached the fifth floor. Floodlight visible in front of a mechanical hoist (left). (Shepherd Construction Limited).

comparison and creating a pool of new ideas. For example, the traditional part of the industry extended greatly the use of plant on site so that heavy machines replaced initially scarce, and later expensive, labour for earth moving, materials handling and concreting. Tractor-diggers, hoists, tower cranes (introduced about 1950; by 1954 200 were in use), and concrete mixers became commonplace, and increasingly hired from specialists rather than acquired. Light equipment such as tubular scaffolding, formwork and power tools made it possible to speed up work without employing more labour and to substitute for scarce or expensive craft skills. Increasing investment which eased the shifting and lifting of heavy weights, making holes, fixing of parts and finishing of surfaces, did not amount to a full-scale revolution; fixed capital employed per worker remained much lower than the level in manufacturing industry.

Increased mechanization and use of small prefabricated components in traditional building did not fundamentally alter the finished products. Compounded by the influence of full employment and higher wages it did call for stronger skills in site management. Old easy-going management flexibility over the use of labour and tolerance of delay declined as building resources became more costly, products more complicated and promoters more time-conscious. Emphasis in management shifted from reacting to slow-moving events to planning and anticipating processes so that they succeeded one another smoothly. In such ways new ideas and approaches were absorbed piecemeal into traditional practice. Change in methods took the form far more of unobtrusive evolution than of dramatic revolution.

Composite goods

A growing number of goods used in building were made of combinations of different materials. Examples of composite goods were: cement, not in bags for mixing on the spot, but in, say, factory-cast, pre-finished concrete units containing steel reinforcement, fixings and perhaps a sandwich of plastic foam insulation and some pipe ducts; timber delivered not rough sawn, but precisely dimensioned and factory assembled into roof trusses complete with metal connectors; prefabricated partitions made of combinations of steel-faced plywood or plastic-faced particle board framed in metal. These examples could be multiplied to include systems of walling, windows, ceilings, roof deckings and so on. This great range of goods was added to and replaced at an accelerating rate. At the same time the traditional materials of brick and timber were still used in enormous quantities as they had been in the past. A result of diverse materials used in different combinations was that competition intensified between firms making dissimilar products for like purposes. To take one of many possible examples, the makers of precast concrete claddings competed against makers of asbestos-cement sheets and metal claddings.

Cement products

Cement-based products moved conspicuously to the centre of accepted practice with increased number and variety. Concrete was sometimes used in place of clay bricks, and in place of timber, when slabs were substituted for joists and boards. It was also used in place of steel, when reinforced concrete frames were substituted for rolled steel members. Development was spurred by wartime steel scarcity, and included improved precasting techniques, pre-stressing and ready-mixed deliveries. Cement production was not too badly affected by war, and later prices changed favourably relative to many other materials. Post, pile, beam, block, screed and slab, cement products all; the demand for concrete increased for goods which were poured, craned and shovelled into place.

Bricks and timber

Brick usage was less buoyant than that of concrete, with reduced wartime production and common bricks losing markets in competition with rival materials. Fletton brick production benefited from low price rises while facing bricks retained an important place, especially in house building. Brickmaking (like cement making) became concentrated so that London Brick in 1973 produced about 43% of British output. Timber supplies also were profoundly affected by war, with imports drastically curtailed and stocks used very frugally indeed. More economical use of the material followed technical advances in stress-grading and new methods of jointing. A more and more widely used cost-saving substitute for solid timber was sheets of reconstituted and composite types such as blockboard and chipboard.

Metals and plastics

Steelwork usage was stimulated by growing numbers of framed buildings on the one hand, but hindered on the other hand by periods of shortage and price rises in excess of those of the rival concrete. Innovations appeared in the form of welded joints and light structural frames of hollow sections and lattices, as used in school building. Aluminium showed great postwar promise which was not fulfilled when later price rises worked against it. Structural applications fell away in favour of its use as cladding, window frames, roof covering and trims. No doubt the use of metals generally widened, and a greater range of different materials was embodied in single buildings than before. There were also losses as, for example, with galvanized sheeting displaced by asbestos-cement, and cast iron displaced by plastics for rainwater and other goods. Plastics appeared in a variety of new and developed forms and soon claimed a substantial market in such varied applications as floor finishes, damp-proof membranes, plumbing, laminated surface finishes, thermal insulation, rooflights and inflatable temporary buildings.

Other goods

Two heavy goods, now produced by monopolies, which continued to hold their own were plasterboard, which progressed relative to traditional plastering, and glass, usage of which benefited from architectural fashion. Other goods, most subject to some level of standardization, included: quarry tiles and glazed tiles; clay and stoneware goods; concrete roof tiles, now dominating their competitors; and asphalt and bituminous felt, increasingly used for flat roofing. Services continued to develop comparatively rapidly with metal, asbestos-cement and pitch fibre pipes and fittings, as well as plastic. Electric, gas and oil heat sources largely superseded solid fuel and were used to power a variety of radiant, convected, underfloor, waterborne and ducted air systems. The development of such systems moved space and water heating further from the realm of hit-or-miss empiricism towards technology and engineering. A similar change was afoot in lighting and ventilation for large buildings. In the extreme cases of laboratories, air-conditioned offices and hospitals, the services installations became very extensive and complicated, so that the associated costs could amount to well over half the total costs of construction.

From the largest buildings to the smallest, the directions of technical development were the same. Most in commercial, institutional and industrial buildings, and least in domestic ones, local and natural materials yielded to universal and highly processed components; from craft to calculation, from wet forms of construction to dry, and from simplicity to complexity.

9

Building in a retreat of big government: after 1973

. . . hitherto 'unthinkable' ideas of the balance between state activity and the free market.

(Harold Perkin (1989) *Rise of Professional Society*)

DEMAND AND BUILDING PROMOTERS

National economy and building activity

At the outset of the period from 1973, promoters were unsettled and their confidence undermined by the OPEC oil crisis. This was followed by fierce inflation (peaking at 28%), political uncertainty and rising unemployment. Amid economic gloom it was apparent that national economic cycles were becoming more strongly linked to international events. Not only was the world shrinking in this way, but British building cycles were becoming more closely integrated with other movements in the national economy. A response to perceived long-term national relative economic decline was ventured in the 1980s with a shift from Keynesian economic orthodoxy to monetarist policies. There followed a programme of privatization and the capping of public spending, which resulted in a less influential public sector. At the same time old heavy industries, outpaced by overseas competition, closed and concern about global resources faded, partly in the face of rising North Sea oil production. There was expansion in the service industries of finance, communications, distribution, entertainment and tourism, so that during the 1980s economic growth proceeded at 3% to reach a climax in 1989.

Construction in 1973 (a peak year) had accounted for about 7.6% of gross domestic product. This fell subsequently, but eventual recovery in some sectors carried total expenditure on new buildings and works in the UK to a peak in 1990 of over

£56,000 m. The next, downswing, stage in the business cycle inevitably followed. Building activity in formerly buoyant service industries sank towards the levels already prevailing in public sector welfare fields. The need for new buildings, and the ability to pay for them, wilted as consumer confidence fell and prolonged recession settled. Total expenditure on new buildings and works dropped back to £46,000 m. in 1993.

Private sector advance

Twin themes affecting promoters were the retreat of government intervention after the stresses of the 1970s, and the associated rise of the private sector. The ebbing of official influence in building procurement was visible in many ways. For example, new towns ceased to be designated and local authority house building was severely trimmed. Again, nationalized industries such as gas and telecommunications were transferred to private ownership, while public authority spending on education and health care was restrained. Among the public sector concerns which were not privatized, most were subjected to spending limits and coaxed towards private sector behaviour. Altogether, between the mid-1970s and the late 1980s, the changes amounted to a revolution in sources of building demand: the value of the public sector share plummeted from just short of 60% of the total to around 25%.

The shift to private sector promotion brought big changes. Fresh importance was imparted to the urgency of projects and to value for money. Earlier, when the public sector had been foremost, leading priorities had been accountability and risk-aversion. The typical promoter of the 1960s (if such a body can be said to have existed) had been a large, rather ponderous organization with numerous committees and advisors. Responsibility was dispersed in such bodies, which had as an aim to optimize between various conflicting claims. Now the typical promoter was large, but faster-moving, with simpler lines of responsibility and more clearly defined objectives. Old-style promoters, such as a county council or health authority, had employed their own building specialists, such as design consultants (and often some direct labour). Newer promoters, such as property development companies and large retailers, preferred to appoint external firms on a project-by-project basis and to minimize their own establishments. In this they gained organizational flexibility and benefited from competition between the firms which they employed. At the same time they gathered experience of the procurement process and often became expert in its intricacies. One sign of this was when a group of promoters set up the British Property Federation in 1974. In general, emergent promoters were better-informed, though more impatient beings than their predecessors had been.

The largest private promoters were multinationals, embracing a whole range of organizational forms and functions. They ranged from Japanese car makers and American toy makers to conglomerate firms and others. Ultimate responsibility for a project was often located in a mass of subsidiary companies, maybe overseas. At the other extreme of scale the far smaller sole proprietor business survived. Between these and the multinationals was a great range of jointly and privately owned businesses working in the full variety of commercial and industrial fields. Speculative building promoters expanded, and more offices, retail units, warehouses and factories were provided that way, and proportionately fewer were custom-built. Smaller local and regional entrepreneurs progressively lost their promoter role, being supplanted by national financial interests of insurance companies, pension funds and the like. Limits on funding and building quality, for large and small private promoters alike, turned ultimately on the competitiveness of the promoters' business and their attitudes to risk.

Private sector promoters worked in direct ways and were able to exercise great discretion over product and process. In contrast, surviving public sector promoters were more indirect and bureaucratic in tone. An example is provided by the housing associations. They were run according to charitable rules, under the close eye of the Housing Corporation which channelled finance and scrutinized product and process. A multi-layered system of project approval and annual budgeting sometimes gave rise to frantic spending programmes alternating with delays [1].

Location

The advance of private sector promoters was most apparent in the South East. Between the early 1970s and the late 1980s the share of national building output in that region increased from rather over 30% to 40%. Some earlier official planning attempts to redirect activity to less prosperous regions were curtailed, although new Enterprise Zones were designated in the early 1980s in which reduced official intervention was intended to stimulate growth. While planning restrictions generally were upheld, edge of town medium-density developments, usually close to motorways, were common.

Prominent examples were the retail Gateshead Metrocentre of 140,000 sq.m floor area of 1986, and the Stockley Park business centre near Heathrow. Elsewhere, run-down docklands, of which London's were the pre-eminent example, were transformed by major commercial and residential redevelopments. In existing town centres, retail expansion took place on back land off high streets and on newly combined street frontage plots. Housing continued to be built on suburban estates and was also increasingly channelled into small urban infill sites in gaps and old gardens. In the countryside, agriculture required buildings, some of which were almost indistinguishable from industrial installations, with large repetitive volumes, engineered silo structures and the like. Where such investments would have been uneconomic, often in upland locations and later in the period, there were new buildings for purposes of recreation. These included scattered holiday cottages, new golf courses and holiday parks. New roads and ever-rising car ownership had further loosened the ancient fetters favouring concentrated location. In consequence promoters now often scrambled to take advantage of newly projected roads which would open up new development opportunities.

Repairs and conservation

New build was only a part of all building activity, and a relatively shrinking part at that. Repairs and maintenance expanded as the existing stock of buildings was enlarged and became older. Here the role of the promoter (for new build, often the dashing risk-bearer) was reduced to a caretaker of assets. But be it only make-do-and-mend, total repair and maintenance work increased strongly: from about 30% of value of all construction output in the early 1970s, to 46% by 1985, although this growth reflected, in part, a fall in new work as well as more repairs.

From repairs and maintenance to conservation and reuse is a short step. Disparate forces combined in the 1970s to greatly stimulate conservation. One force was a public reaction to the perceived excesses of vigorous postwar redevelopment. Another force was new concern about depletion of global resources, said to be being squandered at unsustainable levels on unnecessary new buildings. A third force was high inflation and economic uncertainty which discouraged promoters from major long-term commitments. Conservation and reuse offered several advantages over new build. It saved much-loved old buildings from destruction and replacement by unpopular new ones. It saved global resources and, not least, it could save money. Surviving nineteenth century mass housing, the remains of the coketowns discussed at the outset of this study, underwent large-scale refurbishment. Old warehouses, churches, country houses and much else were converted, often ingeniously. Some commercial promoters were obliged by town planning requirements to retain historic façades when they redeveloped behind them. In all this a rare balance could be struck between a recurring strain in British culture which seemed more committed to the past than to the future, and the contradictory desire to enjoy the fruits of modernity and prosperity.

Pace of change

Quite removed from the relatively sheltered world of historic conservation were major city office developments. Pre-eminent among them was the large Broadgate development in London, by developers Stanhope. It embodied many features which were adopted elsewhere, being built to a high specification in multiple phases, at great speed, in part using air space over a railway. Immense organizational complexity in funding, site acquisition, procurement and marketing were involved. Such undertakings surpassed local authority flat building as the leading sector of activity (generations earlier, church building had been leader).

Changes taking place inside organizations moulded demand for buildings more than hitherto [2]. Most organizations which provided goods and services were affected by a need to respond more quickly to those whom they served, to become more competitive. Pursuit of efficiency led in many directions, but probably that bearing heaviest on promoters was the acceleration of so-called rates of 'churn' in offices. This was movement in the grouping and allocation of workplaces within organizations, so that employees were required to change positions frequently. With movement of people went movement of building interiors, so that many offices became scenes of restless refitting as partitions and facilities were removed from one place to another. Most large firms underwent, in the jargon of their managers, downsizing, delayering and re-engineering. Peripheral business activities were sold off, to be contracted for by outside firms (we shall see below that building contractors shared this idea). New management styles and spiralling provision of computers combined in effect to dissolve and re-erect office walls.

Neither was pervasive change confined to offices, where a

growing proportion of the workforce were now employed. In high street retailing, too, competition was sharp and the search for efficiency relentless. Interior fit-outs here were particularly short-lived as fashions in marketing and corporate identity succeeded one another. Similarly in public houses, restaurants and elsewhere. In manufacturing, where light goods had mostly replaced the old heavy ones, product life cycles shortened and new processes were frequently introduced. Continuous flow line production was adapted towards the idea of the 'project' with a finite life. This not only led to frequent building alterations but, incidentally, created a point of similarity between manufacturing industry and the building industry, which had always thought in terms of 'projects' rather than continuous flows. In higher education (not traditionally host to fast change) new attempts were made to utilize capacity more fully. In health care, organizational change seemed endemic and new medical techniques added their imperatives for building change. Here, for example, hospitals were largely re-cast as short-stay accommodation, as patients returned home after treatment far more quickly than hitherto. In these places and others the impact on building demand was the same: permanence was increasingly a liability; flexibility and adaptability, improvization and short-life were at a premium. The only certainty in detailed building need, it might be said, was that it would soon change [3].

In a climate of quickening change, building users increasingly viewed their buildings as assets to be exploited and adapted, not as fixed 'givens' to be accepted. This was a view that stressed the use-value of buildings more than their exchange-value. The responsibility for matching the ever-changing accommodation needs of an organization with its buildings grew to become a recognized role and specialism. The new profession of facilities manager was imported from the USA and soon took root to meet the new need and to advise or act directly as promoter [4]. The emerging demand for ceaseless building change promised to be something of a godsend to builders: from former once-for-all provision, buildings now were becoming seen as a continuing commitment of work, the provision of an on-going service.

Fluctuations Any smoothing effect on patterns of demand, which sustained change might have had, was not yet apparent in movements in the level of national building output. The aggregate effect of the myriad of decisions to build was a resumption of the old cyclic pattern of output. Although the long postwar expansion based on reconstruction had first faltered in the late 1960s, the first serious check did not occur until 1973. After that, output dropped from a peak, steeply at first then with some recovery around 1976–8, and then again to a trough in 1981. The index for building activity in Great Britain (1985 = 100) fell from 116 in 1973 to 90 in 1981. This bleak time was followed by sustained recovery to notably hectic levels which culminated in 1990. By then the index had reached an all-time high of 126. There followed another decline as promoters withdrew for the duration of a prolonged recession [5]. The time-honoured pattern of boom and slump had returned and it seemed that the two early postwar decades of smoother output had been but an aberration.

ADDITIONS TO BUILDING STOCK

Housing

Housing demand was rooted in demography. Although population growth moderated almost beyond recognition from most earlier periods, a novelty was the formation of more small households. More single people, more old, and more young able to afford their own homes all exerted demand for small dwellings. They included small flats, sheltered housing for the elderly, and timeshare units for leisure purposes. As always, economic and political considerations modified effective demand for housing from the crude totals of household numbers. Here, economic growth made more spending power available for housing and the political shift to a market economy accelerated the move from houses for rental to those for owner occupancy.

The overall trend of housing completions was downward. From 1974 there were two years of modest growth followed by unbroken decline to 1982. Another modest recovery followed until 1988, when decline resumed. Houses completed in Great Britain in 1983 were 199,000, compared with 175,000 in 1993, both totals being a far cry from the peak of the late 1960s. Expressed at constant (1990) prices, the value of housing output was fairly constant until the late 1970s, after which it dipped to a trough in 1981, recovered to a peak in 1988, before dropping back once again. As a proportion of all construction work, housing was fairly constant until the 1988 turning point. It then diverged sharply from other sectors, falling away in the face of a severely depressed housing market, while other sectors went on expanding vigorously for another two years.

Housing promoters followed the broader transfer from public to private sectors. Within an overall housing decline, public sector promotion began to fall steeply from 1977. In 1983 local authorities completed 16.5% of new houses in Great Britain; by 1993 it was down to a mere 1.1%; the days of elected municipal 'housing crusaders' wielding council waiting lists were but a memory. Large parts of local authority stock were transferred to private ownership. Part of the former local authority role in new build was taken over by private house builders, whose output moved up from 74% of new houses in 1983 to 79% in 1993. Housing associations, a minor postwar contributor, began to grow appreciably in the 1990s to reach 19% in 1993. Self-build housing, which combined self-help with an ultimate development of do-it-yourself, also expanded to reach 11,000 houses a year in the late 1980s. This total was more than that produced by any single house building firm [6, 7].

The decline of public sector activity was initially a little less stark than appeared from completion figures. This was because as new build tailed away, so new policy initiatives opened in rehabilitation. By the early 1980s there had been a plethora of improvement grants, intermediate grants, special grants and repair grants as well as General Improvement Areas (GIAs). These were followed by Housing Action Areas (HAAs) and enveloping schemes [8, 9]. Eventually these activities declined just as local authority new build had done, but not before sizeable impact had been made.

Lean numbers were accompanied by lean quality standards. Although typical houses were better insulated and fitted with services for comfort and hygiene, in other ways they were quite spartan. Parker Morris standards for the public sector were abandoned in 1981, permitting smaller floor areas and other economies. Many privately built houses also were subject to similar economies as rising prices threatened sales. One response of the 1980s was new 'starter homes' in which space standards were pared to the bone.

Projects by housing associations reflected growing stress on cost efficiency and standardization. Some house types were developed by private builders and supplied to the associations. This blurred any remaining visible distinction in mass housing between the works of different types of promoter and between different tenures, as befitted a less class-conscious society. At

Figure 44 Cranes above the City. Part of massive Broadgate project well under way in 1990. No doubt many subcontractors are involved. Components are placed ready on floors (centre). There is some temporary weather protection, but scaffolding is mostly unnecessary (Source: Skidmore, Owings & Merrill. Photograph by Ian Clook.)

the upper end of the housing quality range it appeared that upward wealth redistribution (arising largely from taxation policy) had little obvious impact in terms of enhanced conspicuous consumption. Expensive houses did not seem to become, any more than in the recent past, the instruments of display. At the same time, housing in general attracted a notably large slice of national wealth, particularly so in the late-1980s' house price spiral. Arguably this had the effect of depressing investment elsewhere in the economy, particularly in manufacturing, to the detriment of national economic performance.

Costs in 1983 ranged from about £250 per sq.m for local authority suburban houses to £450 to £650 for private houses. By 1995 housing association costs were in the range £290 to £430 and the most costly private houses had reached, and sometimes passed, £700.

Commercial buildings

The commercial sector, of all sectors of output, perhaps best typified the spirit of the age. Here were to be found most of the largest, most costly, quickest built and most novel buildings. Here, too, was activity most closely connected to national and international political and economic change. Here, in short, was to be found the highest pitch of endeavour in building activity. Not that all activity in the sector could claim such distinction, for it also included many unremarkable retail units, say, and much commonplace lettable office space and cut-price accommodation. The claim of the sector to pre-eminence was based on pace-setting office developments.

The value of output of private commercial building activity (at constant 1990 prices) declined steeply at first from about £4,000 m. in 1974 to £3,200 m. in 1977. There then followed almost continuous expansion to a peak of £11,300 m. in 1990. After that, output tailed away quickly in the recession to only £6,600 m. in 1993. Expressed as a percentage of all construction activity, a broadly similar path was followed: in 1974 the proportion was 15% falling for several years, then rising to 37% in 1990, only to slip back to 23% in 1993 [10].

The figures concealed some highly charged dramas when promoters strove first for profit then mere survival. The 1973 property crisis stopped commercial promoters in their tracks so that by the end of the year new projects virtually ceased to appear. Property values fell while interest rates and building costs climbed. The ranks of publicly quoted property companies thinned alarmingly from 110 to 80, and there were spectacular failures such as the Stern Group (debts £100 m.) and the Lyon Group [11, 12]. Developers had seldom enjoyed popularity, but now they plumbed new depths of public and official antipathy.

Recovery from the crisis was slow, but as ever it eventually arrived. Inflation passed its peak in 1975 and within four years the Property Share Index returned to the level of 1973. In the meantime, as a result of the crisis, investors in the forms of large insurance companies and pension funds had become owners of property. They expanded their operations so that the 1982 assets of life insurance companies were £16 bn. and those of pension funds nearly £10 bn. Property had become a major investment outlet alongside gilts and equities [13]. On the way the property market in all its ramifications had developed into one of the most sophisticated in the world, with great resources being wielded, some on a global scale. An oligopolistic commercial property industry, largely composed of major building contractors and investing institutions [14] had largely replaced the earlier and smaller entrepreneurial property industry. A result was that promoters and their backers changed in outlook from an individualistic, swash-buckling search for a financial 'killing' towards a more calculated investment strategy. It was a shift (still incomplete) from raw speculation to orderly investment.

Demand for new offices in the 1980s was for higher-quality buildings than formerly, which were better able to support computer-equipped workforces. The sellers' property market of the 1950s and 1960s which had given rise to indifferent quality buildings was now a buyers' market, to the benefit of quality. Redevelopment or major refurbishment began to be undertaken of offices whose 21-year leases started to fall in. The pattern of office development by the mid-1980s was for projects in the size range 450–10,000 sq.m floor area, with a few over 23,000 sq.m. Rents of the time were of the order of £50 per sq.ft (£540 per sq.m) in the City, down to around £5 (£54 per sq.m) in smaller provincial towns. Building costs in 1983 covered a wide range from about £360 per sq.m for low-rise, naturally ventilated examples up to as much as £1,350 per sq.m for prestige high-rise air-conditioned buildings. This was roughly equivalent to 140 to 540% of local authority housing costs, a wider difference than hitherto.

Retail buildings ranged from regional centres serving populations of 90,000 or more, through smaller district centres, down to modest neighbourhood centres and high street infills. City centre shops ranged from variety stores, often owner-occupied, of 460–2,800 sq.m, to individual units of 90–460 sq.m. Supermarkets and hypermarkets were developed vigorously in the approximate size range 1,900–4,600 sq.m, along with large retail warehouses [15].

Public and social buildings

The field of public and social building retained some of its former variety, but not its volume. A wide range of schools and other educational buildings, defence works, hospitals and other health buildings continued to be built and altered. So, too, were there the smaller volumes of building for police, law courts, fire brigades, public authority administration, public libraries, museums and so on. Yet promoters in the field were increasingly circumscribed in their actions. The older ethos of public service was diluted and outlying parts of the welfare state apparatus were scrutinized and sometimes abandoned or transferred to the private sector. To be sure, there were achievements in building, such as the series of award-winning Hampshire schools, but they became more infrequent with the passing of time. One sign that the tide had turned against public and social building was when school (and housing) consortia of local authorities were disbanded. A more obvious sign was the cutting of building programmes with the privatization of services. Public spending on education and school building plummeted from £1,313 m. in 1972 to only £264 m. in 1982, although private school work no doubt compensated for this in part. Of the services which remained in the public sector many were brought under somewhat closer control of central government.

A large, but static or contracting stock of public sector buildings meant that refurbishment and maintenance took on a relatively greater importance than new build. Responsibility for repair and maintenance, as well as for the design of the shrinking number of new projects, was often passed to the private sector.

The value of output of new public and social buildings (at constant 1990 prices), including expenditure on infra-structure, was £7,700 m. in 1974. The total declined to £6,000 m. by 1979. The following year, but now excluding infrastructure, output had a value of £3,800 m. The total then fell somewhat for the next two years to reach a trough of £3,500 m. in 1982. Output increased thereafter to £5,200 m. by 1993. The proportion of all construction output was the same in 1993 as it had been in 1980 (18%). Of the various major types of buildings, those for education were the ones on which more began to be spent in the 1990s [16]. In 1995 primary schools cost in the range £560 to £760 per sq.m, roughly equivalent to 150 to 200% of housing association house costs, a rather higher proportion than in the early 1980s or, indeed, the 1930s.

Industrial buildings

At one extreme, industrial building activity merged with commercial activity, with little distinction to be drawn between buildings for light industrial processes, research and automated office processes. Buildings for each, or all, could be similar, where not identical. Elsewhere other parts of the industrial sector languished in make-do, low-cost minimal buildings, a result of general under-investment in manu-facturing. Elsewhere again, were some large new plants set up by inward-investing multinational parent concerns, often with financial inducements from government. Here were to be found the likes of Japanese electronic and motor plants such as the Nissan plant at Washington, Tyne and Wear. In this mixed scene a great amount of the new building was on industrial estates and business parks near motorway connections. With the relative decline of manufacturing, many new buildings were for storage and distribution of imported goods. In time, demand for some warehousing of this sort began to decline due to firms cutting inventories by just-in-time deliveries. Physical differences between buildings for manufacture and those for warehousing or, indeed, for retailing were not always obvious. General purpose big box ('crinkly tin') buildings met the needs of a variety of occupiers and functions. They could readily be put up by speculative developers in advance of known demand. The more specialized industrial buildings needed to be custom-built, often with an extensive engineering content, for the specific needs of specialized occupiers.

The value of output of private industrial buildings (at constant 1990 prices), including expenditure on infrastructure, was £3,200 m. in 1974. Progress thereafter followed a switchback which started with a decline to a trough of £3,100 m. two years later, before beginning to recover. Output in 1980, excluding infrastructure, was £2,800 m. falling to another trough in 1983 of £1,900 m. This was the end of a very difficult few years of industrial recession with little confidence for new building. From the 1983 trough there was recovery to a £3,500 m. peak in 1989. By 1993 output had declined once again to £2,600 m. [17].

Industrial building costs in 1995 ranged widely from around £225 per sq.m for basic factories up to £420 to £620 for high-grade buildings also suited for forms of office accommodation. Industrial unit building costs were of the order of 75 to 170% of those of housing association houses.

LOSSES FROM STOCK

Adaptation of the stock of buildings to new needs was more pressing than hitherto. Demolition proposals, often unpopular before 1974, were met with gathering opposition from heritage and green pressure groups. One result, already noted, was more conservation and reuse. Where this was ruled out, conflict could be bitter and prolonged, as in the celebrated case of the City Mappin and Webb building at number one Poultry.

In a society ill at ease with unbridled modernity, obsolescence nevertheless implacably ensnared its victims. Less lamented than some redundant churches, but far more numerous, were the unwanted buildings of dead and declining enterprises:

textile and engineering industries, water and rail transport, small-scale retailing and the like. Some 1960s high flats added to this melancholy catalogue when spectacularly destroyed by planned use of explosives. Their premature departure due to physical inadequacies and doubtful social effectiveness was often greeted with glee. In the commercial sector inflexibility often took a toll, for example in shop units too small and subdivided, and in offices too low in ceiling height to accept modern services. An associated aspect of building loss remains. It was the growing practice of stripping out interiors for subsequent refit. Here was selective demolition of such building elements as services, partitions, surface finishes and sometimes cladding, while retaining the original structure. Such part-demolition of individual buildings was paralleled by what happened in whole towns, where comprehensive urban redevelopment gave way to more selective, plot-by-plot renewal.

BUILDING FORM

Large projects
The quintessential physical form of development of the period was the large group of large buildings of related function. Best-known examples included urban office complexes such as Canary Wharf in London docklands, and urban edge retail complexes such as Merry Hill in the Midlands. Many such physical forms were variations of the deep plan with some natural lighting from atria and arcades, and very heavy building services. Compared with earlier forms, a key feature was high-quality, controlled interior environments on an enormous scale. Projects of this type were few, but their influence on innumerable lesser works was strong and widespread.

Engineered and managed buildings
The broad mass of buildings outside housing were distinguished from earlier work by being more engineered and more managed. Older design rules of thumb about fabric, structure and services yielded somewhat to rational, systematic decisions. The trend was led from the front by the prospect of better-performing buildings at lower cost, and driven from the rear by building codes whose standards were ratcheted upward from time to time. One sense in which buildings were more engineered was that old bulk masonry forms were often replaced by calculated frame construction and light wall cladding. Buildings also were more engineered in the sense

Figure 45 Component building. Prefabricated composite cladding units being placed at Broadgate. Two units in steel cradles wait to be craned (lower right). (Source: Skidmore, Owings & Merrill. Photograph by Ian Clook.)

that thermal, ventilating and lighting provision were the subject of calculation and mechanical plant rather than hit-or-miss guesswork. Where a late 1970s project might have 20 or 30% of total costs devoted to services, by the mid-nineties the proportion could have grown to nearer 50%. Often pulling in the same direction of more plant and equipment (though sometimes in the reverse 'passive design' direction) was rising concern to make buildings 'green' or 'sustainable'. This influenced some building forms, although more often it determined materials specification. Design decisions were profoundly affected by considerations of first cost (as they always had been) but also they were increasingly affected by estimated cost over the building life cycle. This concern was strongest where efficient owner-occupiers held large building stocks, for example retailers Marks and Spencer, who stood to save large sums on running and maintenance over a building life. Life cycle cost concern was weakest where promoters sold their new buildings upon completion, transferring such costs to the buyers.

Figure 46 Heavily serviced space. Mass of pipes, ducts and cables threaded in orderly array through ceiling space on their way to plant rooms at Broadgate. Nothing resembling this scene existed in the nineteenth century. (Source: Skidmore, Owings & Merrill. Photograph by Ian Clook.)

Buildings became more managed in the sense that their condition and performance was more monitored and adjusted from day to day and from hour to hour. This was because the more advanced buildings were becoming too heavily serviced and finely tuned to look after themselves. Extreme examples of this trend were known, perhaps misguidedly, as intelligent buildings. Here the new facilities managers were in demand to ensure good, reliable working conditions and to avoid failures, which for some occupiers such as international banks would be catastrophic. Buildings also were becoming more managed in the already-noted sense that they needed modifying more frequently, for example in the dismantling and re-erection of partitions and lighting to suit fast-changing occupier needs.

The representative building of the period was an increasingly restless, nervous and responsive artefact. Permanent building elements of structure, lifts, stairs and service ducts were increasingly segregated spatially to leave working floorspace unobstructed: the planning principle of shell and core. This separation into discrete elements and systems helped when changing one part of the building without affecting others. In appearance the representative building was lighter, smoother and more colourful than hitherto. Often there was less impression of great weight, and less visible repetition into bays or other units than before. It was notably faster to build, perhaps higher-quality, but probably not cheaper than the buildings of the preceeding period of public sector dominance.

Domestic forms

If what has been written about engineered and managed buildings has overstated the case, parts of what follows will serve to redress the balance. Houses, still a large part of all building, followed their own divergent path of change. Their appearances moved further away from modernity, often towards a superficially simulated impression of antiquity. Spatial arrangements of house groups were influenced in part by planning authority design guides which multiplied in the 1970s [18]. These encouraged enclosed courts and culs-de-sac, and seemed to lead on to traditional features such as heavily textured brickwork, mock timber frames and smaller windows. Demand was firmly conservative, now that innovative local authorities were no longer active promoters. The recession of the 1990s appeared, if anything, to strengthen a wish for yet more traditional appearances. Preferences were for the old or, failing that, something which looked old. Within the house and its fabric, however, matters were different. Here were to be found more building services, airtight room seals, better insulation, wipe-clean finishes and other influences of science and technology. The paradox of demand for old-looking exteriors with modern internal performance and comfort was sharpened by comparing the design of the house with that of another big consumer good, the car standing on the drive. The one looked part old, part new, and the other looked unashamedly new. A muted version of the same contrast could be detected also in the difference between houses and most other building types: in houses, an allusion to tradition; elsewhere, overt modernity.

10

The industry recasts responsibilities: after 1973

. . . the master builder of the present time . . . is aspiring to resolve the problems left by the increasing disintegration of his Victorian predecessors' system by extending his authority and responsibility greatly beyond theirs.

(E.W. Cooney (1993) 'Productivity, Conflict and Order in the British Construction Industry' *Construction History*)

CHARACTER AND INFLUENCES

**Promoters'
attitudes**

In the previous chapter it was noted that the economic context of the industry changed significantly. The years of indifferent national economic performance, particularly after 1973, marked a decline in faith in economic and corporate planning. By the late 1970s opinion was moving towards freer markets and less government intervention, with the result that a series of reforms followed in the 1980s. With the Thatcher era came some renewed sense of dynamism and, for the building industry, a return to old-style fierce workload fluctuations. The long postwar period of mild fluctuations about a rising trend was now over, in retrospect something of a golden era for the industry.

Promoters' expectations of the industry were affected by the changes in the economy. For a start, a greater sense of time-consciousness prevailed. Projects were required with extreme urgency and free of the risk of unexpected delays. Times arose when early completion could be traded for project costs (which nevertheless remained as important as ever). Promoters' priorities about building quality also moved, from fairness and uniformity between projects towards a greater range of quality between one project and another. Private promoters, where they were able, paid extra for high quality in ways seldom open to the public sector in its heyday. In all, the industry faced demand from a society in a greater hurry than before, less tolerant of delays, and sometimes willing to pay more for what it wanted.

Another shift brought by the revival of the market economy was a more critical view taken by major promoters. When considering new projects, they were likely to be less accepting and more sceptical than before of the advice which they received from consultants and the industry. Promoters questioned assumptions and assertions, made comparisons and set targets of their own. In the jargon of the day, they took a more proactive stance, instead of a passive or reactive one. Less prepared to accept the conventional wisdom about what could be done, some promoters were more prone to take a negative attitude.

Doubts and unease

Major promoters and more especially, government, had long been uneasy about some aspects of the performance of the industry. There is evidence of this in a series of official studies such as the Simon Report of 1944 and the Banwell Report of 1964. The idea that the industry was in some sense backward had been current for some time, but now it gained force. At the head of a list of largely familiar doubts and criticisms was the fear that the nation would suffer relative to international trading rivals due to the shortcomings of building. As one official report crisply noted, a 'competitive and thriving construction industry is fundamental to a competitive and thriving economy' [1]. In this respect the productivity and cost record of the industry attracted attention. While productivity in building remained difficult to measure, it was apparent that output per person actually declined in the 1970s (although growth of repairs would inevitably have depressed performance, as would declining levels of output) [2]. After 1981 productivity improved, by 23% between 1981 and 1985, as measured by value added. While this brought a welcome fall in costs in real terms, it was noted [3] that progress was not enough to ease the overall sense of concern.

The relationship between inputs and outputs of the industry was one source of doubt. Another was about the quality of service which was provided. The reliability and durability of products and the extent to which they met promoters' needs was one aspect. There had been failures in the fields of industrialized house building systems (both concrete and timber frame), use of calcium chloride in structural concrete, and deficiencies in much small-scale repair and maintenance work [4]. Added to this was a reputation for project delay and cost overrun [5] (in this respect, perhaps, an unenvied rival for the aerospace industry). At its best the industry performed well and had improved [6], but elsewhere much inadequate work was thought to be taking place.

Beyond the service provided, internal characteristics of the industry also attracted unfavourable comment from without. The industry was said to be damagingly fragmented, with old divisions between design and construction unhealed and very large numbers of separate firms and interest groups, some pulling in opposing directions [7]. Relations between the various parts of the industry were said to suffer from adversarial attitudes and to be prone to damaging disputes and litigation [8]. Communications were thought to be poor and roles and responsibilities remained without clear definition [9]. This led to internal friction and pushed up transaction costs within the industry. Moreover, traditional contract procedures were seen as inappropriate for the new needs of many projects [10]. Innovations which might overcome these problems were restrained by insufficient investment in research and development. All this, together with poor working conditions, made for a poor public image.

The considerable list of criticisms was sharpened by adverse international comparisons, for example with the industries of the USA and Japan [11]. At the same time, in mitigation, the rather loose charge of backwardness of the industry lost force. While many earlier observers of the industry had entertained the idea, they now raised the possibility only to reject it. To ask whether backwardness existed, it was said, was to ask the wrong question. It was to confuse technological efficiency with economic efficiency, and to focus on the supply side at the expense of the demand side [12, 13]. Rather than the industry being condemned as backward, it was recast as a unique response to unique conditions. Some characteristics of buildings as products, which influenced the nature of the industry were pointed out to be fixity to particular sites; uniqueness; weight; bulk or volume; complexity of organization and manufacture; long production time; high initial and running costs; longevity; and often sold before built [14]. Such unusual or unique features of demand made for a unique industry, unsuited to direct comparison with other industries which served quite different patterns of demand. Thus, while the context in which the industry worked was an increasingly critical one, the basis of criticism was changing. It was turning from a narrow focus of alleged technical backwardness, to a broader range of structural problems.

Internal fluidity

Surrounded by an unsympathetic climate of opinion, the industry was far from inactive. While continuity with the past looked strong in some ways, such as technology and scale of operations, there were moves which were as great as, or greater than, any in a similar time span since 1800. Many of the changes were about the division of labour among different firms, about which of them undertook what tasks. Roles and responsibilities held by different parts of the industry began to be reconsidered. At stake were issues of control and independence in the ways in which processes were divided and linked among specialisms and firms. In the vast, restless and loosely linked network of firms making up the industry, from large contractors and skilled consultants down to jobbing builders, new questions of ascendancy arose. In the unaccustomed fluidity among the network of firms, fresh opportunities and threats to established positions loomed. The industry of the 1980s and 1990s began to resemble that of the earlier nineteenth century; who did what was uncertain, and varied from project to project. Circumstances were coming to favour opportunism, ambition and aptitude as much as title and precedent. Tradition was in decay.

One way in which a newly fluid division of labour was apparent was the upsurge of subcontracting and associated self-employment. Leading contractors, formerly able to undertake most (if not all) of the work needed to complete a project, now chose to subcontract [15]. In consequence the proportion of small subcontracting firms increased and the size of contractors' workforces was constrained. Another aspect was that some of the larger firms became parts of parent companies with multiple interests well beyond the field of construction. One example was the firm of Trollope and Colls, which belonged to Trafalgar House. Another aspect of fluidity, to which Ball [16] has drawn attention, was the extent to which large firms had a dual role as merchant-producers. As well as producing buildings they also bought and sold inputs of labour, materials and land, on a big scale. Where they engaged in speculative building they had important functions as land purchasers and owners of land banks. Where they engaged in contracting they dealt with a whole portfolio of contracts. The most successful contractor was the one with the best portfolio, not necessarily the least-cost producer. A further aspect of fluidity was about management responsibility for projects. Coordination and control took on ever greater complexity now that promoters had become so time-conscious and now that the number of subcontracting firms on each project was enlarged. Two kinds of solution emerged. One was a new layer of management between promoter and supply-side interests. This project management role attracted various disciplines, both new, such as professional project managers, and adaptive, such as quantity surveyors. The other solution was for responsibility for design and construction to be concentrated in one organization, thereby placing economic power in the hands of the contractor [17].

Building procurement

Changes in the division of labour were far from the only aspect of change. Closely tied up with them was change affecting building procurement, the procedures and contractual relations of building. The traditional procurement method (design by consultants, lump sum contract awarded on the basis of competitive tender, contractor builds with the assistance of specialist subcontractors) found less favour, though it persisted quite strongly.

One rival of traditional procurement was a form of package deal known as design and build (d. & b.). In this the contractor took the leading role by assuming comprehensive responsibility for the project. There were many variants, as when others produced initial sketch designs for subsequent detailed developments by the d. & b. contractor. Rooted in the experience of 1960s factories and industrialized housing, d. & b. was well suited to providing standard types of buildings where quick delivery and low cost were important. A standard d. & b. form of contract was published in 1981, joining numerous other standard forms. The method grew vigorously to include a widening range and proportion of new buildings.

Another novel procurement method was management contracting. This involved traditional use of design consultants, but early appointment of a management contractor enabled early advice on production to reach the designers. The management contractor took responsibility for site works, carried out through separate subcontracts, on the basis of management contractor's prime cost plus a management fee [18]. Most larger contractors came to offer some form of management contracting service, but only a minority of projects followed the pattern, which appeared to decline over time.

A development of management contracting was construction management. This method introduced the specialist construction management firm, accountable to the promoter, between trade contractors and promoter. Consultants exercised their design responsibilities, while the construction management firm coordinated and supervised the work. Trade contractors had a direct relationship with the promoter [19]. Both management contracting and construction management found most favour among promoters who valued time and quality above costs.

The new procurement methods each had variants, evolved experimentally in the light of experience or to suit some newly emergent circumstances. They added to the impression of fluidity, and were striking evidence of growing openness to new ideas in a hitherto conservative industry.

PROFESSIONS

Position of consultants

The position of consultants, professionals independent of building firms, was somewhat eroded. In society generally, the traditional professions came to be viewed increasingly critically, both by their clients and government. Building professionals sometimes fared badly when confronted by the superior economic force of large contractors. Consultants who were once unchallenged and prestigious leaders might now find themselves answerable to builders and dependent on them for their next commission. But this is to generalize; while one profession or consultant's firm declined in relative position, another ascended. Some were exposed to new pressures more than others and some proved themselves more adaptable than others. The pressures, if anything, intensified with time.

Three features were apparent amid the flux. One was the ascendancy of management skills additional to the central skill of each separate profession. It was no longer enough to be good at designing, or costing, or calculating, alone; effective consultants more than ever had to be able to manage the delivery of their services. With the 'explosion of documentation' [20] needed to get a building built, this became more challenging than ever. The second feature was competition for the ear of the promoter. Whoever became the lead consultant for a project, the promoter's main adviser, was most powerfully placed to influence all subsequent events. The third feature was the proliferation of specialisms within existing professions, and the appearance of new titles such as project manager, value engineer and commissioning engineer.

Architects   The architectural profession was affected by change as much as, or more than, any group, with pressures from several directions. One was from promoters, whose priorities over project timing, cost and building quality did not always accord with the priorities of architects. Many promoters sought a single point of contact with the industry, who would accept full managerial responsibility for their project. Here architects found their traditional lead consultancy role threatened by newcomers with greater management skills, who included project managers and contractors. When relegated to a 'downstream' role more remote from demand, architects were in a more dependent position and hence less able to influence the course of events on a project. They stood to lose influence in the crucial formulation of the project brief and in the choice of procurement method. This weakening of promoters' confidence in architects was epitomized by the Prince of Wales's well-publicized views on the work of the profession [21]. Although his criticism was about architecture rather than architects, the implication was plain.

Another source of pressure came from a migration of some design decisions from the profession to contractors and component manufacturers. Where architects were appointed by contractors rather than by promoters, the profession lost influence (although the rift between design and construction might be narrowed). Again, the technological complexity of building components such as wall cladding and glazing required manufacturers to take a growing design role (as they did in the USA). Here architects often passed responsibility on to manufacturers and suppliers, avoiding some onerous legal liabilities as they did so. The shift of responsibility from designer to producer recalled an earlier one the other way, when craftsmen's autonomy had been usurped by nineteenth-century designers.

A further source of pressure was the government Monopolies and Mergers Commission, which demanded the easing of professional restrictive practices. As a result the mandatory fee scale, related mainly to building cost, was amended in 1982 to permit competition on fees. Other early 1980s relaxations of the architects' code of professional conduct included acceptance of limited liability and advertising.

Severely reduced workload after 1990 exposed the effects of earlier change. Fee income per project appeared to fall, while architects' unemployment and underemployment climbed steeply. Staff of all levels were laid off and many had little alternative but to try to set up their own small independent practices. Former public authority architects' departments were either run down, combined with other professional departments or sold as going concerns, some to large interdisciplinary consultancy firms. Shortly before these retrenchments, in 1988, there were about 5,300 architects' practices in the UK. Of these, 43% were one- or two-person size, 86% were ten persons or smaller, and 1.5% were of 51 or more people. Some of the largest were floated as public companies (with mixed results), some had taken on limited liability, while most retained their partnership or sole practitioner formation. At that time about 50,000 people altogether were employed in architects' practices [22].

The uncomfortable experience of the profession gave rise in 1992 to a penetrating study by the RIBA [23], though other responses from the resourceful minds in the profession remained muted. It was as though the architects' culture acted as an obstacle to their responding to a rising need for strategic management of projects. The idea of the architect as leader looked increasingly anachronistic in an age which conferred responsibility for most projects on the basis of management ability rather than creative ability.

Surveyors and engineers

The position of surveyors and engineers, the two other main professions, also came under some of the pressures which affected architects. They, too, sometimes suffered in relations with contractors over management of larger projects, where legal and financial disputes were frequent. They, too, were affected by the deliberations of the Monopolies Commission, so that quantity surveyors followed the architects and lifted restrictions on fee competition in 1983. RICS members were permitted to assume limited liability and to hold directorships of construction firms several years later. With the business context for professional consultants more commercial and less in their favour than formerly, there were at least some positive signs for surveyors and engineers. The structural engineers were relatively secure in their specialism, without much scope for competition from other groups and with close links to production. By the early 1990s the Institute of Structural Engineers' membership was over 21,000. The building services engineers benefited from an expanding call for their skills and rising status was marked by the granting of a Royal Charter in 1976 to create the Chartered Institute of Building Services Engineers (CIBSE). By the early 1990s membership was about 15,000 [24].

Of all the professions, the quantity surveyors' responded most vigorously to far-reaching changes. Computers and new methods of procurement had jointly threatened to undermine the traditional QS services centred on bills of quantities, variations and final accounts. The profession set about re-casting and relaunching itself to suit new conditions [25] and there was a shift away from simple accounting towards forecasting and broad strategy. New emphasis was placed on financial and management advice of the profession for early development decisions and project management. The new direction suited promoters' needs, with the result that quantity surveyors increasingly took a lead consultant role. Many quantity surveyors worked in small and medium-sized practices, but there was also some concentration. The largest practice, Davis, Langden and Everest, had about 1,500 staff. Total RICS membership reached 86,000 in 1992, of whom 23,000 were quantity surveyors (the Institute of Quantity Surveyors having merged in 1982) and another 5,300 building surveyors. The profession generally was able to benefit from sharply rising repair and maintenance work.

FIRMS

Size and number

The number of building firms steadily increased. There were 114,000 in 1980, rising to a peak of 210,000 in 1990 and then down again to 195,000 in the recession year of 1993. While the upward trend was clear, the exact totals were affected by problems of definition. There was probable undercounting of small firms, some of whose proprietors crossed an indeterminate boundary between employee and self-employed status. Some of these shadowy people enjoyed an ambiguous relationship with taxation law and the black market. The totals of firms conceal important changes in the composition of firm size. Earlier postwar decline of very small firms was reversed and numbers increased unambiguously. One-person firms were 32% of all firms in 1980, rising to 48% in 1993. In the latter year 98.3% of all firms employed fewer than 25 people, and 0.26% of firms employed 115 or more. There had been a strong growth of self-employment and small subcontractors, combined with reduction in employment by the largest firms. The result was that about 82,000 worked in one-person firms, and about 412,000 worked in firms employing fewer than 25. The number of big firms (those employing 115 or more) was about half of that, at 215,000. In all, the industry had become notably less concentrated and at the same time more flexible in coping with unpredictable demand.

Official statistics record 22 different trades among the firms, plus a miscellaneous category. The largest group by a clear margin remained general builders, with 36% of all firms in 1993. The next largest group, which had grown since 1983, was electrical contractors (10.5%). After them came the plumbers (7.1%), carpenters and joiners (6.8%) and painters, now a shrinking group (5.0%) [26].

Figure 47 Operational complexity. Faculty of Engineering building, Bristol University 1995. Many different specialists will have worked on this project which has retained old stone facade (left), in-situ concrete, structural steelwork and heavy services, on a congested sloping urban site.

Liquidations and insolvencies among firms were considerable, with a sharp increase with the onset of the 1990s recession. At the same time the manner of statistical reporting continued to convey a somewhat misleadingly gloomy picture of the industry [27].

Contractors Like consultants, the contractors struggled to adapt to changing circumstances, although more than the consultants they succeeded in turning events to their advantage. The position of larger firms in particular appeared to improve and their power was enhanced. Some of the gains emerged from the uncertainties of the 1970s, when a difficult home market forced contractors to seek work overseas, particularly in the Middle East. There they met unfamiliar and sometimes challenging methods of foreign firms. At home, levels of education and management competence improved so that some long-standing weaknesses in financial control and site management were remedied. Large firms took a bigger share of the smaller national workload, often at the expense of smaller regional contractors. Similarly some regional speculative house builders were bought by national firms, so that housing provision became dominated by big firms. In the more expansionary parts of the 1980s first American, and then Japanese management influences acted as stimuli. The rising position of contractors was further helped by the ascendancy of private sector promoters. Earlier the public sector in its heyday had been more sympathetic to the professional ethic than to the commercial. Now the position was reversed and the private sector was more sympathetic to the commercial ethic, sometimes favouring contractors over professional consultants. Evidence of contractors' growing power ('clout' was the modish word) began to grow: stronger influence on overall management of projects, more responsibility for design, and new procurement methods which reflected contractors' influence. With commercial values of *caveat emptor* in part supplanting professional values, it was suggested that levels of trust between firms were declining [28]. If so, it was the opposite of behaviour among admired and efficient Japanese firms.

Enhanced power was one leading aspect of contractors' experience. The other was the growth of subcontracting. Through the 1970s large contractors progressively divested themselves of large labour forces. By the 1980s they rarely undertook much site work with their own labour, but chose instead to subcontract it. Only in smaller firms and smaller towns were there traditional contractors who directly employed all the main trades. The change was a far-reaching one in which, in Cooney's words [29], subcontracting had 'the objective of turning main contractors into providers of management only, who would specialise in co-ordinating the work of the sub-contractors.' Various benefits of specialization and flexibility followed for the main contractors. More specifically, sub-contracting enabled main contractors to choose specialist trade inputs when they were wanted, from a range of specialists. Competition among subcontractors ensured low prices, while main contractors' own workforces could be kept small, avoiding unemployment, and minimizing working capital requirements. Subcontracting also gave freedom in the types of contract which the main contractor could seek and, finally, the risk associated with workload fluctuations was passed on to the subcontractors. Disadvantages to the main contractor were that negotiating rates for some work was difficult, and that labour costs were high in boom times [30]. Also, coordination of the work of numerous subcontractors on big, fast-track projects made considerable management demands on main contractors. While these could be contained where groups of firms frequently worked together in informal networks, the trend appears to have been towards increasingly formal and legalistic relations.

The identities of the largest firms in construction, by turnover in 1980, appeared to be George Wimpey, John Laing, Trafalgar House (owners of Cementation, Trollope & Colls, Ideal Homes and Willett). Tarmac (owners of Holland, Hannen & Cubitts, Kinear Moodie and McLean Homes), Taylor Woodrow and the Costain Group. Wimpey, the largest, had grown from origins in 1880 as a London mason. Expansion, particularly in the 1940s, had created a firm with interests in contracting, house building, civil engineering and mineral working. By 1990 turnover on Wimpey operations worldwide approached £2 bn. and there were 15,000 employees. Comparisons of size of firms are complicated by their diversity of interests. The largest firms were not only in groups of companies with heavy investment outside construction, such as in hotels and shipping, but were active also in civil engineering and materials production. A sizeable minority of the largest dozen firms were either run by, or had board representation of, the founder's family. This apparently anachronistic feature among large industrial concerns (where separate management and ownership was customary) was due to the modest scale of capital tied up in building, compared with that in manufacturing industry [31]. Amalgamations and mergers between firms were fairly common as a means of growth, diversification or retrenchment, according to market conditions. By 1994 the ten largest contractors in Great Britain, ranked by turnover, were Trafalgar House, Tarmac, Amec, Wimpey, Balfour Beatty, Bovis, Mowlem, Laing, Taylor Woodrow and Costain [32].

The joint interests of the larger firms were represented from 1986 by the Building Employers' Confederation (BEC), as the NFBTE became known. Smaller firms were represented by the Federation of Master Builders. The Chartered Institute of Building (charter granted in 1980) continued to develop the status and position of building as a profession. Among these bodies and the numerous other organized sectional interests in the industry, such as the House Builders' Federation, there were a few signs that some spirit of unity might be taking root.

Sub-contractors
The expanding activities of subcontracting firms extended in two directions. First was technological specialization in fields such as foundation piling, lift installation and asphalting, where subcontractors had gradually proliferated since the late nineteenth century. Now they were joined by new supply and fix specialists in fields as disparate as air conditioning, tension fabric structures, security installations and computer cabling. Some subcontractors let work out to other firms: the sub-subcontract. On some sites all work was subcontracted and the largest subcontractors were bigger than the main contractor who employed them. Most subcontractors were commissioned by main contractors, all the more so with the decline in architects' nomination. The position of subcontractors as dependent on main contractors for work made them vulnerable to main contractors imposing difficult conditions and late payments. Resulting disputes led to increasing dissatisfaction and recognition of a need for sweeping reform [33].

The second direction in which subcontracting extended was labour-only subcontracting. This included individual self-employed operatives as well as large organizations acting as agents in supplying operatives to sites. Labour-only sub-contracting was strongest among the traditional trades of bricklaying, carpentry and joinery, and plastering. Self-employment grew quickly, by 56% between 1970 and 1985, by which time half of all manual building workers were self-employed. However, some of them, at least, were sole principals in jobbing work, rather than labour-only sub-contractors.

Figure 48 Contemporary concerns. Prefinished units have been craned on to floors (upper left). Site trucks and rubbish shutes abound, along with security fencing, safety barriers and discarded component packaging, but operatives are few. All this would have been alien to builders of 1800.

Labour-only subcontracting, springing as it did from the dubious parentage of the 'lump', had mixed associations. Although tax and national insurance malpractices were reduced in the 1970s [34], problems remained. Casual engagement and an elusive, shifting workforce earned the opposition of trade unions and officialdom. Casual self-employed and employee labour working side-by-side at different rates of pay for similar work was bound to create friction. At worst, here was a grey area of the industry which shaded off into a black market fringe. While it was true that casual employment could have short-term efficiency in its favour, it lacked any acceptance of much-needed longer-term reponsibilities for training and safety. It might be viewed either as the natural habitat of cowboys and moonlighters, or alternatively as a cherished opportunity for independent spirits, a nursery for entrepreneurs.

Other agencies

The trajectory traced by local authority direct labour organizations was the opposite of that of subcontracting. For the decade from the early 1970s their output of new work fell, although that of repairs and maintenance increased for a while. Legislation from a government seeking public sector cuts increasingly compelled DLOs to operate more like private firms, and workloads fell away. The value of their new work in Great Britain dropped from £594 m. to £271 m. (at constant 1990 prices) between 1980 and 1993. Similarly, the value of DLO repair and maintenance sank from £4,388 m. to £2,760 m. [35].

One agency of building activity which fared better than DLO was do-it-yourself, the voluntary sector of building, and a leading national leisure pursuit. An idea of the scale of activity comes from the value of materials sold direct to the public, an impressive £1,700 m. in 1980 (an unknown part of which was absorbed by the black economy). Retail outlets, largely edge-of-town warehouse chain premises, offered growing ranges of products and equipment including quite large items for hire. While some DIY activity was work which would otherwise have been undertaken by the industry, much was work which otherwise would have remained undone.

Moving from agencies of direct production to those on the edge of building activity, plant hire firms became more prominent. They undertook over half the total investment in plant used by the industry. Ownership of the hire firms, formerly often the contractors, passed increasingly to independent and centralized firms. Other concerns were builders' merchants, of whom those belonging to the Builders Merchants Federation (over 2,000 outlets) sold about 40% of the value of materials used in the industry. If anything, direct dealing between suppliers and contractors appeared to increase [36].

One other facet of a many-faceted industrial entity was research and development. Having always been small and poor, in comparison with equivalent undertakings in the manufacturing sector as a whole, it remained so. Construction industry spending on research and development (including that of materials producers) in the UK declined steadily from around 0.3% of value added to around 0.25% between 1980 and 1988. Two years later spending was £329 m., of which construction firms contributed 10%. Funding also came from various government agencies, public utility companies and trade associations. The dominant role for building, as distinct from branches of engineering, was played by the Building Research Establishment. The former Cement and Concrete Association took on a modified role as the British Cement Association from 1987 and other leading centres continued to include TRADA and CIRIA.

LABOUR

Composition, recruitment and training

Unemployment returned with some severity after relative freedom from it through the period of postwar reconstruction. Bad though it was for individuals and some regions, many of the hardships of prewar unemployment happily remained absent. In the mid-1980s up to 0.5 m. people were thought to be affected, although reliable figures remained wanting, in a field where casual employment prevailed.

Self-employment, it was noted above, greatly increased. The other side of this was a fall in the number of employed operatives, from 59% in 1975 to only 35% in 1993. Among those directly employed, the proportion of administrative, professional, technical and clerical staff (APTCs) remained fairly stable at between 18 and 20% of the total workforce (though a rising proportion of those were directly employed) [37]. Within the APTC class, managers and to a lesser extent technical staff multiplied, while foremen, and clerical and sales staff became fewer. The class was relatively strongest in larger firms and in those working in technically more advanced fields such as environmental engineering.

About 70% of manual employees in the private sector possessed some sort of recognized skill. The six largest trades in 1989, in descending order of size (after the labourers, with 31%) were carpenters and joiners, 13.7%; electricians, 9.8%; painters, 6.1%; mechanical equipment operatives, 5.8%; bricklayers, 5.2%; and plumbers, 4.2% [38].

Recruitment was restrained by the image of a 'difficult, demanding and unbecoming occupation with an adversarial culture . . .' [39]. Added to this were insecurity and casual employment, and a poor safety record. Presumably the image explained the persistent unattractiveness of the industry to women, who accounted for only about one in ten of the workforce [40]. Typical operatives were younger rather than older, with a rapid turnover of people and many leaving the industry before full retirement age. Craft training by day or block release expanded in the 1980s, but was affected by budgetary cuts. Technicians were recruited largely from diploma and higher diploma construction courses, and professionals were recruited from degree courses. Overall the workforce was reckoned to be poorly qualified in comparison with that of Europe; in boom times there were skill shortages, at their worst in the South East.

Wages

Although wages and conditions continued to be negotiated between representatives of employers and unions, the terms were not followed closely in practice. Bonuses and self-employment caused divergences from agreements, so that self-employed earnings were said to be two, three or more times higher than negotiated rates. However, statistics were unreliable and the self-employed would need to make their own provisions for pensions, sickness and so on.

Average wages in the early 1970s were a little above those for all industries and services. This relationship then deteriorated, so that by 1993 average gross weekly earnings of manual construction workers were £274.3 for a 44.7 hour week (including overtime), compared with similar earnings for a week of only 44.3 hours in all industries. Non-manual construction workers earned a weekly average of £401.0 for 40 hours, compared again adversely with £418.2 for 38.6 hours in all industries. These figures conceal differences by region and by craft. Differentials between crafts in the mid-1980s ranged from £187.8 for foremen at one extreme, £153.3 for carpenters and joiners and a little less for bricklayers, and at the other extreme down to £134.6 for mates and labourers. At that time average gross weekly earnings of all manual construction workers were £156.8 [41].

Organization

Building had seldom been a very fertile ground for trade unions and they now found themselves caught between two opposing forces. On one side was growing self-employment and subcontracting, and on the other was the rightward national political shift and associated employment legislation. The result was an ebbing of power and membership, from 430,000 members in 1980 to 306,000 by 1987. This last was equivalent to about 20% of all workers in the industry (but of course a higher proportion of the directly employed). Membership was dominated by two unions, UCATT with 278,000 in 1983 and the T&GWU with 65,000 in construction (it had many more in other industries). Stoppages were relatively few and well below the rate in industry in general. Exceptional disruptions took place during the wide conflicts of the 1979 'winter of discontent' and the 1984 miners' strike. Waning union power meant a weakening in the general bargaining position of the workforce, as much for the APTC class as for manual employees. At the same time there was not a simple transfer of power to the contractor employers. They, too, had lost influence over site labour because of widespread subcontracting [42].

MATERIALS, COMPONENTS AND PROCESSES

Prices

Building prices over the period were carried up relentlessly by inflation. The tender price index [43] reflected also the state of demand on the industry, with depressed prices in slack times and higher prices when demand was strong. Using as a base year 1976, with a price index of 100, tender prices advanced to 170 in 1980, then climbed onwards to reach 248 in 1985, and 337 in 1990. By 1993, when demand was depressed, the index stood at 372.

The rise reflected high output costs compared with those of building in other developed countries, while input costs of labour were relatively low [44]. The proportion of materials costs varied widely from well over 40% for many projects down to as little as 15% for some repairs and maintenance.

Conditions for innovation

Generation and diffusion of innovations, in building processes and products, offered a possible escape from charges of backwardness and high output costs. However, progress was retarded, not only by the indifference which was apparently a characteristic of parts of British manufacturing culture, but by the fragmentation and division of responsibilities in building. With relations between designers, manufacturers and builders being distant and temporary (usually no more than the duration of one project), the opportunities for innovation were hampered. Designers lacked production expertise, manufacturers lacked a comprehensive view of the whole building task and product, and builders had transformed their role from practical building to management and the coordination of subcontractors. All had partial views; no one could take responsibility for a process from beginning to end. Neither was there any formal mechanism for feedback on success or failure.

Conditions favourable to innovation were further stunted by the disappearance of large, coordinated demand for buildings which followed the run-down of the public sector. Large long-term programmes of work, which might have encouraged investment in innovation, were no longer assembled and coordinated by public authorities. With this, the government impulse to modernize building production, which had arisen from time to time since the First World War, was apparently extinguished. All that replaced it in the official view seemed to be a rather unfocused wish, noted above, that building would not hinder national economic competitiveness. Remedies were discussed, but at the time of writing had not been implemented [45].

Despite this unpromising climate, four main incentives for innovation at the level of individual firms were apparent. One was to accelerate building processes so as to meet demand for rapid delivery. An example was by telescoping, or overlapping, the successive stages of a project rather than proceeding with them sequentially. Builders would build foundations and ground floors while designers were still at work designing the upper floors. Another incentive was to reduce risk inherent in large projects, for example by organizing work into independent packages so as to improve control and cut the dependence of one subcontractor on the work of others. A further incentive was the time-honoured one of reducing production costs, for example by substituting slow, wet brick house carcass construction with faster, dry timber frames. Finally there was the incentive of enhancing the value of outputs, for example by improving the performance of buildings in, say, environmental aspects. These incentives led to short incremental step improvements to building, rather than revolutionary changes. They also seemed to lead as much or more to management innovations as to technological ones.

Examples and effects of innovation

Other examples of technological innovation and diffusion of processes included improved means of handling materials with wheel-mounted plant and equipment and simple demountable rubbish shutes. Methods of joining components together were speeded up with the use of power tools and fixings. Temporary site accommodation was more readily stacked up into multi-storeys and moved about to save precious site working space. Bulk materials were more often delivered packaged and palletted, and complicated services units were prefabricated for craning directly into place. Robot applications viewed on Japanese study tours were more talked about than applied; higher labour costs would probably be needed to justify such investments. Also in the future was the impact of EC legislation on health and safety. On the product side the increased use of heavily processed materials was sustained. Examples were where aluminium sheet replaced brick and blockwork, and stainless steel roofs replaced tiles and asphalt. Another example was where complicated precision assemblies of glass, metal and plastics replaced wet site construction of wall masonry and plaster. With growing site assembly of pre-finished components there was rising interest in joints and connections. This stimulated attempts by the British Standards Institution and government departments to standardize leading dimensions and performance, and some limited progress was made. A growing proportion of high-value components arrived on site from overseas sources, with some of them said to be of higher quality than home-produced ones. Literally beneath many of these changes in products and materials, much remained as it had been for a generation or two. Most heavy structures and work below ground continued to use concrete, brick and structural steel, largely untouched by changes affecting more visible and lighter parts of buildings.

Beyond the growing substitution of traditional heavy and wet materials by light and dry ones was the addition of more 'bolt-on' assemblies which had not been provided at earlier times. They included advanced controls for intelligent buildings, provisions for planned maintenance, communications and data systems, security monitors and the like.

The flow of innovations, each to take its chance and succeed or fail, put pressure on many traditional ways. Some, such as wet plastering and timber-boarded cladding, suffered in the competiton with, respectively, dry lining and plastics. Yet few traditional materials and crafts were pushed to extinction. Certainly some became rare, but a large building stock to maintain, together with sentimental appeal, meant that they mostly survived in some form or another, if much reduced. At one end the industry spawned new processes while at the other, old ones like thatching and dry stone walling refused to disappear. Instead they passed by stages to a state where they were sustained by their power to confer satisfaction in the doing, as well as in the finished product. They were kept for their own sakes, visible on historic conservation projects and open-air museum demonstrations. In earlier, poorer and less sentimental times they would have been consigned to oblivion without much thought.

Thus building activity stretched in a long unbroken line. At one extreme were capital-intensive activities which embraced tower cranes, robotics and information technology. They were essential in helping to efficiently shelter society. At the other extreme were labour-intensive and quasi-voluntary activities which embraced do-it-yourself and the preservation of obsolescent crafts. They were wanted largely because they gave people satisfaction and helped to lend meaning to their lives. Building activities had always been remarkable for their diversity.

Afterword

Almost two centuries of a vast industry has produced in-numerable far-reaching changes as well as some recurring themes. Taking first the context and demand for buildings, there has been a change among promoters. Typically, they evolved from inexperienced individuals to well-informed organizations, as solitary entrepreneurs yielded to expert committees. The context in which they worked was also transformed: from *laissez-faire* to interventionist; from rapid population growth to moderate; from manufacturing economy to service economy; and from slow social and economic change to rapid.

Over the two centuries the total provision of buildings has extended from small-scale to very large. In the process the relationship of building stock to building need has improved from absolute scarcity to relative adequacy; few people today work outdoors in all weathers as they once did, or contrive to live in one room. Another change is that the volume of repairs and maintenance has risen greatly, like the effort put into updating quite young buildings to match new needs. In this, building provision moves haltingly from once-for-all products towards indeterminate process. Amid the restless shifts of demand some events remain familiar. Most notable of these are fluctuations of activity. The building cycle, with its twin torments of overheating and over-capacity, predates our period and looks set to outlive it.

The forms of building reflect many of the changes in society. Two centuries ago most new single buildings and whole projects were relatively small; now many are far bigger. The growth has been from terrace of houses to whole estate, and from high street plot to city block. Building fabrics have become less bulky (usable space for usable space) over time, and more filled with building services. Here the shift has been from outdoor sanitation to full air conditioning and permanent artificial lighting. The distribution of building quality was once pyramid-shaped, with a few high-quality buildings at the top and many low-quality ones at the base. This has now been altered, by redistribution of national wealth, coupled with tighter building codes, to a squat diamond shape resting on one of its points. Now most buildings are medium quality, with only a few exceptionally high- and low-quality examples: few new country houses, turf hovels or flimsy back-to-backs, very many mid-range surburban blocks.

To move to the industry itself is to see superficial long-term continuity. As ever, building sites are muddy scenes of apparent chaos of scaffold and trench peopled by the bluff and sometimes rough. As ever, the industry has the look of a restless, heavy undertaking. Paradoxically perhaps, historical continuity here is in the interminable cycle of movement from site to site, and the repeated imposition of change on the appearance of places and things. A closer look at the industry also reveals the existence of discontinuities, first in terms of prestige. Early in the period the rising new contracting firms gained prestige by operating at an impressive scale at or near the forefront of the technology of the time. Early in the period, too, the many smaller firms endured a poor reputation: the scamping subcontractor and the speculative builder who 'found a solitude and left a slum'. In short, the great and good of building coexisted side-by-side with a very mixed bunch of smaller men. Now the industry leaders appear to experience lessened prestige for, by the standards of other industries, they no longer command notably great or advanced resources; in point of investment, at least, progress has passed them by. At the same time the 'tail' of small firms has perhaps redeemed itself somewhat in public esteem. In terms of prestige, the industry has been subject to levelling up as well as levelling down. As with building quality, the distribution of firms according to prestige has moved from pyramid to squat diamond.

Within the industry much has changed. Ownership of firms has extended by stages from sole proprietor to conglomerates (for example, Trafalgar House) with interests extending well outside construction. Fields of operation have grown from parochial to global scales although (another continuity here) local jobbing firms remain unscathed by the growth of markets for big projects. Division of labour among firms has advanced, for example with the production of materials passing from builders to specialist firms. Among subcontractors, and designers and advisers, the range of specialist skills and firms has multiplied. In the emergent building world of the early nineteenth century questions of who, or which firm, did what on a project had been open. Then for a century or more there was growing hierarchical order and consolidation of roles and responsibilities. Latterly the old fluidity has returned, conferring historical symmetry on the period as a whole. Now, once again, the balance of responsibility between builder and consultant, and the independence or integration of firms doing different tasks, is unsettled. Is design and build or construction management the preferred procurement method? What skills and responsibilities should be held by the firms which exercise overall management of projects? Amid flux, the fragmentation of the industry which was apparent at the outset still remains today. And now, as then, it helps the onerous, ever-present task of matching capacity to fluctuating demand.

Life among the operatives has been transformed. Once, sites swarmed with poor, largely unskilled men toiling manually for long hours. Now they are better paid, far fewer, site for site, and they work shorter hours with the help of rather more, formally recognized, skills and much more powered equipment. They are directed in their efforts by more numerous managers. Once, the operatives' task had been to create on the spot a simple, but unique and partly *ad hoc* artefact from raw materials. Wet trades using locally won ingredients and timber were fashioned by muscle-power and craft skill quite slowly into buildings. Now, in large measure, heavily processed dry components of diverse materials, brought from distant factories, are fitted together quickly into more complicated, calculated, standardized and pre-planned buildings. Digging, hewing and smoothing have given way to steering, bolting and sealing.

Of the many changes which the industry has undergone over two centuries, most were evolutionary rather than revolutionary. Of all the new ways of doing things which were tried out, ways of managing and controlling the means of production now seem as prominent as the applications of technology (though less visible and less understood). In the introduction of new ways, also, interaction with the rest of society has been crucial to change in the industry. The shifting demands of promoters have ultimately been the critical force in moulding the industry. For example, unrestrained nineteenth century growth and inexperienced, once-in-a-lifetime promoters at the mercy of an industry mysterious in its ways, gave rise to a stratum of building professionals. They mediated between builders and promoters and, in doing so, created a lasting hierarchical set of roles and relationships. Another example came much later when the age of total war gave rise to the novelties of central planning, control, direction and cost indifference. The industry worked closely with government, adapted to licensing and in the process became an instrument of the command economy. Again, the succeeding postwar mixed economy with heavy public sector building (and higher labour costs) brought promoters concerned with public accountability, costs, standardization and large building programmes. The industry responded to sustained heavy demand with improved management and investment in industrialized production. Yet again, the rise of private sector promoters in the 1980s brought fresh priorities of urgency and value-for-money to the fore. Responses to these are still maturing in a welter of uncertainty.

Building promoters of every age have each had their own characteristic priorities which left their mark on an ever-flexible industry. The result was that the industry has been a sort of microcosm of the society which it has served and influenced. The industry, like the architecture which it produced, was eloquent of its age. In this sense, we get the industry which we deserve.

References

1 BUILDING COKETOWN: 1800–1850

[1] Cleary, E.J. (1965) *The Building Society Movement*, Elek, p. 44.

[2] Price, S.J. (1959) *Building Societies: Their Origin and History*, Franey.

[3] Clarke, L. (1992) *Building Capitalism: Historical Change and the Labour Process in the Production of the Built Environment*, Routledge.

[4] Olsen, D.J. (1973) in *Victorian City: Images and Realities* (eds Dyos, H.J. and Wolff, M.), Routledge & Kegan Paul.

[5] Treen, C. (1982) Process of Suburban Development in North Leeds 1870–1914, in *Rise of Suburbia* (ed. Thompson, F.M.L.), Leicester University Press, pp. 158–209.

[6] Chalklin, C.W. (1974) *The Provincial Towns of Georgian England: a Study of the Building Process 1740–1820*, Arnold, p. 311.

[7] Brunskill, R.W. (1971) *Illustrated Handbook of Vernacular Architecture*, Faber, p. 27.

[8] Flinn, M.W. (ed.) (1965) *Report on the Sanitary Condition of the Labouring Population of Gt. Britain by Edwin Chadwick 1842*, Edinburgh University Press, p. 83.

[9] Feinstein, C.H. and Pollard, S. (eds) (1988) *Studies in Capital Formation in the United Kingdom 1750–1920*, Clarendon, Table X, p. 446.

[10] e.g. Shannon, H.A. (1966) Bricks – a Trade Index 1785–1849, in *Essays in Economic History* (ed. Carus-Wilson, E.M.), Arnold, Vol. 3.

[11] Lewis, J.P. (1965) *Building Cycles and Britain's Growth*, Macmillan, p. 192.

[12] Sheppard, F., Belcher, V. and Cottrell, P. (1979) Middlesex and Yorkshire Deeds Registries and the Study of Building Fluctuations, *London Journal*, **5** (2).

[13] Mitchell, B.R. and Deane, P. (1962) *Abstract of British Historical Statistics*, Cambridge University Press, pp. 20, 24, 26.

[14] Feinstein and Pollard, *op. cit.*, pp. 387, 446.

[15] Treble, J.H. (1971) Liverpool Working Class Housing 1801–51, in *The History of Working Class Housing: a Symposium*, (ed. Chapman, S.D.), David & Charles.

[16] Aspin, C. (1969) *Lancashire: the First Industrial Society*, Helmshore Local History Society, p. 93.

[17] Olsen, D.J. (1976) *The Growth of Victorian London*, Batsford, p. 191.

[18] Chapman, S.D. and Bartlett, J.N. Contribution of Building Clubs and Freehold Land Societies to Working Class Housing in Birmingham, in Chapman, *op. cit.*, p. 228.

[19] Burnett, J. (1986) *A Social History of Housing 1815–1985*, Methuen, p. 51.

[20] Pollard, S. (1959) *A History of Labour in Sheffield*, Liverpool University Press, pp. 18–20.

[21] Rubinstein, D. (1974) *Victorian Homes*, David & Charles, pp. 260–2.

[22] Smith, L.D.W. (1976) Textile Factory Settlements in the Early Industrial Revolution, Ph.D. thesis, University of Aston, pp. 137–8.

[23] Hitchcock, H.-R. (1972) *Early Victorian Architecture in Britain*, Trewin Copplestone, Vol. 2, pp. XIII, 17, 18, 22.

[24] Flinn, M.W. *op. cit.*, p. 5.

[25] Deane, P. and Cole, W.A. (1967) *British Economic Growth 1688–1959*, Cambridge University Press, p. 213.

[26] Tann, J. (1970) *The Development of the Factory*, Cornmarket, p. 147.

[27] Mathias, P. (1972) *The First Industrial Nation*, Methuen, p. 283.

[28] *The Builder*, 29 July 1843.

[29] Howell, P. (1968) *Victorian Churches*, Country Life.

[30] Chalklin, C.W. (1980) Capital Expenditure on Building for Cultural Purposes in Provincial England 1730–1830, *Business History*, **XXII** (1).

[31] Hitchcock, *op. cit.*, Vol. 1 pp. 97 *et seq.*

[32] Spencer-Silver, P. (1993) *Pugin's Builder: the Life and Work of George Myers*, University of Hull Press, pp. 211–59.

[33] Seaborne, M. (1971) *English School: Its Architecture and Organisation 1370–1870*, Routledge & Kegan Paul, pp. 131–41.

[34] Nicholson, P. (1823) *New Practical Builder and Workman's Companion*, Kelly, pp. 576 *et seq.*

[35] Dixon, R. and Muthesius, S. (1978) *Victorian Architecture*, Thames & Hudson, p. 110.

[36] Mumford, L. (1961) *The City in History*, Secker & Warburg, p. 449.

[37] Girouard, M. (1971) *The Victorian Country House*, Clarendon, pp. 19–20.

[38] Pevsner, N. (1976) *A History of Building Types*, Thames & Hudson, p. 289.

[39] Herbert, G. (1978) *Pioneers of Prefabrication: the British Contribution in the Nineteenth Century*, Johns Hopkins University Press.

2 THE INDUSTRY FORGES THE MEANS: 1800–1850

[1] Aston, M.A. (1974) *Stonesfield Slate*, Oxfordshire County Council, p. 32.

[2] Clapham, J.H. (1950) *An Economic History of Modern Britain: the Early Railway Age 1820–1850*, Cambridge University Press, p. 72.

[3] Pollard, S. (1978) Labour in Gt. Britain, in *Cambridge Economic History of Europe. Vol. VIII Industrial Economies: Capital, Labour and Enterprise* (eds Mathias, P. and Postan, M.M.), Cambridge University Press, pp. 97–164.

[4] Elsam, R. (1826) *The Practical Builder's Perpetual Price Book*, Kelly, p. vii.

[5] Nisbet, J. (1993) *Fair and Reasonable: Building Contracts from 1550, a Synopsis*, Stoke Publications, p. 45.

[6] Port, M.H. (1967) Office of Works and Building Contracts in Early Nineteenth Century England, *Economic History Review* 2nd series, **20** (1).

[7] Cooney, E.W. (1955–56) Origins of the Victorian Master Builders, *Economic History Review* 2nd series, **8** (2).

[8] Cooney, E.W. (1980) Building Industry, in *The Dynamics of Victorian Business: Problems and Perspectives to the 1870s* (ed. Church, R.), Allen and Unwin, pp. 142–60.

[9] Nisbet, *op. cit.*, pp. 33–46.

[10] Bowyer, J. (1973) *History of Building*, Crosby Lockwood Staples, p. 240.

[11] Nisbet, J. (1951–52) Quantity Surveying in London During the Nineteenth Century, *J. of the Royal Institution of Chartered Surveyors*, **31**.

[12] Thompson, F.M.L. (1968) *Chartered Surveyors: the Growth of a Profession*, Routledge & Kegan Paul, pp. 88–91.

[13] Hobhouse, H. (1971) *Thomas Cubitt: Master Builder*, Macmillan.

[14] Spencer-Silver, P. (1993) *Pugin's Builder: The Life and Work of George Myers*, University of Hull Press.

[15] Clarke, L. (1992) *Building Capitalism: Historical Change and the Labour Process in the Production of the Built Environment*, Routledge.

[16] Sigsworth, E.M. (1958) *Black Dyke Mills: a History*, Liverpool University Press, pp. 169–71.

[17] Powell, C.G. (1985) Case Studies and Lost Tribes: the Bristol Firm of James Diment and Stephens, Bastow & Co., *Construction History*, **1**.

[18] Olsen, D.J. (1976) *The Growth of Victorian London*, Batsford, pp. 265–6.

[19] Powell, C.G. (1986) He That Runs Against Time: Life Expectancy of Building Firms in Nineteenth Century Bristol, *Construction History*, **2**.

[20] Nenadic, S. (1993) The Small Family Firm in Victorian Britain, *Business History*, **35** (4).

[21] Brown, E.H.P. and Hopkins, S.V. (1955) Seven Centuries of Building Wages, *Economica* New Series, **XXII** (87).

[22] Elsam, *op. cit.*

[23] Postgate, R.W. (1923) *Builders' History* Nat. Fed. of Building Trade Operatives, Appendix I.

[24] Hobsbawm, E.J. (1964) *Labouring Men: Studies in the History of Labour*, Weidenfeld & Nicolson, p. 81.

[25] Burnett, J. (ed.) (1977) *Useful Toil*, Penguin, p. 267.

[26] Burnett, *op. cit.*, pp. 274–5, 312 *et seq.*

[27] Thompson, E.P. (1968) *The Making of the English Working Class*, Penguin, pp. 285–6.

[28] Crook, J.M. and Port, M.H. (1973) *The History of the King's Works*, HMSO, Vol. VI, p. 129.

[29] Hilton, W.S. (1963) *Foes to Tyranny: a History of the Amalgamated Union of Building Trade Workers*, AUBTW, pp. 34–49, 74–85.

[30] Postgate, *op. cit.*, pp. 26 *et seq.*

[31] Gayer, A.D., Rostow, W.W. and Schwarz, A.J. (1953) *Growth and Fluctuations of the British Economy 1790–1850*, Oxford University Press, p. 417.

[32] Chalklin, C.W. (1974) *The Provincial Towns of Georgian England: a Study of the Building Process 1740–1820*, Arnold, pp. 192–3.

[33] Bowley, M. (1960) *Innovations in Building Materials*, Duckworth, p. 62.

[34] Clifton-Taylor, A. (1962) *The Pattern of English Building*, Batsford.

[35] McCann, J. (1983) *Clay and Cob Buildings*, Shire.

[36] Louw, H. (1992) Mechanisation of Architectural Woodwork in Britain from the Late-Eighteenth to the Early Twentieth Century, and its Practical, Social and Aesthetic Implications Pt. I, *Construction History*, **8**.

[37] Davey, N. (1961) *A History of Building Materials*, Phoenix, pp. 98 *et seq.*

[38] Hudson, K. (1972) *Building Materials*, Longman, p. 49.

[39] Smeaton, A.C. (1835) *The Builder's Pocket Manual*, Taylor, p. 122.

[40] Sheppard, R. (1945) *Cast Iron in Building*, Allen & Unwin.

3 BUILDING AND THE TRIUMPH OF URBANIZATION: 1851–1914

[1] Daunton, M.J. (1977) *Coal Metropolis: Cardiff 1870–1914*, Leicester University Press, pp. 75–118.

[2] Jenkins, S. (1975) *Landlords to London: the Story of a Capital and its Growth*, Constable, p. 99.

[3] Bell, C. and Bell, R. (1972) *City Fathers*, Penguin, p. 262.

[4] Dyos, H.J. (1968) Speculative Builders and Developers of Victorian London, *Victorian Studies*, **XI** Summer supplement.

[5] Cleary, E.J. (1965) *The Building Society Movement*, Elek, pp. 45–152.

[6] Marriott, O. (1967) *The Property Boom*, Hamish Hamilton, p. 19.

[7] Ashworth, W. (1972) *The Genesis of Modern British Town Planning*, Routledge & Kegan Paul, p. 8; quotes Local Government Board (1909) *Statistical Memoranda and Charts Relating to Public Health and Social Conditions* BPP, CIII.

[8] Mitchell, B.R. and Deane, P. (1962) *Abstract of British Historical Statistics*, Cambridge University Press, p. 6.

[9] Based on Feinstein, C.H. and Pollard, S. (eds) (1988) *Studies in Capital Formation in the United Kingdom 1750–1920*, Clarendon, p. 446.

[10] Cooney, E.W. (1960–61) Long Waves in Building in the British Economy of the Nineteenth Century, *Economic History Review* 2nd series, **13** (2).

[11] Mackay, D.I. (1967) Growth and Fluctuations in the British Building Industry, *Scottish J. of Political Economy*, **14**.

[12] Lewis, J.P. (1965) *Building Cycles and Britain's Growth*, Macmillan, pp. 301 *et seq.*

[13] Saul, S.B. (1962) House Building in England 1890–1914, *Economic History Review* 2nd series, **15** (1).

[14] Kenwood, A.G. (1963) Residential Building Activity in North Eastern England 1853–1913, *Manchester School of Economic and Social Studies*, **XXXI**.

[15] Cairncross, A.K. (1953) *Home and Foreign Investment 1870–1913*, Cambridge University Press, p. 110.

[16] Feinstein and Pollard, *op. cit.*, p. 387.

[17] Gauldie, E. (1974) *Cruel Habitations*, Allen & Unwin, p. 172.

[18] Hole, J. (1866) *The Homes of the Working Classes with Suggestions for their Improvement*, Longmans Green, p. 71.

[19] Webb, C.A. (1913) *Valuation of Real Property*, Crosby Lockwood, pp. 42 *et seq.*

[20] Wohl, A.S. (1977) *The Eternal Slum: Housing and Social Policy in Victorian London*, Arnold, p. 294.

[21] Birch, J. (1892) *Examples of Labourers' Cottages &c*, Blackwood.

[22] Girouard, M. (1971) *The Victorian Country House*, Clarendon, pp. 5–6.

[23] Service, A. (1977) *Edwardian Architecture: a Handbook to Building Design in Britain 1890–1914*, Thames & Hudson, pp. 128 *et seq.*

[24] Winter, J. (1970) *Industrial Architecture: a Survey of Factory Building*, Studio Vista.

[25] Lawrence, J.C. (1990) Steel Frame Architecture Versus the London Building Regulations: Selfridges, the Ritz and American Technology, *Construction History*, **6**.

[26] Sachs, E.O. and Woodrow, E.A.E. (1968) *Modern Opera Houses and Theatres*, Blom, Vol. I, pp. 37–46 and Vol. II, pp. 35–45.

[27] Lady Bell (1969) *At the Works*, David & Charles, p. 8.

[28] Taylor, J. (1991) *Hospital and Asylum Architecture in England 1840–1914*, Mansell.

[29] Pinker, R. (1966) *English Hospital Statistics 1861–1938*, Heinemann, p. 56.

[30] Feinstein and Pollard, *op. cit.*, p. 362.

[31] Seaborne, M. (1971) *English School: its Architecture and Organisation 1370–1870*, Routledge & Kegan Paul.

[32] Robson, E.R. (1972) *School Architecture*, Leicester University Press, pp. 2, 291–350.

[33] Robins, E.C. (1887) *Technical School and College Building*, Whittaker, p. 75, Appendix.

[34] Clarke, B.F.L. (1938) *Church Builders of the Nineteenth Century*, SPCK, p. 223.

[35] Micklethwaite, J.T. (1874) *Modern Parish Churches*, King, p. 339.

[36] Cunningham, C. (1981) *Victorian and Edwardian Town Halls*, Routledge & Kegan Paul, p. 254.

[37] Ashburner, E. (1946) *Modern Public Libraries: Their Planning and Design*, Grafton, p. 20.

[38] Cowan, P. *et al.* (1969) *The Office: a Facet of Urban Growth*, Heinemann, p. 157.

[39] Kellet, J.R. (1969) *The Impact of Railways on Victorian Cities*, Routledge & Kegan Paul, p. 327.

[40] Knowles, C.C. and Pitt, P.H. (1972) *The History of Building Regulations in London 1189–1972*, Architectural Press, pp. 60–4.

[41] Gaskell, S.M. (1985) *Building Control: National Legislation and the Introduction of Local Bye-Laws in Victorian England*, Bedford Square Press.

[42] Harper, R. (1977) Conflict Between English Building Regulations and Architectural Design: 1890–1918, *J. of Architectural Research*, **6** (1).

[43] Lawrence, *op. cit.*

[44] Harper, R.H. (1985) *Victorian Building Regulations*, Mansell.

[45] Markus, T.A. (1993) *Buildings and Power: Freedom and Control in the Origins of Modern Building Types*, Routledge, p. xixi.

[46] Vaughan, A. (1977) *A Pictorial Record of Great Western Architecture*, Oxford Publishing, pp. 8–9, 192, 334, 376.

[47] *Kelly's Directory of the Building Trades* (1886), Kelly.

[48] Hamilton, S.B. (1956) *A Note on the History of Reinforced Concrete in Buildings*, HMSO.

[49] Hamilton, S.B. (1958) *A Short History of the Structural Fire Protection of Buildings*, HMSO.

[50] Port, M.H. (1995) *Imperial London: Civil Government Building in London 1850–1915*, Yale University Press, p. 145.

[51] Banham, R. (1969) *The Architecture of the Well-Tempered Environment*, Architectural Press, pp. 39, 45–6.

[52] Middleton, G.A.T. (n.d.; *c.* 1905) *Modern Buildings: Their*

Planning, Construction and Equipment, Caxton, pp. 119 *et seq.*

[53] Derry, T.K. and Williams, T.I. (1960) *Short History of Technology from the Earliest Times to AD 1900*, Clarendon, pp. 508–13.

[54] Banham, R. (1975) *Mechanical Services: History of Architecture and Design 1890–1939*, Open University Press.

[55] Wright, L. (1960) *Clean and Decent: the Fascinating History of the Bathroom and the Water Closet*, Routledge & Kegan Paul.

4 THE INDUSTRY CONSOLIDATES: 1851–1914

[1] Mitchell, B.R. and Deane, P. (1962) *Abstract of British Historical Statistics*, Cambridge University Press, p. 60.

[2] Gotch, J.A. (1934) *The Growth and Work of the Royal Institute of British Architects*, RIBA, pp. 121–3.

[3] Kaye, B. (1960) *The Development of the Architectural Profession in Britain*, Allen & Unwin, p. 64.

[4] Micklethwaite, J.T. (1874) *Modern Parish Churches*, King, p. 236.

[5] Trowell, F. (1985) Speculative Housing Development in Leeds and the Involvement of Local Architects in the Design Process 1866–1914, *Construction History*, **1**.

[6] Summerson, J. (1973) *The London Building World of the Eighteen-Sixties*, Thames & Hudson, p. 20.

[7] Nisbet, J. (1951–52) Quantity Surveying in London during the Nineteenth Century, *J. of the Royal Institution of Chartered Surveyors*, **31**.

[8] Doughty, M. (ed.) (1986) *Building the Industrial City*, Leicester University Press, pp. 5–17.

[9] Aspinall, P.J. (1982) Internal Structure of the House-building Industry in Nineteenth Century Cities, in *Structure of Nineteenth Century Cities* (eds Johnson, J.H. and Pooley, C.G.), Croom Helm, p. 77.

[10] Dyos, H.J. (1968) Speculative Builders and Developers of Victorian London, *Victorian Studies*, **XI** Summer supplement.

[11] Doughty, *op. cit.*

[12] Bowley, M. (1966) *The British Building Industry: Four Studies in Response and Resistance to Change*, Cambridge University Press, p. 339.

[13] Spencer-Silver, P. (1993) *Pugin's Builder: The Life and Work of George Myers*, University of Hull Press, p. 84.

[14] Port, M.H. (1995) *Imperial London; Civil Government Building in London 1850–1915*, Yale University Press, p. 140.

[15] Cooney, E.W. (1980) Building Industry, in *The Dynamics of Victorian Business: Problems and Perspectives to the 1870s* (ed. Church, R.), Allen & Unwin, pp. 142–60.

[16] Powell, C.G. (1985) Case Studies and Lost Tribes: the Bristol Firm of James Diment and Stephens, Bastow and Co., *Construction History*, **1**.

[17] Home, R.K. (1982) A Nineteenth Century Macclesfield Builder: Some Notes on George Roylance (1836–92), *Trans. Lancs. & Ches. Antiq. Soc.*, **81**.

[18] Crouch, P. (1983) Walter Mason and the Late Nineteenth Century Building Industry in Haverhill, *Suffolk Review*, **5** (4).

[19] Louw, H. (1993) Mechanisation of Architectural Woodwork in Britain from the Late-Eighteenth to the Early Twentieth Century, and its Practical, Social and Aesthetic Implications Pt. II: Technological Progress *c.* 1860 to *c.* 1915, *Construction History*, **9**.

[20] Dyos, H.J. (1966) *Victorian Suburb: a Study of the Growth of Camberwell*, Leicester University Press, pp. 122 *et seq.*

[21] Sheppard, F.H.W. (ed.) (1973) *Survey of London. Vol. XXXVII Northern Kensington*, Athlone, p. 8.

[22] Dyos (1968) *op. cit.*

[23] Belcher, V. (1982) Records of a London Building Firm, *Business Archives*, **48** (Nov.).

[24] Benson, J. (1983) Building, in *Penny Capitalists: a Study of Nineteenth Century Working Class Entrepreneurs*, Gill & Macmillan, pp. 50–4.

[25] *Kelly's Directory, op. cit.*

[26] Muthesius, S. (1982) *The English Terraced House*, Yale University Press, p. 30.

[27] Rose, W. (1952) *Village Carpenter*, Country Book Club.

[28] Tressel, R. (1965) *The Ragged Trousered Philanthropists*, Panther.

[29] Clapham, J. (1963) *An Economic History of Modern Britain: Free Trade and Steel 1850–1886*, Cambridge University Press, p. 120.

[30] Samuel, R. (ed.) (1975) *Village Life and Labour*, Routledge & Kegan Paul, pp. 164, 175, 230.

[31] Jones, G.T. (1933) *Increasing Return*, Cambridge University Press, p. 270.

[32] Maiwald, K. (1954) An Index of Building Costs in the

United Kingdom 1845–1938, *Economic History Review* 2nd series, **VII**, (2).

[33] Brown, E.H.P. and Hopkins, S.V. (1955) Seven Centuries of Building Wages. *Economica* New Series, **XXII** (87).

[34] Levi, L. (1867) *Wages and Earnings of the Working Classes*, Murray, p. 65.

[35] Usill, G.W. (ed.) (1885) *Builders' and Contractors' Price Book and Guide to Estimating*, Scientific Publishing.

[36] Routh, G. (1965) *Occupation and Pay in Great Britain 1906–1960*, Cambridge University Press, p. 88.

[37] Postgate, R.W. (1923) *Builders' History*, Nat. Fed. of Building Trade Operatives, p. 181.

[38] Hilton, W.S. (1963) *Foes to Tyranny: A History of the Amalgamated Union of Building Trade Workers*, AUBTW, p. 165.

[39] Maiwald, *op. cit.*

[40] Springett, J. Land Development and House-Building in Huddersfield, 1770–1911, in Doughty, *op. cit.*

[41] Barker, T.C. and Savage, C.I. (1974) *Economic History of Transport in Britain*, Hutchinson, pp. 105, 141.

[42] Laxton, W. (1894) *Laxton's Builders' Price Book*, Kelly.

[43] Jones, *op. cit.*, pp. 66, 83, 94.

[44] Louw (1993), *op. cit.*

[45] Skyring, W.H. (1856) *Skyring's Builders' Prices*, Skyring.

[46] Slater, E.A. (1912) *Structural Economy*, St Bride's Press, pp. 21, 23, 32.

5 BUILDING THE SUBURBS: 1915–1939

[1] Richardson, H.W. and Aldcroft, D.H. (1968) *Building in the British Economy Between the Wars*, Allen & Unwin, p. 43.

[2] Bowley, M. (1966) *The British Building Industry: Four Studies in Response and Resistance to Change*, Cambridge University Press, pp. 368–9.

[3] Jackson, A.A. (1973) *Semi-Detached London*, Allen & Unwin, pp. 121–2.

[4] Robinson, H.W. (1939) *The Economics of Building*, King, pp. 9–10.

[5] Young, G.M. (1943) *Country and Town: a Summary of the Scott and Uthwatt Reports*, Penguin, pp. 35–6.

[6] Priestley, J.B. (1934) *English Journey*, Heinemann, pp. 398–9, 401.

[7] Bowley, M. (1937–38) Some Regional Aspects of the Building Boom, 1924–36, *Review of Economic Studies*, **5**.

[8] Burnett, J. (1986) *A Social History of Housing 1815–1985*, Methuen, p. 246.

[9] Powell, C.G. (1986) Some Trends in Relative Costs of Building Types: Description and Interpretation, *Construction Management and Economics*, **4**.

[10] Wright, H.M. (1946) *Small Houses £500–£2,500*, Architectural Press.

[11] Bowley, M. (1947) *Housing and the State 1919–1944*, Allen & Unwin.

[12] Marriner, S. (1976) Cash and Concrete: Liquidity Problems in the Mass-Production of 'Homes for Heroes', *Business History*, **XVIII** (2).

[13] Local Government Board (1918) *Report of the Committee . . . to Consider Questions of Building Construction in Connection with the Provision of Dwellings for the Working Classes . . .* (Tudor Walters Report), HMSO.

[14] Swenarton, M. (1981) *Homes Fit for Heroes: the Politics and Architecture of Early State Housing in Britain*, Heinemann.

[15] Sayle, A. (1924) *The Houses of the Workers*, Unwin, p. 153.

[16] Hole, W.V. and Attenburrow, J.J. (1966) *Houses and People*, HMSO, p. 49.

[17] Ravetz, A. (1974) From Working-class Tenement to Modern Flat: Local Authorities and Multi-Storey Housing Between the Wars, in *Multi-Storey Living: the British Working-Class Experience* (ed. Sutcliffe, A.), Croom Helm.

[18] *Architects' Journal*, 16 July 1930.

[19] Kahn, M. (1917) *The Design and Construction of Industrial Buildings*, Technical Journals, p. 11.

[20] Kohan, C.M. (1952) *History of the Second World War: Works and Buildings*, HMSO, p. 278.

[21] Harvey, N. (1970) *History of Farm Buildings in England and Wales*, David & Charles, pp. 170–1.

[22] Whitehand, J.W.R. (1992) Makers of British Towns: Architects, Builders and Property Owners, *c.* 1850–1939, *J. of Historical Geography*, **18** (4).

[23] Orwell, G. (1963) *The Road to Wigan Pier*, Penguin, p. 58.

[24] White, R.B. (1965) *Prefabrication: a History of its Development in Great Britain*, HMSO, p. 103.

[25] Nuffield Foundation, Division of Architectural Studies (1961) *Design of Research Laboratories*, Oxford University Press, p. 19.

6 THE INDUSTRY AS A FORCE FOR STABILITY: 1915–1939

[1] Richardson, H.W. and Aldcroft, D.H. (1968) *Building in the British Economy Between the Wars*, Allen & Unwin, p. 269.

[2] Robinson, H.W. (1939) *The Economics of Building*, King, pp. 5–6.

[3] Gotch, J.A. (1934) *The Growth and Work of the Royal Institute of British Architects*, RIBA, pp. 121–3.

[4] Nisbet, J. (1993) *Fair and Reasonable: Building Contracts from 1550, a Synopsis*, Stoke Publications.

[5] *The Times* (1938) *British Homes: the Building Society Movement*, The Times, p. 68.

[6] Kaye, B. (1960) *The Development of the Architectural Profession in Britain*, Allen & Unwin, pp. 151–6, 174.

[7] Cresswell, H.B. (1972) *Honeywood File: an Adventure in Building*, Faber.

[8] Whitehand, J.W.R. (1992) Makers of British Towns: Architects, Builders and Property Owners *c.* 1850–1939, *J. of Historical Geography*, **18** (4).

[9] Bowley, M. (1966) *The British Building Industry: Four Studies in Response and Resistance to Change*, Cambridge University Press, pp. 78 *et seq.*

[10] Davey, N. (1964) *Building in Britain*, Evans, p. 101.

[11] Marriner, S. (1979) Sir Alfred Mond's Octopus: a Nationalised House-Building Business, *Business History*, **XXI** (1).

[12] Richardson and Aldcroft, *op. cit.*, pp. 157–8.

[13] Whitehand, *op. cit.*

[14] Robinson, *op. cit.*, p. 15.

[15] Coad, R. (1992) *Laing: the Biography of Sir John W. Laing, CBE (1879–1978)*, Hodder & Stoughton.

[16] Burnett, J. (1986) *A Social History of Housing 1815–1985*, Methuen, p. 257.

[17] Bowley (1966) *op. cit.*, p. 382.

[18] Maiwald, K. (1954) An Index of Building Costs in the United Kingdom 1845–1938, *Economic History Review* 2nd series, **VII** (2).

[19] Chapman, A.L. and Knight, R. (1953) *Wages and Salaries in the UK 1920–1938*, Cambridge University Press, p. 27.

[20] Kingsford, P.W. (1973) *Builders and Building Workers*, Arnold, p. 175.

[21] Hilton, W.S. (1968) *Industrial Relations in Construction*, Pergamon, pp. 161–2.

[22] Maiwald, *op. cit.*

[23] White, R.B. (1965) *Prefabrication: a History of its Development in Great Britain*, HMSO, pp. 73–4.

[24] Gunn, E. (1932) *Economy in House Design*, Architectural Press, p. 36.

[25] Young, C. (ed.) (1924) *Spons' Architects' and Builders' Price Book*, Spon.

[26] Stobart, T.J. (1927) *Timber Trade of the United Kingdom*, Crosby Lockwood, Vol. I table facing p. 1, pp. 1–2, 91; Vol. II table facing p. 2.

[27] Bowley, M. (1960) *Innovations in Building Materials*, Duckworth, pp. 133, 151, 263–5.

[28] Bowley (1960) *op. cit.*, pp. 279–85.

7 BUILDING IN CRISIS AND RECONSTRUCTION: 1940–1973

[1] Higgin, G. and Jessop, N. (1965) *Communications in the Building Industry: the Report of a Pilot Study*, Tavistock, p. 16.

[2] Emmerson, H. (1956) *The Ministry of Works*, Allen & Unwin, p. 20.

[3] Kohan, C.M. (1952) *History of the Second World War: Works and Buildings*, HMSO, pp. 353 *et seq.*

[4] Rosenberg, N. (1960) *Economic Planning in the British Building Industry 1945–49*, University of Pennsylvania Press, p. 135.

[5] Cullingworth, J.B. (1966) *Housing and Local Government in England and Wales*, Allen & Unwin, p. 67.

[6] Sharp, E. (1969) *The Ministry of Housing and Local Government*, Allen & Unwin, p. 26.

[7] Needleman, L. (1965) *The Economics of Housing*, Staples, pp. 135, 138.

[8] Layton, E. (1961) *Building by Local Authorities*, Allen & Unwin, p. 72.

[9] Balchin, P.N. and Kieve, J.L. (1977) *Urban Land Economics*, Macmillan, p. 91.

[10] Cadman, D. and Austin-Crowe, L. (1978) *Property Development*, Spon, pp. 174, 176–7.

[11] Cowan, P. *et al.* (1969) *The Office: a Facet of Urban Growth*, Heinemann, p. 127.

[12] Cullingworth, J.B. (1970) *Town and Country Planning in England and Wales: the Changing Scene*, Allen & Unwin.

[13] English, J. *et al.* (1976) *Slum Clearance: the Social and*

Administrative Context in England and Wales, Croom Helm, pp. 36–7.

[14] Sugden, J.D. (1975) Place of Construction in the Economy, in *Aspects of the Economics of Construction* (ed. Turin, D.A.), Godwin.

[15] Hancock, W.K. and Gowing, M.M. (1949) *History of the Second World War: British War Economy*, HMSO, pp. 174–5, 321.

[16] Central Statistical Office (1973) *Annual Abstract of Statistics 1973*, HMSO, p. 191.

[17] Donnison, D.V. (1967) *The Government of Housing*, Penguin, p. 167.

[18] Vipond, M.J. (1969) Fluctuations in Private Housebuilding in Great Britain 1950–1966, *Scottish J. of Political Economy*, **16**.

[19] Ministry of Housing and Local Government (various dates) *Housing Statistics: Great Britain*, HMSO.

[20] Dept. of the Environment (various dates) *Housing and Construction Statistics*, HMSO.

[21] Central Housing Advisory Committee (1944) *Design of Dwellings*, HMSO.

[22] Ministry of Health and Ministry of Works (1944) *Housing Manual 1944*, HMSO.

[23] Forshaw, J.H. and Abercrombie, P. (1943) *County of London Plan*, Macmillan, p. 78.

[24] Burnett, J. (1986) *A Social History of Housing 1815–1985*, Methuen, pp. 299–300.

[25] Ministry of Housing and Local Government (1961) *Homes for Today and Tomorrow*, HMSO.

[26] Stone, P.A (1973) *Structure, Size and Costs of Urban Settlements*, Cambridge University Press, p. 104.

[27] Seaborne, M. and Lowe, R. (1977) *English School: Its Architecture and Organisation Vol. II 1870–1970*, Routledge & Kegan Paul, p. 155.

[28] Saint, A. (1987) *Towards a Social Architecture: the Role of School Building in Post-War England*, Yale University Press.

[29] Ward, C. (ed.) (1976) *British School Buildings: Designs and Appraisals 1964–74*, Architectural Press.

[30] Berriman, S.G. and Harrison, K.C. (1966) *British Public Library Buildings*, Deutsch.

[31] Incorporated Church Building Society (n.d., *c.* 1956) *Sixty Post-War Churches*, ICBS, p. 11.

[32] Harvey, N. (1970) *History of Farm Buildings in England and Wales*, David & Charles, pp. 212–48.

[33] Cowan *et al., op. cit.*, pp. 112, 181.

[34] National Economic Development Office (1978) *How Flexible is Construction? A Study of Resources and Participants in the Construction Process*, HMSO, p. 75.

[35] Harrison, D. (1947) *Introduction to Standards in Building*, E & FN Spon.

[36] *Building Regulations 1965* (1965), HMSO.

8 THE INDUSTRY FIGHTS FOR FREEDOM AND GROWTH: 1940–1973

[1] Matthews, R.C.O., Feinstein, C.H. and Odling-Smee, J.C. (1982) *British Economic Growth 1856–1973*, Clarendon, pp. 228–9, 236.

[2] Nisbet, J. (1993) *Fair and Reasonable: Building Contracts from 1550, A Synopsis*, Stoke Publications, pp. 74–5.

[3] Dow, J.C.R. (1965) *Management of the British Economy 1945–1960*, Cambridge University Press, pp. 149–51.

[4] Smyth, H. (1985) *Property Companies and the Construction Industry in Britain*, Cambridge University Press, pp. 117–19.

[5] Rosenberg, N. (1960) *Economic Planning in the British Building Industry 1945–49*, University of Pennsylvania Press.

[6] Ministry of Works (1962) *Survey of Problems Before the Construction Industry*, HMSO.

[7] Bowley, M. (1966) *The British Building Industry: Four Studies in Response and Resistance to Change*, Cambridge University Press, p. 441.

[8] Higgin, G. and Jessop, N. (1965) *Communications in the Building Industry, the Report of a Pilot Study*, Tavistock.

[9] Ministry of Public Building and Works (1964) *Placing and Management of Contracts for Building and Civil Engineering Work*, HMSO.

[10] Ministry of Works (1944) *Placing and Management of Contracts in the Building Industry*, HMSO.

[11] National Economic Development Office (1974) *Before You Build: What a Client Needs to Know About the Construction Industry*, HMSO, pp. 26–7.

[12] Royal Institute of British Architects (1962) *The Architect and His Office*, RIBA, p. 26.

[13] Jenkins, F. (1961) *Architect and Patron: a Survey of Professional Relations and Practice in England from the*

Sixteenth Century to the Present Day, Oxford University Press, p. 236.

[14] Bowley (1966) *op. cit.*, p. 279.

[15] MacEwen, M. (1974) *Crisis in Architecture*, RIBA.

[16] Hillebrandt, P.M. (1974) *Economic Theory and the Construction Industry*, Macmillan, p. 157.

[17] Forster, G. (1978) *Building Organisation and Procedures*, Longman, pp. 72–7.

[18] Gaskell, M. (1989) *Harry Neal Ltd.: a Family Firm of Builders*, Granta, pp. 64–72.

[19] Turner, G. (1971) *Business in Britain*, Penguin, pp. 292, 296–300.

[20] Foster, C. (1969) *Building With Men*, Tavistock.

[21] National Economic Development Office (1978) *How Flexible is Construction? A Study of Resources and Participants in the Construction Process*, HMSO, p. 21.

[22] Gray, H. (1968) *The Cost of Council Housing*, Institute of Economic Affairs, p. 65.

[23] *Report of the Committee of Inquiry Under Professor E.H. Phelps Brown into Certain Matters Concerning Labour in Building and Civil Engineering* (1968), HMSO.

[24] Cheetham, J.H. (ed.) (1970) *House's Guide to the Building Industry*, House.

[25] Parlett, D.S. (ed.) (1976) *Construction Industry UK*, House.

[26] White, R.B. (1965) *Prefabrication: a History of its Development in Great Britain*, HMSO, pp. 123, 137, 152 *et seq.*

[27] Grossmith, G. and Grossmith, W. (1964) *Diary of a Nobody*, Dent, pp. 57 *et seq.*

[28] Hobbs, E.W. (1926) *House Repairs: a Practical Guide for the House-Holder & Amateur Craftsman*, The Architectural Press.

[29] Design Council (1977) *Leisure in the Twentieth Century*, Design Council.

[30] Office of Population Censuses and Surveys, Social Survey Division (1976) *General Household Survey 1973*, HMSO, p. 80.

[31] Department of the Environment (various dates) *Housing Statistics: Great Britain*, HMSO.

[32] Thomas, G. (1968) *Operatives in the Building Industry*, HMSO, pp. 2, 5–6, 42.

[33] Zweig, F. (1952) *The British Worker*, Penguin, pp. 35–6.

[34] Wallis, L. (1945) *Building Industry: its Work and Organisation*, Dent, p. 17.

[35] National Board for Prices and Incomes (1968) *Report No.*

92: Pay and Conditions in the Building Industry, HMSO, pp. 8, 39–40.

[36] Prest, A.R. and Coppock, D.J. (1976) *UK Economy: a Manual of Applied Economics*, Weidenfeld & Nicolson, pp. 38, 44.

[37] Central Statistical Office (1975) *Monthly Digest of Statistics No. 349*, HMSO, pp. 146–7.

[38] Stone, P.A. (1966) *Building Economy*, Pergamon, p. 158.

[39] White, *op. cit.*, pp. 138–49.

[40] Barham, H. (1947) *Building Industry: a Criticism and a Plan for the Future*, St. Botolph, p. 6.

[41] Finnimore, B. (1985) A.I.R.O.H. House: Industrial Diversification and State Building Policy, *Construction History*, **1**.

[42] Saint, A. (1987) *Towards a Social Architecture: the Role of School-Building in Post-War England*, Yale University Press.

[43] Finnimore, B. (1989) *Houses from the Factory: System Building and the Welfare State*, Rivers Oram.

9 BUILDING IN A RETREAT OF BIG GOVERNMENT: AFTER 1973

[1] Rougvie, A. (1987) *Project Evaluation and Development*, Mitchell, pp. 107–11.

[2] Duffy, F. (1992) *Changing Workplace*, Phaidon.

[3] Brand, S. (1994) *How Buildings Learn*, Viking.

[4] Becker, F. (1990) *Total Workplace*, Van Nostrand Reinhold.

[5] Department of the Environment (1991) *Housing and Construction Statistics 1980–1990*, (1994) *Housing and Construction Statistics 1983–1993*, HMSO.

[6] Sim, D. (1993) *British Housing Design*, Longman.

[7] Department of the Environment (1994) *op. cit.*

[8] Balchin, P.N. (1985) *Housing Policy: an Introduction*, Croom Helm.

[9] Short, J.R. (1982) *Housing in Britain: the Post-War Experience*, Methuen.

[10] Department of the Environment (1994) *op. cit.*, Table 1.6.

[11] Rose, J. (1985) *Dynamics of Urban Property Development*, E & FN Spon, p. 169.

[12] Harvey, J. (1981) *Economics of Real Property*, Macmillan, p. 117.

[13] Fraser, W.D. (1984) *Principles of Property Investment and Pricing*, p. 399.

[14] McIntosh, A.P.J. and Sykes, S.G. (1985) *Guide to Institutional Property Investment*, p. 25.

[15] McIntosh and Sykes, *op. cit.*, p. 150.

[16] Department of the Environment (1994) *op. cit.*, Tables 1.6, 1.10.

[17] Department of the Environment (1994) *op. cit.*, Table 1.6.

[18] Essex County Council (1973) *Design Guide for Residential Areas*, Essex County Council.

10 THE INDUSTRY RECASTS RESPONSIBILITIES: AFTER 1973

[1] *Technology Foresight: Progress Through Partnership: 2. Construction* (1995), Office of Science & Technology, pp. 1, 14.

[2] Hillebrandt, P.M. (1984) *Analysis of the British Construction Industry* (1984), Macmillan, pp. 221–6.

[3] Cooney, E.W. (1993) Productivity, Conflict and Order in the British Construction Industry: a Historical View, *Construction History*, **9**.

[4] Ball, M. (1988) *Rebuilding Construction: Economic Change and the British Construction Industry*, Routledge, pp. 7–10.

[5] Hillebrandt, *op. cit.*, pp. 59–60.

[6] Centre for Strategic Studies in Construction (1988) *Building Britain 2001*, University of Reading, p. 8.

[7] Harvey, R.C. and Ashworth, A. (1993) *Construction Industry of Great Britain*, Newnes, p. 189.

[8] Cooney (1993) *op. cit.*

[9] Rougvie, A. (1987) *Project Evaluation and Development*, Mitchell, pp. 195–6.

[10] Nisbet, J. (1993) *Fair and Reasonable: Building Contracts from 1550, A Synopsis*, Stoke Publications, p. 85.

[11] Bennett, J. (1993) Managing Construction, *Building Special Supplement Anniversary Issue 150 Years 1843–1993*, Feb.

[12] Harvey, J. (1981) *Economics of Real Property*, Macmillan, p. 163.

[13] Smyth, H. (1985) *Property Companies and the Construction Industry in Britain*, Cambridge University Press, p. 59.

[14] Groak, S. (1992) *Idea of Building*, E & FN Spon, p. 126.

[15] Cooney (1993) *op. cit.*

[16] Ball, *op. cit.*, pp. 37–9.

[17] Nisbet (1993) *op. cit.*, p. 87.

[18] Nisbet (1993) *op. cit.*, pp. 99–100.

[19] Rougvie, *op. cit.*, pp. 143–4.

[20] Gray, C., Hughes, W. and Bennett, J. (1994) *Successful Management of Design*, University of Reading, pp. 9–14.

[21] Charles Prince of Wales (1989) *Vision of Britain: a Personal View of Architecture*, Doubleday.

[22] RIBA (1988) *Census of Private Architectural Practices*, RIBA.

[23] RIBA (1992) *Strategic Study of the Profession: Phase 1 Strategic Overview*, RIBA.

[24] Harvey and Ashworth, *op. cit.*, pp. 179–81.

[25] Rougvie, *op. cit.*, p. 178.

[26] Department of the Environment (1994) *op. cit.*, Table 3.4.

[27] Hillebrandt (1984) *op. cit.*, p. 138.

[28] Nisbet (1993) *op. cit.*, p. 92.

[29] Cooney (1993) *op. cit.*

[30] Hillebrandt (1984) *op. cit.*, pp. 119–20.

[31] Ball, *op. cit.*, pp. 123–4.

[32] Top 50 Contractors, *Building*, 14 July 1995.

[33] Latham, M. (1994) *Constructing the Team: Joint Review of Procurement and Contractual Arrangements in the Construction Industry*, Dept. of the Environment.

[34] Smithies, E. (1984) *The Black Economy in England Since 1914*, Gill & Macmillan, pp. 134–6.

[35] Department of the Environment (1994) *op. cit.*, Table 1.8.

[36] Harvey and Ashworth, *op. cit.*, pp. 81–2.

[37] Department of the Environment (1994) *op. cit.*, Table 2.1.

[38] Department of the Environment (1994) *op cit.*, Table 2.2

[39] Harvey and Ashworth, *op. cit.*, p. 192.

[40] *Building*, 5 May 1995.

[41] Department of the Environment (1994) *op. cit.*, Tables 2.5, 2.6 and 2.7.

[42] Ball, *op. cit.*, pp. 198–204.

[43] Davis, Belfield and Everest (eds) (1995) *Spon's Architects' and Builders' Price Book 1995*, Spon, p. 785.

[44] *Technology Foresight . . .*, *op. cit.*, p. 9.

[45] Latham, *op. cit.*

Further reading

BOOKS

Ashburner, E. (1946) *Modern Public Libraries: Their Planning and Design*, Grafton.

Ashworth, W. (1972) *Genesis of Modern British Town Planning*, Routledge and Kegan Paul.

Aspin, C. (1969) *Lancashire: the First Industrial Society*, Helmshore Local History Society.

Aspinall, P.J. (1982) Internal Structure of the Housebuilding Industry in Nineteenth Century Cities, in *Structure of Nineteenth Century Cities* (eds Johnson, J.H. and Pooley, C.G.), Croom Helm.

Aston, M.A. (1974) *Stonesfield Slate*, Oxfordshire County Council, Dept. of Museum Services

Balchin, P.N. (1985) *Housing Policy: an Introduction*, Croom Helm.

Balchin, P.N. and Kieve, J.L. (1977) *Urban Land Economics*, Macmillan.

Bales, T. (1904) *Builder's Clerk*, E & FN Spon.

Ball, M. (1988) *Rebuilding Construction: Economic Change and the British Construction Industry*, Routledge.

Banham, R. (1969) *Architecture of the Well-Tempered Environment*, Architectural Press.

Banham, R. (1975) *Mechanical Services: History of Architecture and Design 1890–1939*, Open University Press.

Barham, H. (1947) *Building Industry: a Criticism and a Plan for the Future*, St Botolph.

Barker, T.C. and Savage, C.I. (1974) *Economic History of Transport in Britain*, Hutchinson.

Barr, A.W.C. (1958) *Public Authority Housing*, Batsford.

Becker, F. (1990) *Total Workplace*, Van Nostrand Reinhold.

Bell, C. and Bell, R. (1972) *City Fathers*, Penguin.

Bell, Lady (1969) *At the Works*, David & Charles.

Benson, J. (1983) Building, in *Penny Capitalists: a Study of*

Nineteenth Century Working Class Entrepreneurs, Gill & Macmillan.

Berriman, S.G. and Harrison, K.C. (1966) *British Public Library Buildings*, Deutsch.

Birch, J. (1892) *Examples of Labourers' Cottages &c.*, Blackwood.

Bowley, M. (1947) *Housing and the State 1919–1944*, Allen & Unwin.

Bowley, M. (1960) *Innovations in Building Materials*, Duckworth.

Bowley, M. (1966) *British Building Industry: Four Studies in Response and Resistance to Change*, Cambridge University Press.

Bowyer, J. (1973) *History of Building*, Crosby Lockwood Staples.

Braithwaite, D. (1981) *Building in the Blood: The Story of Dove Brothers of Islington 1781–1981*, Godfrey Cave.

Brand, S. (1994) *How Buildings Learn*, Viking.

British Standards Institution (1951) *Fifty Years of British Standards 1901–1951*, BSI.

Brunskill, R.W. (1971) *Illustrated Handbook of Vernacular Architecture*, Faber.

Builder Ltd. and Roskill, O.W. (1962) *Building Industry – 1962 Onwards*, Builder.

Building Regulations 1965 (1965), HMSO.

Burnett, J. (1977) *Useful Toil*, Penguin.

Burnett, J. (1986) *Social History of Housing 1815–1985*, Methuen.

Cadman, D. and Austin-Crowe, L. (1978) *Property Development*, E & FN Spon.

Caffyn, L. (1986) *Workers' Housing in West Yorkshire 1750–1920*, HMSO.

Cairncross, A.K. (1953) *Home and Foreign Investment 1870–1913*, Cambridge University Press.

Central Housing Advisory Committee (1944) *Design of Dwellings*, HMSO.

Central Statistical Office (1973) *Annual Abstract of Statistics 1973*, HMSO.

Centre for Strategic Studies in Construction (1988) *Building Britain 2001*, University of Reading.

Chalklin, C.W. (1974) *Provincial Towns of Georgian England: a Study of the Building Process 1740–1820*, Arnold.

Chapman, A.L. and Knight, R. (1953) *Wages and Salaries in the UK 1920–1938*, Cambridge University Press.

Chapman, S.D. and Bartlett, J.N. (1971) Contribution of Building Clubs and Freehold Land Societies to Working

Class Housing in Birmingham, in *History of Working Class Housing: a Symposium* (ed. Chapman, S.D.), David & Charles.

Charles, Prince of Wales (1989) *Vision of Britain: a Personal View of Architecture*, Doubleday.

Cheetham, J.H. (ed.) (1970) *House's Guide to the Building Industry 1970*, House.

Cherry, G.E. (1988) *Cities and Plans: the Shaping of Urban Britain in the Nineteenth and Twentieth Centuries*, Arnold.

Clapham, J.H. (1950) *Economic History of Modern Britain: the Early Railway Age 1820–1850*, Cambridge University Press.

Clapham, J.H. (1963) *Economic History of Modern Britain: Free Trade and Steel 1850–1886*, Cambridge University Press.

Clarke, B.F.L. (1938) *Church Builders of the Nineteenth Century*, SPCK.

Clarke, L. (1980) Organisation of the Labour Process in Construction, in *Production of the Built Environment: Proceedings of the Bartlett Summer School 1980*, Bartlett School of Architecture & Planning, University College London.

Clarke, L. (1992) *Building Capitalism: Historical Change and the Labour Process in the Production of the Built Environment*, Routledge.

Cleary, E.J. (1965) *Building Society Movement*, Elek.

Clifton-Taylor, A. (1962) *Pattern of English Building*, Batsford.

Coad, R. (1992) *Laing: the Biography of Sir John W. Laing CBE (1879–1978)*, Hodder & Stoughton.

Colclough, J.R. (1965) *Construction Industry of Great Britain*, Butterworths.

Cole, G.D.H. (1945) *Building and Planning*, Cassell.

Cooney, E.W. (1980) Building Industry, in *Dynamics of Victorian Business: Problems and Perspectives to the 1870s* (ed. Church, R.), Allen & Unwin.

Cowan, P. *et al.* (1969) *The Office: a Facet of Urban Growth*, Heinemann.

Cresswell, H.B. (1972) *Honeywood File: an Adventure in Building*, Faber.

Crook, J.M. and Port, M.H. (1973) *History of the King's Works* Vol. VI, HMSO.

Crossick, G. (1978) *Artisan Elite in Victorian Society: Kentish London 1840–1880*, Croom Helm.

Cullingworth, J.B. (1966) *Housing and Local Government in England and Wales*, Allen & Unwin.

Cullingworth, J.B. (1970) *Town and Country Planning in England and Wales: the Changing Scene*, Allen & Unwin.

Cunningham, C. (1981) *Victorian and Edwardian Town Halls*, Routledge & Kegan Paul.

Daunton, M. J. (1977) *Coal Metropolis: Cardiff 1870–1914*, Leicester University Press.

Daunton, M.J. (1983) *House and Home in the Victorian City*, Arnold.

Davey, N. (1961) *History of Building Materials*, Phoenix.

Davey, N. (1964) *Building in Britain*, Evans.

Davis, Belfield and Everest (eds) (Various years) *Spons' Architects' and Builders' Price Book*, E & FN Spon.

Deane, P. and Cole, W.A. (1967) *British Economic Growth 1688–1959*, Cambridge University Press.

Derry, T.K. and Williams, T.I. (1960) *Short History of Technology from the Earliest Times to AD 1900*, Clarendon.

Design Council (1977) *Leisure in the Twentieth Century*, Design Council.

Dixon, R. and Muthesius, S. (1978) *Victorian Architecture*, Thames & Hudson.

Dobson, E. (1891) *Foundations and Concrete Works*, Crosby Lockwood.

Dolan, D. (1979) *British Construction Industry*, Macmillan.

Donnison, D.V. (1967) *Government of Housing*, Penguin.

Doughty, M. (ed.) (1986) *Building the Industrial City*, Leicester University Press.

Dow, J.C.R. (1965) *Management of the British Economy 1945–1960*, Cambridge University Press.

Duffy, F. (1992) *Changing Workplace*, Phaidon.

Dyos, H.J. (1966) *Victorian Suburb: a Study of the Growth of Camberwell*, Leicester University Press.

Elsam, R. (1826) *Practical Builder's Perpetual Price Book*, Kelly.

Emmerson H. (1956) *Ministry of Works*, Allen & Unwin.

English, J. *et al.* (1976) *Slum Clearance: the Social and Administrative Context in England and Wales*, Croom Helm.

Essex County Council (1973) *Design Guide for Residential Areas*, Essex County Council.

Feinstein, C.H. and Pollard, S. (eds) (1988) *Studies in Capital Formation in the United Kingdom 1750–1920*, Clarendon.

Finnimore, B. (1989) *Houses from the Factory: System Building and the Welfare State*, Rivers Oram.

Fleming, M. (1988) Construction, in *Structure of British Industry* (ed. Johnson, P.), Unwin Hyman.

Flinn, M.W. (ed.) (1965) *Report on the Sanitary Condition of the Labouring Population of Gt. Britain by Edwin Chadwick 1842*, Edinburgh University Press.

Forshaw, J.H. and Abercrombie, P. (1943) *County of London Plan*, Macmillan.

Forster, G. (1978) *Building Organisation and Procedures*, Longman.

Foster, C. (1969) *Building With Men*, Tavistock.

Fraser, W.D. (1984) *Principles of Property Investment and Pricing*, Macmillan.

Gaskell, M. (1989) *Harry Neal Ltd.: a Family Firm of Builders*, Granta.

Gaskell, S.M. (1985) *Building Control: National Legislation and the Introduction of Local Bye-Laws in Victorian England*, Bedford Square Press.

Gauldie, E. (1974) *Cruel Habitations*, Allen & Unwin.

Gayer, A.D., Rostow, W.W. and Schwarz, A.J. (1953) *Growth and Fluctuations of the British Economy 1790–1850*, Oxford University Press.

Girouard, M. (1971) *Victorian Country House*, Clarendon.

Glasstone, V. (1975) *Victorian and Edwardian Theatres: an Architectural and Social Survey*, Thames & Hudson.

Glendinning, M. and Muthesius, S. (1994) *Tower Block: Modern Public Housing in England, Scotland, Wales and Northern Ireland*, Yale University Press.

Gotch, J. A. (1934) *Growth and Work of the Royal Institute of British Architects*, RIBA.

Gray, C., Hughes, W. and Bennett, J. (1994) *Successful Management of Design*, University of Reading.

Gray, H. (1968) *Cost of Council Housing*, Institute of Economic Affairs.

Groak, S. (1992) *Idea of Building*, E & FN Spon.

Grossmith G. and Grossmith, W. (1964) *Diary of a Nobody*, Dent.

Gunn, E. (1932) *Economy in House Design*, Architectural Press.

Hall, D. (1948) *Cornerstone: a Study of Britain's Building Industry*, Lawrence & Wishart.

Hamilton, S.B. (1956) *Note on the History of Reinforced Concrete in Buildings*, HMSO.

Hamilton, S.B. (1958) *Short History of the Structural Fire Protection of Buildings*, HMSO.

Hancock, W.K. and Gowing, M.M. (1949) *History of the Second World War: British War Economy*, HMSO.

Harper, R.H. (1985) *Victorian Building Regulations*, Mansell.

Harrison, D. (1947) *Introduction to Standards in Building*, E & FN Spon.

Harvey, J. (1981) *Economics of Real Property*, Macmillan.

Harvey, N. (1970) *History of Farm Buildings in England and Wales*, David & Charles.

Harvey, R.C. and Ashworth, A. (1993) *Construction Industry of Great Britain*, Newnes.

Herbert, G. (1978) *Pioneers of Prefabrication: the British Contribution in the Nineteenth Century*, Johns Hopkins University Press.

Higgin, G. and Jessop, N. (1965) *Communications in the Building Industry: the Report of a Pilot Study*, Tavistock.

Hillebrandt, P.M. (1974) *Economic Theory and the Construction Industry*, Macmillan.

Hillebrandt, P.M. (1984) *Analysis of the British Construction Industry*, Macmillan.

Hilton, W.S. (1963) *Foes to Tyranny: a History of the Amalgamated Union of Building Trade Workers*, AUBTW.

Hilton, W.S. (1968) *Industrial Relations in Construction*, Pergamon.

Hitchcock, H.-R. (1972) *Early Victorian Architecture in Britain* Vols. 1 and 2, Trewin Copplestone.

Hobbs, E.W. (1926) *House Repairs: a Practical Guide for the House-Holder & Amateur Craftsman*, Architectural Press.

Hobhouse, H. (1971) *Thomas Cubitt: Master Builder*, Macmillan.

Hobsbawm, E.J. (1964) *Labouring Men: Studies in the History of Labour*, Weidenfeld & Nicolson.

Hole, J. (1866) *Homes of the Working Classes with Suggestions for Their Improvement*, Longmans Green.

Hole, W.V. and Attenburrow, J.J. (1966) *Houses and People*, HMSO.

Holloway, S.J. (1924) *Ancient and Modern Building: Being Some Notes on the Craft of the Builder with Special Reference to the Work of Holloway Brothers . . . .*, Holloway Bros.

Howell, P. (1968) *Victorian Churches*, Country Life.

Hudson, K. (1972) *Building Materials*, Longman.

Incorporated Church Building Society (n.d.; *c.* 1956) *Sixty Post-War Churches*, ICBS.

Jackson, A.A. (1973) *Semi-Detached London*, Allen & Unwin.

Jeffreys, J.B. (1954) *Retail Trading in Britain 1850–1950*, Cambridge University Press.

Jenkins, F. (1961) *Architect and Patron: a Survey of Professional Relations and Practice in England from the Sixteenth Century to the Present Day*, Oxford University Press.

Jenkins, S. (1975) *Landlords to London: the Story of a Capital and its Growth*, Constable.

Jones, G.T. (1933) *Increasing Return*, Cambridge University Press.

Jones, J.R. (1946) *Welsh Builder on Merseyside: Annals and Lives*, J.R. Jones.

Kahn, M. (1917) *Design and Construction of Industrial Buildings*, Technical Journals.

Kaye, B. (1960) *Development of the Architectural Profession in Britain*, Allen & Unwin.

Kellet, J.R. (1969) *Impact of Railways on Victorian Cities*, Routledge & Kegan Paul.

Kelly's Directory of the Building Trades (1886), Kelly.

Kingsford, P.W. (1973) *Builders and Building Workers*, Arnold.

Knowles, C.C. and Pitt, P.H. (1972) *History of Building Regulations in London 1189–1972*, Architectural Press.

Kohan, C.M. (1952) *History of the Second World War: Works and Buildings*, HMSO.

Latham, M. (1994) *Constructing the Team: Joint Review of Procurement and Contractual Arrangements in the Construction Industry*, DOE.

Laxton, W. (1894) *Laxton's Builders' Price Book*, Kelly.

Layton, E. (1961) *Building by Local Authorities*, Allen & Unwin.

Levi, L. (1867) *Wages and Earnings of the Working Classes*, Murray.

Lewis, J.P. (1965) *Building Cycles and Britain's Growth*, Macmillan.

Local Government Board (1918) *Report of the Committee . . . to Consider Questions of Building Construction in Connection with the Provision of Dwellings for the Working Classes . . .* (Tudor Walters Report), HMSO.

Long, H. (1993) *Edwardian House*, Manchester University Press.

Lowe, J.B. (1987) *Welsh Industrial Workers Housing 1775–1875*, National Museum of Wales.

McCann, J. (1983) *Clay and Cob Buildings*, Shire.

MacEwen, M. (1974) *Crisis in Architecture*, RIBA.

McIntosh, A.P.J. and Sykes, S.G. (1985) *Guide to Institutional Property Investment*, Macmillan.

Markus, T.A. (1993) *Buildings and Power: Freedom and Control in the Origins of Modern Building Types*, Routledge.

Marks, P.L. (1905) *Principles of Planning*, Batsford.

Marriott, O. (1967) *Property Boom*, Hamilton.

Masterman, J. (1992) *Introduction to Building Procurement Systems*, E & FN Spon.

Mathias, P. (1972) *First Industrial Nation*, Methuen.

Matthews, R.C.O., Feinstein, C.H. and Odling-Smee, J.C. (1982) *British Economic Growth 1856–1973*, Clarendon.

Micklethwaite, J.T. (1874) *Modern Parish Churches*, King.

Middleton, G.A.T. (n.d.; *c.* 1905) *Modern Buildings: Their Planning, Construction and Equipment*, Caxton.

Ministry of Health and Ministry of Works (1944) *Housing Manual 1944*, HMSO.

Ministry of Housing and Local Government (1961) *Homes for Today and Tomorrow* (Parker Morris Report), HMSO.

Ministry of Public Building and Works (1964) *Placing and Management of Contracts for Building and Civil Engineering Work* (Banwell Report), HMSO.

Ministry of Works (1944) *Placing and Management of Contracts in the Building Industry* (Simon Report), HMSO.

Ministry of Works (1962) *Survey of Problems Before the Construction Industry* (Emmerson Report), HMSO.

Mitchell, B.R. and Deane, P. (1962) *Abstract of British Historical Statistics*, Cambridge University Press.

Mumford, L. (1961) *City in History*, Secker & Warburg.

Muthesius, S. (1982) *English Terraced House*, Yale University Press.

National Board for Prices and Incomes (1968) *Report No. 92: Pay and Conditions in the Building Industry*, HMSO.

National Economic Development Office (1974) *Before You Build: What a Client Needs to Know About the Construction Industry*, HMSO.

National Economic Development Office (1978) *How Flexible is Construction: a Study of Resources and Participants in the Construction Process*, HMSO.

Needleman, L. (1965) *Economics of Housing*, Staples.

Nicholson, P. (1823) *New Practical Builder and Workman's Companion*, Kelly.

Nisbet, J. (1993) *Fair and Reasonable: Building Contracts from 1550, a Synopsis*, Stoke Publications.

Nuffield Foundation, Division of Architectural Studies (1961) *Design of Research Laboratories*, Oxford University Press.

Office of Population Censuses and Surveys, Social Survey Division (1976) *General Household Survey 1973*, HMSO.

Olsen, D.J. (1973) House Upon House, in *Victorian City: Images and Realities* (eds Dyos, H.J. and Wolff, M.), Routledge & Kegan Paul.

Olsen, D.J. (1976) *Growth of Victorian London*, Batsford.

Orwell, G. (1963) *Road to Wigan Pier*, Penguin.

Parlett, D.S. (ed.) (1976) *Construction Industry UK*, House.

Pevsner, N. (1976) *History of Building Types*, Thames & Hudson.

Pinker, R. (1966) *English Hospital Statistics 1861–1938*, Heinemann.

Pollard, S. (1959) *History of Labour in Sheffield*, Liverpool University Press.

Pollard, S. (1978) Labour in Gt. Britain, in *Cambridge Economic History of Europe. Vol. VIII Industrial Economies: Capital, Labour and Enterprise* (eds Mathias, P. and Postan, M.M.), Cambridge University Press.

Port, M.H. (1995) *Imperial London: Civil Government Building in London 1850–1915*, Yale University Press.

Postgate, R.W. (1923) *Builders' History*, NFBTO.

Prest, A.R. and Coppock, D.J. (1976) *UK Economy: a Manual of Applied Economics*, Weidenfeld & Nicolson.

Price, R. (1980) *Masters, Unions and Men: Work Control in Building and Rise of Labour 1830–1914*, Cambridge University Press.

Price, S.J. (1959) *Building Societies: Their Origin and History*, Franey.

Priestley, J.B. (1934) *English Journey*, Heinemann.

Ravetz, A. (1974) From Working-class Tenement to Modern Flat: Local Authorities and Multi-Storey Housing Between the Wars, in *Multi-Storey Living: the British Working-Class Experience* (ed. Sutcliffe, A.), Croom Helm.

Report of the Committee of Inquiry Under Professor E.H. Phelps Brown into Certain Matters Concerning Labour in Building and Civil Engineering (1968), HMSO.

Richardson, H.W. and Aldcroft, D.H. (1968) *Building in the British Economy Between the Wars*, Allen & Unwin.

Robins, E.C. (1887) *Technical School and College Building*, Whittaker.

Robinson, H.W. (1939) *Economics of Building*, King.

Robson, E.R. (1972) *School Architecture*, Leicester University Press.

Roger, R. (1989) *Housing in Urban Britain 1780–1914*, Macmillan.

Rose, J. (1985) *Dynamics of Urban Property Development*, E & FN Spon.

Rose, W. (1952) *Village Carpenter*, Country Book Club.

Rosenberg, N. (1960) *Economic Planning in the British Building Industry 1945–49*, University of Pennsylvania Press.

Rougvie, A. (1987) *Project Evaluation and Development*, Mitchell.

Routh, G. (1965) *Occupation and Pay in Great Britain 1906–1960*, Cambridge University Press.

Royal Institute of British Architects (1962) *Architect and His Office*, RIBA.

Royal Institute of British Architects (1988) *Census of Private Architectural Practices*, RIBA.

Royal Institute of British Architects (1992) *Strategic Study of the Profession: Phase 1 Strategic Overview*, RIBA.

Rubinstein, D. (1974) *Victorian Homes*, David & Charles.

Ruddock, L. (1992) *Economics for Construction and Property*, Arnold.

Sachs, E.O. and Woodrow, E.A.E. (1968) *Modern Opera Houses and Theatres*, Blom, Vols. I and II.

Saint, A. (1987) *Towards a Social Architecture: the Role of School Building in Post-War England*, Yale University Press.

Samuel, R. (ed.) (1975) *Village Life and Labour*, Routledge & Kegan Paul.

Sayle, A. (1924) *Houses of the Workers*, Unwin.

Seaborne, M. (1971) *English School: its Architecture and Organisation 1370–1870*, Routledge & Kegan Paul.

Seaborne, M. and Lowe, R. (1977) *English School: its Architecture and Organisation. Vol. II 1870–1970*, Routledge & Kegan Paul.

Service, A. (1977) *Edwardian Architecture: a Handbook to Building Design in Britain 1890–1914*, Thames & Hudson.

Shannon, H.A. (1966) Bricks – a Trade Index 1785–1849, in *Essays in Economic History* (ed. Carus-Wilson, E.M.), Arnold, Vol. 3.

Sharp, E. (1969) *Ministry of Housing and Local Government*, Allen & Unwin.

Sheppard, F.H.W. (ed.) (1973) *Survey of London. Vol. XXXVII Northern Kensington*, Athlone.

Sheppard, R. (1945) *Cast Iron in Building*, Allen & Unwin.

Short, J.R. (1982) *Housing in Britain: the Post-War Experience*, Methuen.

Shutt, R. (1982) *Economics for the Construction Industry*, Longman.

Sigsworth, E.M. (1958) *Black Dyke Mills: a History*, Liverpool University Press.

Sim, D. (1993) *British Housing Design*, Longman.

Simon, E.D. (1945) *Rebuilding Britain: a Twenty Year Plan*, Gollancz.

Simon, J.D. (1875) *House-Owner's Estimator: or What Will It Cost to Build, Alter or Repair?*, Lockwood.

Skyring, W.H. (1856) *Skyring's Builders' Prices*, Skyring.

Slater, E.A. (1912) *Structural Economy*, St Bride's Press.

Smeaton, A.C. (1835) *Builder's Pocket Manual*, Taylor.

Smithies, E. (1984) *Black Economy in England Since 1914*, Gill & Macmillan.

Smyth, H. (1985) *Property Companies and the Construction Industry in Britain*, Cambridge University Press.

Spencer-Silver, P. (1993) *Pugin's Builder: the Life and Work of George Myers*, University of Hull Press.

Springett, J. (1986) Land Development and House-Building in Huddersfield, 1770–1911, in *Building the Industrial City* (ed. Doughty, M.), Leicester University Press.

Stillman, C.G. and Cleary, R.C. (1949) *Modern School*, Architectural Press.

Stobart, T.J. (1927) *Timber Trade of the United Kingdom*, Crosby Lockwood, Vols. I and II.

Stone, P.A. (1966) *Building Economy*, Pergamon.

Stone, P.A. (1973) *Structure, Size and Costs of Urban Settlements*, Cambridge University Press.

Sugden, J.D. (1975) Place of Construction in the Economy in *Aspects of the Economics of Construction* (ed. Turin, D.A.), Godwin.

Summerson, J. (1973) *London Building World of the Eighteen-Sixties*, Thames & Hudson.

Swenarton, M. (1981) *Homes Fit for Heroes: the Politics and Architecture of Early State Housing in Britain*, Heinemann.

Swift, G.A. (1930) *Steel Framed Works Buildings*, Draughtsman Publishing.

Tann, J. (1970) *Development of the Factory*, Cornmarket.

Taylor, J. (1991) *Hospital and Asylum Architecture in England 1840–1914*, Mansell.

Technology Foresight. Progress Through Partnership: 2. Construction (1995), Office of Science & Technology.

Thomas, G. (1968) *Operatives in the Building Industry*, HMSO.

Thomas, P.E. (ed.) (n.d.; *c.* 1938) *Modern Building Practice*, Newnes.

Thompson, A. (1963) *Library Buildings of Britain and Europe*, Butterworths.

Thompson, E.P. (1968) *Making of the English Working Class*, Penguin.

Thompson, F.M.L. (1968) *Chartered Surveyors: the Growth of a Profession*, Routledge & Kegan Paul.

The Times (1938) *British Homes: The Building Society Movement*, The Times.

Treble, J.H. (1971) Liverpool Working Class Housing 1801–51, in *History of Working Class Housing: a Symposium* (ed. Chapman, S.D.), David & Charles.

Treen, C. (1982) Process of Suburban Development in North Leeds 1870–1914, in *Rise of Suburbia* (ed. Thompson, F.M.L.), Leicester University Press.

Tressel, R. (1965) *Ragged Trousered Philanthropists*, Panther.

Turner, G. (1971) *Business in Britain*, Penguin.

Usill, G.W. (ed.) (1885) *Builders' and Contractors' Price Book and Guide to Estimating*, Scientific Publishing.

Vaughan, A. (1977) *Pictorial Record of Great Western Architecture*, Oxford Publishing.

Wallis, L. (1945) *Building Industry: its Work and Organisation*, Dent.

Ward, C. (ed.) (1976) *British School Buildings: Designs and Appraisals 1964–74*, Architectural Press.

Weaver, L. (1913) *Country Life Book of Cottages Costing from £150 to £600*, Country Life.

Webb, C.A. (1913) *Valuation of Real Property*, Crosby Lockwood.

White, R.B. (1965) *Prefabrication: a History of its Development in Great Britain*, HMSO.

Whitehand, J.W.R. (1992) *Making of the Urban Landscape*, Blackwell.

Winter, J. (1970) *Industrial Architecture: a Survey of Factory Building*, Studio Vista.

Wohl, A.S. (1977) *Eternal Slum: Housing and Social Policy in Victorian London*, Arnold.

Wright, H.M. (1946) *Small Houses £500–£2,500*, Architectural Press.

Wright, L. (1960) *Clean and Decent: the Fascinating History of the Bathroom and the Water Closet*, Routledge & Kegan Paul.

Young, C. (ed) (various years) *Spons' Architects' and Builders' Pocket Price Book*, E. & F.N. Spon.

Young, G.M. (1943) *Country and Town: a Summary of the Scott and Uthwatt Reports*, Penguin.

Zweig, F. (1952) *British Worker*, Penguin.

JOURNALS AND PERIODICALS

Architects' Journal, 16 July 1930.

Belcher, V. (1982) Records of a London Building Firm, *Business Archives*, **48**, Nov.

Bennett, J. (1993) Managing Construction, *Building Special Supplement Anniversary Issue 150 Years 1843–1993*, Feb.

Bowley, M. (1937–38) Some Regional Aspects of the Building Boom 1924–36, *Review of Economic Studies*, **5**.

Brown, E.H.P. and Hopkins, S.V. (1955) Seven Centuries of Building Wages, *Economica* New Series, **XXII** (87).

The Builder, 29 July 1843.

Building, 5 May 1995.

Central Statistical Office (1975) *Monthly Digest of Statistics* 349.

Chalklin, C.W. (1980) Capital Expenditure on Building for Cultural Purposes in Provincial England 1730–1830, *Business History*, **XXII** (1).

Cooney, E.W. (1955–56) Origins of the Victorian Master Builders, *Economic History Review* 2nd series, **8** (2).

Cooney, E.W. (1960–61) Long Waves in Building in the British Economy of the Nineteenth Century', *Economic History Review* 2nd series, **13** (2).

Cooney, E.W. (1987) Innovation and Contracts in the Postwar British Building Industry, *Construction History* **3**.

Cooney, E.W. (1993) Productivity, Conflict and Order in the British Construction Industry: a Historical View, *Construction History*, **9**.

Crouch, P. (1983) Walter Mason and the Late Nineteenth Century Building Industry in Haverhill, *Suffolk Review*, **5** (4).

Department of the Environment (various dates) *Housing and Construction Statistics*.

Dyos, H.J. (1968) Speculative Builders and Developers of Victorian London, *Victorian Studies*, **XI**, Summer supplement.

Finnimore, B. (1985) A.I.R.O.H. House: Industrial Diversification and State Building Policy, *Construction History*, **1**.

Harper, R. (1977) Conflict Between English Building Regulations and Architectural Design: 1890–1918, *J. of Architectural Research*, **6** (1).

Home, R.K. (1982) Nineteenth Century Macclesfield Builder: Some Notes on George Roylance (1836–92), *Trans. Lancs. & Ches. Antiq. Soc.*, **81**.

Kenwood, A.G. (1963) Residential Building Activity in North Eastern England 1853–1913, *Manchester School of Economic and Social Studies*, **XXXI**.

Lawrence, J.C. (1990) Steel Frame Architecture Versus the London Building Regulations: Selfridges, the Ritz and American Technology, *Construction History*, **6**.

Locock, M. (1992) Development of the Building Trades in the West Midlands 1400–1850, *Construction History*, **8**.

Louw, H. (1991) Window Glass Making in Britain c. 1660–c. 1860 and its Architectural Impact, *Construction History*, **7**.

Louw, H. (1992) Mechanisation of Architectural Woodwork in Britain from the Late-Eighteenth to the Early Twentieth Century, and its Practical, Social and Aesthetic Implications Pt. I, *Construction History*, **8**.

Louw, H. (1993) Mechanisation of Architectural Woodwork . . . Pt. II, *Construction History*, **9**.

Mackay, D.I. (1967) Growth and Fluctuations in the British Building Industry, *Scottish J. of Political Economy*, **14**.

Maiwald, K. (1954) Index of Building Costs in the United Kingdom 1845–1938, *Economic History Review* 2nd Series, **VII** (2).

Marriner, S. (1976) Cash and Concrete: Liquidity Problems in the Mass-Production of 'Homes for Heroes', *Business History*, **XVIII** (2).

Marriner, S. (1979) Sir Alfred Mond's Octopus: a Nationalised House-Building Business, *Business History*, **XXI** (1).

Ministry of Housing and Local Government (various dates) *Housing Statistics: Great Britain*.

Nenadic, S. (1993) Small Family Firm in Victorian Britain, *Business History*, **35** (4).

Nisbet, J. (1951–52) Quantity Surveying in London During the Nineteenth Century, *J. of the Royal Institution of Chartered Surveyors*, **31**.

Port, M.H. (1967) Office of Works and Building Contracts in Early Nineteenth Century England, *Economic History Review* 2nd series, **20** (1).

Potter, J. (1955) British Timber Duties 1815–60, *Economica*, **22**.

Powell, C.G. (1985) Case Studies and Lost Tribes: the Bristol Firm of James Diment and Stephens, Bastow & Co., *Construction History*, **1**.

Powell, C.G. (1986) He That Runs Against Time: Life Expectancy of Building Firms in Nineteenth Century Bristol, *Construction History*, **2**.

Powell, C.G. (1986) Some Trends in Relative Costs of Building Types: Description and Interpretation, *Construction Management and Economics*, **4**.

Powell, C.G. (1990) 'Widows and Others' on Bristol Building Sites: Some Women in Nineteenth Century Construction, *Local Historian*, **20** (2).

Roskill, O.W. (1938) Economics of the Building Industry, *Architects J.*, 1 Dec.

Saul, S.B. (1962) House Building in England 1890–1914, *Economic History Review* 2nd series, **15** (1).

Sheppard, F., Belcher, V. and Cottrell, P. (1979) Middlesex and Yorkshire Deeds Registries and the Study of Building Fluctuations, *London Journal*, **5** (2).

'Top 50 Contractors', *Building*, 14 July 1995.

Trowell, F. (1985) Speculative Housing Development in Leeds and the Involvement of Local Architects in the Design Process 1866–1914, *Construction History*, **1**.

Vipond, M.J. (1969) Fluctuations in Private Housebuilding in Great Britain 1950–1966, *Scottish J. of Political Economy*, **16**.

Whitehand, J.W.R. (1992) Makers of British Towns: Architects, Builders and Property Owners, c. 1850–1939, *J. of Historical Geography*, **18** (4).

UNPUBLISHED THESIS

Smith, L.D.W. (1976) Textile Factory Settlements in the Early Industrial Revolution, Ph.D. University of Aston.

Index

Page numbers appearing in **bold** refer to figures.